Good Intentions

PHILANTHROPIC AND NONPROFIT STUDIES

Dwight F. Burlingame and David C. Hammack, general editors

EDITED BY DAVID H. SMITH

Good Intentions

Moral Obstacles and Opportunities

INDIANA UNIVERSITY PRESS
Bloomington and Indianapolis

This book is a publication of

Indiana University Press
601 North Morton Street
Bloomington, IN 47404-3797 USA

http://iupress.indiana.edu

Telephone orders   800-842-6796
Fax orders   812-855-7931
Orders by e-mail   iuporder@indiana.edu

The paper used in this publication meets the minimum requirements of American National Standard for Information Sciences—Permanence of Paper for Printed Library Materials, ANSI Z39.48-1984.

Manufactured in the United States of America

Library of Congress Cataloging-in-Publication Data

Good intentions : moral obstacles and opportunities / edited by David H. Smith.
p. cm. — (Philanthropic and nonprofit studies)
Includes bibliographical references and index.
ISBN 0-253-34531-6 (cloth : alk. paper) 1. Ethics. 2. Generosity. 3. Justice.
I. Smith, David H., 1939-II. Series.
BJ1531.G59 2005
177′.7—dc22

                                                          2004020309

1 2 3 4 5   10 09 08 07 06 05

Contents

Acknowledgments

This book is the result of a seminar funded by the Center on Philanthropy at Indiana University-Purdue University in Indianapolis. The seminar was convened over the two-year duration of its existence by the Poynter Center for the Study of Ethics and American Institutions. Funding came from research support provided to the Center on Philanthropy by the Lilly Endowment, Inc. Thus the Poynter Center's greatest debts are to the Center on Philanthropy, particularly its Director of Research Patrick Rooney and Associate Executive Director and Director of Academic Programs Dwight Burlingame, both of whom participated in the seminar, and to Craig Dykstra, Vice President for Religion at the Lilly Endowment, Inc. On another level we are deeply indebted to the participants whose essays are collected here and whose eager, candid, and judicious seminar participation made the meetings and editing a joy from beginning to end. This is a diverse group of scholars, all of whom came to the table prepared to listen and learn as well as to speak.

We have other debts as well. Before other commitments supervened, Judith Failer contributed enormously to our discussions. At various stages of the project's gestation Judith Granbois and Glenda Murray improved our prose, participated in our conversations, and made sure our small ship stayed afloat. Carol Bland kept our financial world in order. Mark Wilson and Jae Chung read drafts of the Introduction, made helpful comments, and served as intellectual prods to the editor. At a seminar discussion of the next-to-last draft of the book, we received helpful comments from Constance Baker, Joann Campbell, Lawrence J. Friedman, Robert Katz, Richard B. Miller, Michael Reinke, and Robert Sloan, as well as many of the people mentioned before. Errors and limits that remain are, of course, the responsibility of the authors and editor.

Good Intentions

Introduction: Doing Good

David H. Smith

We all face questions about whom to help and how to help long before national crises or natural disasters occur. Should I give money to my church, the United Way, the local homeless shelter, or a political party that I think will take the country in the right direction? Should I vote to preserve or increase government action to help the unfortunate, or volunteer and contribute to welfare and the public good through nonprofit organizations? Sometimes I may need or mean to help but in fact only get in the way; at other times my help seems patronizing and disrespectful to those I mean to help. Sometimes I am offered help from someone I cannot respect or trust, and I have to decide whether to take the gift, or how to refuse it appropriately. I can't possibly meet all the needs of members of my family or friends, or of persons in other parts of the world who are much worse off. How should I set my priorities? How should we set our priorities?

Giving Is Good

Strange as it seems, it is important to begin with the apparently obvious assertion that giving is a good thing. We honor people who give; we are grateful for gifts; institutions that have done remarkable amounts of good have been enabled by gifts. It seems perverse to be critical or cynical about a kind of behavior that has done so much for so many of us.

But there are profound arguments against a social stress on giving. A great deal of the social and political philosophy of the past four hundred years can be seen as a series of meditations on the theme that the inevitable neediness of human beings is best responded to with a focus on justice. Justice is understood to be an alternative to generosity, and a superior alternative at that. The language of justice is the language of rights and claims, but gifts are not the sort of thing that anyone has a right to.

Much moral philosophy has stressed justice because of the high value we all place on self-respect. When my needs for education or health care are regarded as something I have a *right* to have met, then I do not have to plead or beg or feel inferior to someone who finds herself in a less needy position. When we think in terms of justice, we think of problems that might befall any one of us, and we agree to use our resources to help out ourselves and each other. The fact that we are all actually or potentially needy is made very clear. When we rely on *giving* to meet need, we too easily assume that the world can be divided into those who are needy and those who are not.

I will not attempt a full response to this argument here; indeed, I think it makes an irrefutable claim—that justice is a fundamental virtue of social institutions. The harder issue is to determine whether our acknowledgement of the importance of self-respect should lead us to jettison a stress on giving as one of the social values we treasure and hope to inculcate. I don't think we should draw that conclusion or despise giving.

To start with, the need for assistance is simply there. Six thousand people die from AIDS each day in Africa, and one need only read any day's newspaper to learn of a litany of natural or human disasters, the suffering caused by human indifference and ambition. Given the magnitude of human need in the world, it seems foolish to despise any program or gift that might help. Moreover, it is clear that resources are there to be tapped. Two thirds of U.S. households contributed a total of $2.1 billion to help after the September 11, 2001, disaster. Paul Schervish and his colleagues speak of an expected transfer of $44.8 trillion of funds from one generation to another within the next fifty years. Within a shorter time frame of twenty years (1998 to 2017), the total will be $12.8 trillion. Even within the lifetimes of readers of this book, these conservative estimates amount to a substantial amount of money and the stakes for how it is used to affect the human prospect are enormous.[1] *Perhaps* in an ideal world, this money would be equitably redistributed, but it seems sensible to put some effort into a strategy that presumes the transfer will proceed as scheduled and suggests to persons the magnitude of the responsibility that they have inherited.

Moreover, justice is blind. The statue of justice that is found over many courthouses shows her blindfolded. And she is cold. Justice is impartial and impersonal. These are important qualities in a system of allocation, but they are insufficient as specifications for the moral requirement of helping each other out in a community. This is clear to us in families. Justice in the family is important, but a family in which justice is the only value observed is a caricature. Social life would be flat if justice were our only standard; we need wiggle room for love and for giving, for spontaneity and indeed partiality.

We can see one illustration of this difference between justice and giving if we compare the roles of charity in the United States and the United Kingdom. In the U.K., the state is called "the crown," and citizens assume that the corporate body will take care of many basic needs. A welfare-based conception of justice has been adopted. Its features include comprehensive education, a national health service, and significant government subvention of arts and culture. Ironically, the effect is to minimize the role of charity, or organized giving. Fewer citizens give, they give less, and they give less frequently than in the United States. By contrast, U.S. citizens have always been suspicious of government. Our philanthropies are larger, better organized for fund raising, and more numerous. We give more, and most of our giving flows through religious institutions. In the United States, we try to accomplish with a combination of justice and charity what people in Great Britain think of strictly as a matter of justice.

Limits on what we do are obvious. Our provision is uneven, often unfair, and frequently uncaring. We have a lot of free riders. But we also have an admirable sense that all people need to pitch in and help out as best they can. We have a healthy resistance to the idea that we can simply leave problems to public officials and the public purse. Nothing reveals that notion more clearly than our responses after the 9/11 disaster. On the one hand, the chaos of those responses makes clear the need for a more coherent public policy concerning disaster in particular and for helping each other in general. On the other hand, the overwhelming outpouring of generosity takes one's breath away. A polity that fosters what Americans did then cannot be all bad.

What Is a Gift?

Giving is a much studied term that means different things to different people. In our ordinary usage we think of a gift as spontaneous, a surprise and unnecessary. When I was a Divinity School student at Yale in the early 1960s, my wife and I had little money. One cold December night we stood in line outside Woolsey Hall hoping to buy balcony tickets for a recital by the great cellist Rostropovich. A large man in a huge coat and wearing a Russian hat approached us, asked us if we hoped to buy tickets to the recital, and—when we said we did—gave us two tickets—indeed two of the best seats I have ever had in a major hall. It was the then Yale Chaplain William Sloane Coffin.

That remarkable act beautifully illustrates our usual concept of the gift. The gift is contrasted with what we are obliged to provide. Think of the statement "I will give you my basketball tickets." That means that I choose to give them; I did not "have to" or owe them to you, and I am not selling them to you. On these terms, what we might call the *pure gift* is spontaneous, uncoerced, and for those reasons often received with surprise. The essence of the gift is its voluntariness, the freedom with which it is offered. The gift is unexpected by the recipient, completely voluntary and unnecessary by the giver. It is a Romantic notion of gift, nurtured in an individualist society.

In contrast to this stands a more classical concept of gift as a distinctive form of social relation, a relation insightfully studied by Marcel Mauss, Lewis Hyde, and others. These writers identify a form of social exchange that contrasts with market exchanges. On these terms gift giving is obligatory, not optional. Gifts are transactions that knit a social group together; they establish personal relations; not giving a gift can cause a major social rupture. We are all familiar with this form of giving as well as the more romantic and individualistic gift. Failing to provide a gift for an anniversary, birthday, Christmas, or bar mitzvah is to default on an obligation. This kind of gift is expected, and so is reciprocation of some sort.

This form of giving is the life blood of traditional societies. I receive a gift and am expected to pass it on; if I cannot literally pass it on, then I should give something else. In its most rigorous form, the notion that many, if any, items are my personal and private possession is called into question. Provision of such gifts is a very important component in sustaining the web of social relations that holds a society together.

For us, a gift "economy" parallels the market economy of buying and selling. Though we distinguish the two kinds of transactions sharply, we tend to devalue the obligatory nature and importance of our own gift economies, perhaps because they seem less tangible and quantifiable than market exchanges. In fact, they are not really optional or voluntary; the omission of a wedding or birthday gift makes a statement, whether one wants it to or not. To be sure, the form of coercion involved is not the long arm of the law. It is internalized and socially reinforced. But the social force is nevertheless real and powerful.

Other characteristics of gifts come to mind. Jesus praises what is often called the "widow's mite."[2] The penurious widow makes a small contribution, but Jesus says that her gift has greater value than the larger contributions of others who are wealthier. Her giving represents a larger fraction of what she has than the others have offered. It holds more consequences for her than their larger donations hold for them. Whether the gift is customary or free, we think of gifts as more valuable if they are precious or close to the self or identity of the giver; indeed, their value increases as they approximate or symbolize a gift of oneself.

The social or moral compulsion associated with gifts reflects the extent to which they are perceived as gifts of self, or gifts that establish or seal a relationship between selves. After the tragedy of September 11, many people felt that they had no choice but to give after they had seen what they had seen. Of course, in one sense they had a choice; no one was forcing them. In that sense, their contributions were pure gifts. But in a more profound sense they had to give out of a sense of identification with victims and a need to identify with those who were heroically helping. They gave because of who they were and wanted to be.[3]

Thus on the surface, it seems that at least three types of exchange exist: buying and selling in the market, providing the free or pure gift, and offering the customary or obligatory gift. The difficult issue is to assess how many of the apparently spontaneous gifts are—from the standpoint of the giver—matters of obligation, conscience, or a search for meaning. In any case, gifts seem closer to the self, more a reflection of someone's identity than the demands of justice. We can be just for diverse reasons and without really committing ourselves in heart and mind. But giving requires an engagement of the self, no matter how much we may wish it didn't.

Giving Is Fraught with Moral Perils

The fact that gifts are a special and powerful mode of exchange should not lead us to idealize giving as a form of caring or as a measure of human relations. For example, givers expect gifts to be received with gratitude. When the sign of appreciation isn't up to standard, givers feel betrayed. The result is what has been called the "tyranny of the gift," for the act of giving creates an unequal relationship, a relationship that, when it goes wrong, leads to disrespect by the giver, loss of self-respect by the recipient, and a souring of genuine community. Apart from recognition of reciprocity, giving corrupts equality. And the act of giving can be intrusive.

I have already suggested why meeting social needs through giving is morally risky. If we don't let those worries dissuade us from stressing the importance of giving, there are still many serious problems to resolve. I will identify two such situations.

Whose need is being met when I give a gift? I may think someone who lives in another neighborhood needs education; he may think he needs food. Conflicts between the vision of a donor and that of a recipient are recurrent in the world of organized giving. For example, on learning that the Red Cross had followed its usual practice and held back some of the money donated for assistance after the 9/11 disaster, one of my oldest friends remarked, "I'll never give to the Red Cross again." Participation in that particular rescue effort there and then was essential to him. He didn't want generally to be a helpful person, but wanted to do something to help with that particular tragedy. With the best will in the world, his need to be involved overwhelmed sober judgment about what was needed. I will argue later that there is nothing wrong with the giver acknowledging her or his neediness—to the contrary. But sorting out the differences between the donor's needs and vision and the real needs of the moment can be difficult.

More troublesome are those situations in which a desire to control or correct is masquerading as a desire to give or to help. The giver begins with a full outline of what the good life entails; he or she wants to help the recipient live up to those specific standards. This is what one moral theologian calls the philanthropy of patronage, rather than the philanthropy of humility. It is a desire to dominate, not to empower, through love. C. S. Lewis captured the problem in his phrasing of an imaginary epitaph:

> Erected by her sorrowing brothers,
>   in memory of Martha Clay.
> Here lies one who lived for others.
> Now she has peace,
>   And so have they.

Patronizing intrusiveness like this arises from self-satisfaction and self-righteousness on the part of donors. Psychologically, the way to head it off is for all givers to acknowledge their own neediness and dependence. No one is really self-made. Everyone has been the beneficiary of individual assistance and of social structures that enable even the most self-directed of ascents to power. Moreover, one's own powers of intellect or will have scarcely been earned or designed. They are the product of the genetic and social lottery, of fate or the enabling grace of God. The granting of humility, reciprocal giving, is impossible without a sense of neediness. Authentic giving is only possible for people who have internalized the sense that they have been given to.

The sense of donor finitude and gratefulness must, in authentic giving, be coupled with a sense of respect for the identity and particularity of those whom the donor wants to help. In the film version of *Seabiscuit*, Red Pollard's boss doesn't want to let Red ride again after a terrible accident and injury. Red's friend and fellow jockey, George Wolfe, intercedes with the owner, saying that it is "better to let a man break his leg than to break his heart." Paternalistic attacks on self-respect are patronizing and insulting. Respecting dignity is a necessary condition of morally worthy giving.

Philanthropy

Philanthropy is only one kind of giving. Mother Teresa was widely regarded as a saint, but it strains our ordinary usage of words to call her a *philanthropist*. Her deeds fit the etymology of the word—a lover of humankind—but not the connotations that the term *philanthropy* has in ordinary speech. At another extreme, if I call myself a philanthropist after dropping ten dollars in the Salvation Army bucket at Christmas time, my words can be understood only as an attempt at a joke. Rather, *philanthropy* connotes a kind of scale or magnitude that is in some way unusual. An act of philanthropy makes a splash; it makes a noticeable difference. Moreover, in contrast to the work of Mother Theresa, *philanthropy* entails mediation—it implies working through others who administer, design, serve, minister, or help. We remember Mother Teresa because she was an active and involved caregiver herself. Philanthropists may want to get involved (and I think that is not a bad thing), but the distinctive task of philanthropy is enabling, providing resources. Philanthropists must work through others on the basis of a personal or institutional policy or plan.

There are other puzzles. Robert Payton, founder of the Indiana University Center on Philanthropy, has often defined philanthropy as "voluntary action for the public good." This definition distinguishes philanthropy from government action (which from the point of individual citizens is involuntary) and private actions (which are assumed to be in the interest or for the good of individuals themselves). The world of philanthropy is distinguished from government, on the one hand, and business, on the other. This straightforward definition is clear and very useful, but not uncontroversial. On these terms, how should we describe the Victims' Compensation Fund established by Congress after the 9/11 disaster? The financial assistance cannot be called philanthropy, for it is public action supported by tax dollars. Yet it somehow seems more like what the private foundations have traditionally been doing than like the conventional provision of education, welfare, or health care.

Another definition, consistent with the etymology of the word *philanthropy*, is to understand it to be love of humankind. Phillip Turner uses this definition in his essay in this volume. On Turner's reading, *philanthropy* denotes love for all humans, regardless of their religious, ethnic, or political identities. It is a term from the Enlightenment, meant to go beyond tribalism and religious conflict. Whereas Payton's definition focuses on the source of the gift or who the giver is, Turner's calls attention to the recipient. Philanthropic giving is impartial in the sense that ties of love or kinship or other communities are irrelevant. Turner argues that there is tension between the choice of religious giving, which may suggest preference for some recipients over others, and philanthropy properly understood. In fact, readers of this volume will see that several of the essays stipulate different meanings for the term *philanthropy*.

Giving Takes Work

Nonphilanthropic giving certainly requires work. Knowing what to give, when to give, and then finding the right gift requires energy, insight, imagination, and patience. I am regularly reminded of these facts, as I am married to a mother of three and grandmother of five who expends countless hours of effort in trying (with great success) to identify appropriate gifts for birthdays and holidays. The fundamental problem really isn't money; it's making the fact of love tangible. Indeed, diverting attention to money may lead the dedicated giver astray. Of course, not all persons are such careful and committed givers; I have been known to do considerable shopping in haste, which has resulted in less appropriate gifts than my wife's carefully chosen selections. Tangible gifts are not the only, or perhaps the most important, things people give to each other, but such gifts are not as trivial as some of us would like to pretend. They are sacramental tokens of love and friendship.

Philanthropic giving requires virtues much like those of the committed shopper. On the one hand, giving requires the ability to understand, listen, and learn. It calls for discernment. Without the giver's willingness to learn about the reality of the lives of recipients, many a well-intentioned gift will fall off target. Patience—which listening requires—goes hand in hand with self-discipline. The hasty shopper lunges at the first attractive item he or she sees in the store. The careful shopper does not. Impulse may have a part to play in the careful shopper's actions, but it is impulse schooled by experience and observation. Good philanthropic giving requires knowledge of the self and a commitment to a set of priorities. It is thought out and based in a knowledge of the world into which the philanthropist hopes to enter.

Moreover, to be all it should be, philanthropy requires self-involvement. To be sure, objectives may be attained if the donor's self is kept completely in the background, but a price is paid for that (perhaps it would be better to say *an opportunity is lost*) for the donor. To take a terribly unflattering instance, Scrooge is helped by helping Bob Cratchit. In another example, the late New York philanthropist Brooke Astor was famous (infamous to some) for showing up among people in trouble wearing her best clothes and pearls. She was criticized for being patronizing, but I think it might have been worse for Astor to have pretended to be something or someone she was not. And she was surely right—perhaps within her rights—to want to show up. The philanthropist who keeps too great a distance between herself and the actions done on her behalf protects herself from criticism and misunderstanding at a cost of learning, enjoying herself, and the chance at doing better.

Why Bother?

If anyone takes seriously what I have said so far, a natural response is to say that giving is a morally ambiguous act, an act that both diverts money from good uses within my own family and takes a lot of time. Why do I bother with it? I've got better things to do with my life. There are two powerful responses to this understandable point of view.

First, we need to involve ourselves in giving because we realize that we are part of something larger: a family, city, congregation, state, or nation. Or we do so because we are among those persons dedicated to the cultural benefits of art and music; we are alumni of a college or professional school, or people who have been helped by a hospital. A surprising number give because they consider themselves to have been befriended by a loving God. In any case, we realize that *we are not alone, not unaffected by what happens to others.* We are parts of communities of memory and communities of shared hopes.

Thus we give so as to acknowledge that we are not alone, not radically independent. We give from gratitude, to meet need, and to express gratefulness for the chances we have had and the opportunities we see.

We give philanthropically because we need help to show adequately that gratitude. We have finite strength, vision, and time. Given the scope of human need, we have to work cooperatively, empowering others as best we can. We provide that help by setting an example, by teaching, and by providing resources. What do we get out of it? An entirely legitimate sense of enjoying ourselves, maybe a whiff of transcendence, and a kind of awareness that we have made a difference over the long haul.

Love

Many readers of this book will want to find a justification for offering gifts or seeking justice in the responsibility to be loving or a duty to love one's neighbor. However, as Paul Tillich noted, the concept of love is the most misused and ambiguous in the English language. It may mean affection or duty; and it may or may not require radical altruism. Still, *justice* doesn't fully capture what we mean when we think of our responsibility to help, and *giving* may seem either too routine or, on the pure gift conception, too unreliable and patronizing. Love of others seems at once more constant and more personal.

In the middle of the twentieth century, much Protestant thought, under the influence of Soren Kierkegaard and Anders Nygren, adopted a radically altruistic conception of love. In its most rigorous terms, love meant an exclusive focus on the needs of others. Love for oneself had no legitimate role. Love *meant* radical altruism, and any whiff of self-interest was thought to be corrupting. The roots of this rigorous conception were theological. God's gracious love and acceptance provided security and hope for the anxious soul. Thanks to the miracle of faith in one's acceptance by God, individuals were freed from anxiety and freed to love a neighbor, as persons normally love themselves. As one writer put it, whatever the neighbor needs, that thing love seeks for her.

The most radical altruism implicit in this rigor could not be sustained. Concern for oneself might be justified on instrumental grounds—if I or my projects are necessary for meeting the needs of others, concern for self becomes legitimate. Or on utilitarian grounds—if love is interpreted to mean concern for all humankind, then the self can count as one, but no more than one, member of the human family. An alternative conception of love, in which love is understood to mean a quest for fulfillment, has been of renewed importance in the last quarter century. The idea, in theological terms, is that love requires trust and commitment to God and God's cause; and that love for God entails love for the friends of God—including not only humankind but others of God's creatures as well. Seeking joy for oneself is not viewed as corrupt, but great stress is laid on *what one loves*, on having one's priorities straight. A distinction is made between loving the self as the most important thing in the world (which is rejected) and the happiness that comes to the self from loving the right thing. We should care about more than ourselves, but the fact that we care and seek to rejoice in the triumph of the right is not just another perversely refined form of corrupt egoism. It is a symptom of a well-ordered soul.

Love understood in either of these ways may lend support to securing justice and the making of gifts. Our lives are seen as gifts; they are not our own but we hold them in trust from God to be used for the accomplishment of God's purposes, or to bring joy to ourselves and to all creation. Love entails a duty to meet basic needs and to recognize the binding quality of commitments made to each other in trust. It requires development of a plausible conception of justice.

But love does not require a distinctive sorting out of the role of gifts and justice in the provision of welfare or the meeting of needs. That sorting may appropriately vary from time to time and place to place. The loving form of social, economic, and political organization for the United States in the early twenty-first century may not be right for the United Kingdom—to say nothing of China, Kenya, or Mexico. But it seems probable that love would require attention both to justice and to the role of giving in any society.

Religion

A stress on love, on justice, and on giving is certainly possible without bringing religion into the conversation. Many persons are not religious in any conventional sense, let alone members of the Abrahamic faiths of Judaism, Christianity, and Islam. Hindus and Buddhists, self-described atheists and agnostics, have embraced many of these concepts in different ways, times, and places. They are not the exclusive property of any one tradition. Yet it is very hard, if not impossible, to work out a tradition-neutral articulation of them—a fact that has led some philosophers to adopt a phrase such as "overlapping consensus."

The basic problem of relating religious traditions to this modern age in which great stress is laid on individual rights and freedom remains. Traditional religion characteristically de-centers the human soul and sets human life in some larger context. This is most easily seen in the monotheistic traditions of the West with their preoccupation with the transcendent God who is creating, covenanting, and saving. Whatever and whomever God may be, God is not simply identical to but is more important than the individual soul. In Hinduism and Buddhism, the self or soul is also considered in a larger context or worldview, and compassion may become a prominent requirement. One way or another, the question of how to reconcile the de-centered self with the modern worldview focused on individual rights and freedom has to be faced. Any vital religion will have something to say about this question. The important concepts of love, justice, and giving are worthwhile starting points for the conversation.

Our Essays

The essays that follow take stands on the issues raised so far, and open others. They are diverse in what they advocate, in how they analyze the facts, and in their styles. In short, they represent a sample of a conversation or "recital" among thoughtful persons concerned with the moral problems of doing good.

Part I of our book concerns the important roles that individuals can play in the world of giving and helping. Amy Kass calls attention to the exemplary work of Booker T. Washington, an out-of-favor hero. Washington was exemplary in the responsibility he took for himself, in the creation of institutions that encouraged others to do the same, and as a public embodiment of responsible care for the self and for others. Born into abject poverty, he took initiative and received several lessons in what we now call "tough love." The lesson he learned was to "put down your bucket where you are," that is, to draw on the resources at hand, your own, and those who will work with you. He wanted to empower African-Americans to take responsibility for themselves, to think first of self-help and then to think of help from others as an important tool or resource in that effort. His major gift to the world was his own example and institutions that enabled others to follow that example. Respect for people in trouble meant treating them as humans with the power to do things for themselves.

Jane Addams stressed the social dimension of the helping process, as Paul Pribbenow points out. She encouraged those who wanted to support her work to come to Hull House to observe and to get personally involved. She needed and wanted monetary contributions, but her basic idea was to encourage human community and reciprocity. Addams believed that membership in the community and philanthropy rightly understood went hand in hand. The alternative—external giving—was inevitably patronizing and in the long run ineffective. Helping each other was a common task for both the poor and those with resources. Pribbenow argues that Addams's conception of philanthropy remains insightful. He sketches the implications for nonprofit organizations and fundraising professionals.

Part II contains two essays that raise the question of justice and giving in different ways. David Craig argues that the best motivation for giving is to make a better life possible for another person. To specify the vague term *a better life*, he draws on the work of Martha Nussbaum and her appeal to human "capabilities." Identification of those capabilities provides a set of standards for measuring the worth of various causes. If we secure the advancement of those capabilities, we can have confidence that our gifts are working for justice. Some gifts may help those in trouble; others may allow individuals or groups to attain true excellence. Either is compatible with justice.

Patricia Werhane goes at the problem in a different way. Drawing on the work of Immanuel Kant and Adam Smith, she argues that the pursuit of justice always obliges us, whereas helping others does not. Neither requires radical altruism, she contends, and both are vague. To specify what justice and love may require of me now, I must "focus" my personal choices on a limited pool of possible recipients. Then I should evaluate the levels of need involved, the difference my personal contribution may make, and the extent to which my contribution may have ripple effects. The result is not an arithmetic formula, but it does advance us in the quest for guidance.

Much the largest percent of personal giving in the United States goes to religious organizations. In Part III of this collection, we consider some specific problems faced by churches and synagogues. Elliot Dorff considers three of these within the context of Conservative Judaism. How should Jewish institutions respond to gifts of "tainted money"—money that was acquired in illegal or immoral ways? Under what circumstances, if any, can these funds be accepted? Secondly, how should synagogue dues, which are not gifts, be adjusted for differing circumstances? Third, what special treatment should generous donors receive? Dorff's method of reasoning is clearly founded in rabbinic argumentation.

By contrast, Phillip Turner suggests that there is at least one problem in Christian ethics of giving that is a matter of character, not casuistry. Do Christians have special duties to fellow Christians just because they are Christians? In much of twentieth-century Christian ethics, that idea seemed mistaken, as it confused the reason for loving (salvation in Christ) with the parties Christians should love (the world for which the Christ died). Turner argues that this universalistic idea is too simple. He concedes that Christians have duties to all people, no matter what their religion, but he argues that they have special duties to fellow Christians who are all members of the communal body of Christ. For example, partly because of a shared religious alliance, Christians in the developed world have special responsibilities to come to the assistance of Christians in Africa who are in trouble. The tension between duties to all and duties to fellow Christians can, he concludes, be relaxed, but it can never be eliminated.

In Part IV, we turn from this discussion to consider the relationship of love and giving to justice. Paul Schervish sketches a way of looking at ourselves and our relationships with others that is coherent with his many years of ethnographic work. People are always in some form of development, beginning with a sense of their past and relying on a moral compass to chart their futures. Our moral biographies are stories about what we do with this situation; Schervish thinks that care is a natural and familiar component of our lives and that as we become more discerning, we learn how to care more fully both for others and for ourselves. Identification with others is the moral prerequisite for care. Caring in this sense is the core of moral citizenship; *philanthropy* on these terms is a special form of caring because it is not refracted through economic or political pressures. It opens the opportunity for an unmediated and reciprocal relationship in which the needs of another are addressed because of the intrinsic value of the person in need.

John Langan shifts our focus to the social institutions and dimensions of care and charity. He contrasts the New Testament ideal of charity with the contemporary practice of philanthropy, and offers a sympathetic critique of the notion of charity. He then turns to discuss subsidiarity and solidarity, two concepts of great importance in papal social teaching over the past century or more. Those concepts, Langan suggests, provide a corrective and context in which individual charity and institutional philanthropy make sense and, indeed, are of extraordinary value.

With Part V, the book concludes with two discussions that place our arguments in context, relating directly to the United States in the early twenty-first century. David Hammack explains the actual structures of giving in the United States. Giving in the nineteenth century stressed responsible self-sufficiency on the part of recipients; donations by individuals of time and money were central to the life of most nonprofit organizations. Charitable organizations were quite autonomous, able morally to debate about and to chart their own course, whether it was evangelical, rationalistic, or Catholic. Yet increasingly, persons concerned with the common good began to see charity as inadequate. In the twentieth century, the nonprofit world expanded enormously. The American concept of welfare changed dramatically with the New Deal and federal commitment to assure welfare for all citizens. This commitment entailed a public–nonprofit partnership; that meant more regulation of nonprofit boards whose moral autonomy was, for better or worse, constrained. Money flowed from the government directly to nonprofits, and indirectly through payment for client services.

The effect was to increase the market force of nonprofits. Giving became an institutional matter in which public and private resources are closely intertwined. Of course individual decisions matter, but they are dwarfed by policy choices. In fact, nonprofit organizations earn half of their income in the market, receiving about a third of it from the federal government, and less than a sixth from private donors.

William Sullivan concludes the volume with a prophetic overview of the changing role of philanthropy in American culture, past and future. Philanthropy, he notes, has meant different things at different times. Americans have difficulty reconciling the increasingly collective, often governmental sources of philanthropic funds with the growing emphasis upon individual donor choice. The deeper problem is a profound ambivalence about institutions, particularly those connected to the government. This ambivalence makes today's philanthropic involvement less than effective in countering the tendency toward an enclave society of greater social inequality and income segregation. People are, unfortunately, less communally involved than Jane Addams would have tolerated, as is illustrated by the widespread replacement of Parent Teacher Associations (part of a national organization) by local Parent Teacher Organizations. Giving after 9/11 has become a "diagnostic moment" in which generosity is tapped in response to the crisis, but chronic problems continue to go unanswered.

We hope these essays will contribute to thoughtful discussions of ways of helping each other. We assume that our readers are persons of good faith, aware of the needs both of others and of at least some of their own needs for help. We are persuaded that really doing good things is not as easy as it may seem, that it calls for judgment, self-discipline, and perhaps restraint as well as generosity and concern for others. From the Grand Inquisitor's commitment to keep people happy by shielding them from the cruel truth of the universe, through the desire of parents to help their children avoid mistakes that will lead to pain, well-intentioned beneficence has led to tragedy. Our individual and collective problem at root is how to nurture and educate the impulse to help, without starving it or so confining it that the miracle of love or care is routinized out of all recognition. We urge reflection, conversation, and civil inquiry into the issues we raise—and others. The extent of human need and the resources at our disposal are almost without measure. Let us seize the opportunities for doing good.

Notes

1. John J. Havens and Paul Schervish, Boston College Social Welfare Institute Working Paper, *Forthcoming Wealth Transfer in 2002 Dollars.*
2. Luke 21:1–4.
3. When we speak of "gifted persons" we refer in a different way to a connection between gifts and identity. Referring to intelligence or athletic talent as a "gift" has a theological connotation. It implies that the quality is not something that the person invented or originated, although it might require cultivation. God or some power beyond the person's control is the source of the gift, but we naturally say that the person "has" the gift. It is an essential component of who he or she is.

Part One: Important Exemplars

1   The Invisible Gifts of Booker T. Washington

Amy A. Kass

> No man whose vision is bounded by colour can come into contact with what is highest and best in the world.[1]
>
> —Booker T. Washington

Everywhere in our country, the vast consequences of September 11th continue, still, to unfold. Conspicuous among them has been the reawakening of our philanthropic imaginations. There is a new moral seriousness abroad, manifested by a redoubled desire to give and to serve, and by new efforts to contribute to the common good. Fueled further by President George W. Bush's "Call to Service," and his creation of the USA Freedom Corps to help foster a "culture of citizenship, service and responsibility" in communities throughout our country, the outpouring of personal and civic benevolence may well become more than a fleeting response to the grim atrocities.

But as everyone knows, benevolence is not yet beneficence. Good will needs both knowledge and effort if it is to issue in genuinely beneficial deeds.[2] Even for someone eager to give, figuring out what to give, be it time, talent, or treasure, is seldom self-evident. A particularly thorny difficulty concerns a gift's effects on the recipient. It is often difficult to know what to give somebody—and how to give it—so that the gift does not accentuate the recipient's sense of neediness, inferiority, or indebtedness. This general problem is made far worse when the beneficiaries start out in a humiliated, debased, or depressed condition, as is often the case with the disabled, the poor, or those permanently bereft as a result of catastrophe. It is made worse still when giving is practiced not to individuals one-on-one in private but is based on lumping people into groups defined solely in terms of their need for generosity. Giving to groups can cause the donor to overlook the fact that each beneficiary is first of all an individual, with personal hopes and fears, joys and sorrows, concerns and circumstances.

Concerns of this sort have long been central in discussions about private charitable giving. But they have acquired special poignancy in our political debates about welfare and affirmative action. Would-be benefactors are struggling to figure out what to do for people whose immiseration has apparently resisted the best efforts of private and governmental programs, which, though well intentioned, have effected no enduring change in these individuals' conditions. In the public and private sectors, there is a growing suspicion that both the content and the manner of past philanthropic efforts may in fact have exacerbated the problem. Not only have these programs done little to enable their beneficiaries to help themselves, but they have also undermined the self-respect of their recipients by making them dependent on forms of assistance that define them solely in terms of their neediness or their inclusion in a group designated as victims. As we search for a wiser and more effective philanthropic approach that will not diminish those it seeks to help, especially in matters involving race and poverty, we should perhaps spend less time looking to Washington the city and more time revisiting Washington the man. Not George, but Booker T.

Why Booker T. Washington?

Booker T. Washington is today largely ignored. He has been pigeonholed as a black thinker concerned only with issues of race, and his teachings on this subject are thought to be, at best, outdated. It is true that he was most emphatically concerned with issues of race. Washington was founder, executive director, prime fundraiser, educational leader, and chief teacher of the all-black Tuskegee Institute, and mastermind of its vast outreach program, the "Tuskegee Machine," a nationwide network of black supporters and black leaders active in every aspect of black life. It is also true that, viewed from the perch of the twenty-first century, many of Washington's teachings seem passé. His insistence on industrial training, for example, seems too narrow, his faith in economic activity too one-sided, and his insistence that blacks eschew the pursuit of political power downright foolish. Everyone knows that many advances in civil rights and equality for blacks in this country were made, and continue to be made, through the pursuit of educational, economic, and political strategies very different from Washington's.

These complaints about Washington are nothing new. In fact, early in the twentieth century, even at the peak of his national prominence, even as he was widely acknowledged as the most respected and most influential black man in America, Washington was himself well aware of the opposition mounting against him. As more and more white Southerners began to regain their lost dominion, as more and more anti-Negro legislation was being passed, criticism, especially from within the black community, became louder and louder.[3] Yet, Washington nonetheless stood firm. Not from narrowness, or naiveté, or, as many increasingly insisted, from fear or servility, but from conviction. For Washington's vision was never "bounded by colour," and however retrograde the particular tactics he advocated seemed back then, or to us today, the idea that informed them—his core teaching—is surely not irrelevant. Not then, not today, not ever.

Most of Washington's critics seem consistently to overlook, neglect, or dismiss Washington's main and enduring insight. Ironically, it was not missed by W. E. B. DuBois, one of Washington's earliest and most severe critics:

> The industrial training of Negro youth was not an idea originating with Mr. Washington, nor was the policy of conciliating the white South wholly his. But he first put life, unlimited energy, and perfect faith into this programme; he changed it from an article of belief into a whole creed; he broadened it from a by-path into a veritable Way of Life.[4]

Behind Washington's much decried tactics was Washington's commitment to a "Way of Life," informed by his singular faith in the importance of self-acceptance, self-knowledge, and above all, self-help.

In his "Atlanta Compromise Speech" (September 1895), the speech that instantly hurled him into fame (and subsequent infamy), Washington conveyed the essence of his teaching about how to live in a parable:

> A ship lost at sea for many days suddenly sighted a friendly vessel. From the mast of the unfortunate vessel was seen a signal, "Water, water; we die of thirst!" The answer from the friendly vessel at once came back, "Cast down your bucket where you are." A second time the signal, "Water, water; send us water!" ran up from the distressed vessel, and was answered, "Cast down your bucket where you are." And a third and fourth signal for water was answered, "Cast down your bucket where you are." The captain of the distressed vessel, at last heeding the injunction, cast down his bucket, and it came up full of fresh, sparkling water from the mouth of the Amazon River.[5]

Washington enjoined his fellow Americans, whites and blacks, to avail themselves of the opportunities before them, not to succumb to past grievances. He urged them to find their bearings by looking to themselves and to one another, not to faraway people or faraway lands. He exhorted them to build up from what they had in hand, not from what they longed someday to have. In short, he called on people to begin now, at home: know where you are, who you are. "Cast down *your* bucket where *you* are." Don't wait for the *Deus ex machina*. Don't ask others to save you. No one can save you if you will not try to save yourself.

At first glance, Washington's teaching might seem to imply, as a corollary, a rejection of philanthropy altogether. The doctrine of self-help might be taken as a warning to any would-be do-gooder to restrain a desire to offer help to others. But a careful study of his autobiographical narrative, *Up from Slavery,* shows that this view is mistaken. For the autobiography not only shows the ground of his faith in self-help and its role in his own remarkable development, but it also makes vivid the way in which the idea of self-help informed his school and the many efforts he made on behalf of others. Thus, it enables us to realize that Washington's insight about how to live is, in effect, also an insight about how—and what—to give. Furthermore, it appears that Washington subscribes to a manner of giving in which recipients are not only not humiliated but are not even compelled to feel indebtedness or to express gratitude, as they sense that the source of the gift comes not from without but from within.

But Washington and his autobiographical narrative commend themselves to us for yet another, perhaps even more compelling, reason. Though he emphasized, in word and deed, the importance of self-help, especially economic and material self-help, Washington's greater gift may well be his invisible gift of hope or inspiration. For this spiritual benefaction, his autobiography is the major vehicle. It enables us not only to behold the great man from afar but also to identify with the young man who pulled himself up from slavery, despite his many trials, *both* inner and outer. As a result, we, Washington's countless readers, are encouraged to believe that we too, with our own power, can liberate ourselves from irrational prejudices, within and without. Like Washington, we too can become truly free and independent. We too can live well and give well. We too can become truly philanthropic—literally, lovers of human beings virtuously disposed to promote the dignity and well-being of our fellows—as well as clearsighted about how to do so. By trying to understand Washington's vision and, better, following his lead, perhaps we too "can come into contact with what is highest and best in the world."

The cynical reader will, likely, sneer at Washington's seemingly unqualified optimism; the sophisticated will no doubt find him quaint; and the academic will look down on his seeming lack of theory or method. But we should all try to resist these prejudices.[6] The stakes are great and the cause is urgent. Since Washington has something important to teach us, we ignore him to our detriment. I shall consider first his view about self-help, then his teachings about helping others, and finally, what his lessons might mean for us today.

Washington's Teaching: Helping Oneself

Washington tells his life story simply and straightforwardly—in fact, so simply and so straightforwardly that one might well have the impression that his rise from the "miserable, desolate, and discouraging surroundings" of his birth to his position of prominence in 1900 was pretty much inevitable. True, he gives us more than occasional glimpses of the struggles he had to endure. But the lack of affect in his retelling takes the sting out of those terrible experiences. Washington seems never to have experienced either the despair or the inner torment that so often accompany hardship and struggle. Once, and on my reading only once, toward the very end of his narrative, does he jar his readers' expectations. Washington, the protagonist of the tale, is here already a man of fame and substance, yet toward the end of the chapter about his success in public speaking, Washington, the autobiographer, inserts a most revealing anecdote.

Commenting first on the kind of audience that he likes best to address, "an organization of strong, wide-awake, business men," he then makes, as we might expect, a brief reference to his own vast and impressive experience: "Within the last few years I have had the privilege of speaking before most of the leading organizations of this kind in the large cities of the United States." This leads him to offer a bit of advice for successful fund raising: "The best time to get hold of an organization of business men is after a good dinner." But then, as we anticipate a lesson about how to speak successfully after dinner to businessmen, he suddenly changes his tone and mood: "I think that one of the worst instruments of torture that was ever invented is the custom which makes it necessary for a speaker to sit through a fourteen-course dinner, every minute of the time feeling sure that his speech is going to prove a dismal failure and disappointment." [7]

Reminded of food, Washington abruptly interrupts his account of public speaking. Quite suddenly, and unexpectedly, he is transported, and the reader with him, back to his life on the Virginia plantation, to his life as a slave:

> I rarely take part in one of these long dinners that I do not wish that I could put myself back in the little cabin where I was a slave boy, and again go through the experience there—one that I shall never forget—of getting molasses to eat once a week from the "big house." ... [o]n Sunday morning my mother was permitted to bring down a little molasses ... for her three children, and when it was received how I did wish that every day was Sunday! [8]

To drive home his point, Washington becomes unusually expansive and, for a brief moment, almost poetic. He provides vivid details about how he held up his tin plate "for the sweet morsel," how he shut his eyes while the molasses was being poured out, how he spread out his two spoonfuls over his plate so that there would be more of it, and so on. At the very end of his reverie, he assures us again that the Sunday special while in servitude was far more enjoyable than "a fourteen-course dinner after which I am to speak." [9]

Washington's sudden nostalgia and uncharacteristic sentimentality, appearing here at the end of his narrative where he is describing the peak of his career in public life, make us acutely aware that Washington the autobiographer wants us to know that Washington the national celebrity never could and never did forget Washington the slave boy. Further, he never took his own celebrity for granted. Where he came from was a permanent and ever-present part of his consciousness. Washington the autobiographer thus tacitly warns the reader not to be taken in by his largely simple, straightforward, and emotionally muted prose. Though the story of his rise from slavery and subsequent success occupies most of his narrative, we are invited to take our bearings, as he continues to take his own, from his slave beginnings and from what it means to be a slave.

Slave Beginnings

Washington the autobiographer begins his narrative in a most conventional way with an account of the time and place of his birth, his ancestry, and his early habits. He seems at first just like many other autobiographers, but his words quickly betray his difference. The very conventionality of the topics he addresses alerts us to the radical unconventionality of Washington, the slave boy.

First of all, he knows precious little about either the place or the time of his birth. There are no records:

> I was born a slave on a plantation in Franklin County, Virginia. I am not quite sure of the exact place or exact date of my birth, but at any rate I suspect I must have

been born somewhere and at some time. As nearly as I have been able to learn, I was born near a crossroads post-office called Hale's Ford, and the year was 1858 or 1859. I do not know the month or the day.[10]

Second, he knows virtually nothing about his family: "Of my ancestry I know almost nothing."[11] That is, he knows nothing beyond his mother and nothing at all about his father. Third, he recalls how, as a young boy, he knew no habits. Not of bathing, nor sleeping, nor eating. He slept together with his siblings on dirty rags on the dirt floor, whenever, wherever. He took his food very much as "dumb animals" take theirs, eating whatever he could find: "It was a piece of bread here and a scrap of meat there. It was a cup of milk at one time and some potatoes at another."[12] Washington shows us, without having to say so, that to be a slave meant living with no name, definition, direction, laws, habits, or conventions. To be a slave meant to be radically rootless and utterly nonconventional. But there was more.

Young Booker lived not only at the behest of his own appetites, but also at the behest of others. He lived in perpetual fear—fear of his own weakness, fear of real and apparent dangers, fear of his master's wrath. Not old enough to perform the regular jobs on the plantation, he did auxiliary service, such as cleaning the yards, carrying water, and taking corn to the mill to be ground. The last left an especially deep impression on him:

> The heavy bag of corn would be thrown across the back of the horse, and the corn divided about evenly on each side; but in some way, almost without exception, on these trips, the corn would so shift as to become unbalanced and would fall off the horse, and often I would fall with it. As I was not strong enough to reload the corn upon the horse, I would have to wait, sometimes for many hours, till a chance passer-by came along who would help me out of my trouble. The hours while waiting for some one [sic] were usually spent in crying. The time consumed in this way made me late in reaching the mill, and by the time I got my corn ground and reached home it would be far into the night.[13]

Traveling home after dark often took him through a dense forest, reputed to be full of army deserters who cut off the ears of young black boys. Arriving home late meant facing the wrath of his master: "I would always get a severe scolding or a flogging."[14]

Fear was the primary passion of the slave boy, but not his only passion. Young Booker also aspired to the goods enjoyed by his masters. His cravings went hand-in-hand with his fears. Indeed, he had two rather focused ambitions. The first, to go to school, he thought well beyond the pale of reasonable earthly expectations, tantamount to going to heaven:

> [O]n several occasions I went as far as the schoolhouse door with one of my young mistresses to carry her books. The picture of several dozen boys and girls in a schoolroom engaged in study made a deep impression upon me, and I had the feeling that to get into a school house and study in this way would be about the same as getting into paradise.[15]

The second, securing for himself the delicacies he saw his young mistresses eat, came to represent the meaning and lure of freedom itself, the sum of all ambition:

> I remember that at one time I saw two of my young mistresses and some lady visitors eating ginger-cakes. . . . At that time those cakes seemed to me to be absolutely the most tempting and desirable things that I had ever seen; and I then and there resolved that, if I ever got free, the height of my ambition would be reached if I could get to the point where I could secure and eat ginger-cakes in the way that I saw those ladies doing.[16]

Such, then, was the meaning and legacy of slavery: anonymity and anomie, fear and envy. True, the "school of slavery" taught young Washington to yearn for freedom, but his diploma signified little about what freedom meant or how to obtain it. By revealing the state of his soul under servitude, Washington, the now free and thoughtful autobiographer, makes abundantly clear to his readers the necessity, but also the insufficiency, of political Emancipation. For the young slave to become truly free would take much more than a legislative enactment. It would require healing the real wounds of slavery that lay deep in the soul.

Up from Slavery

After emancipation, Washington, along with his mother and siblings, traveled by foot to Malden, West Virginia, a distance of several hundred miles. Young Booker passed from the "school of slavery" to the West Virginia Salt Furnaces, from frightening and difficult work to exceedingly frightening and difficult work, from bad living conditions to conditions that were far worse—more crowded, filthy, oppressive, and "shockingly immoral."[17] Though he was no doubt natively curious, it is little wonder that under such wretched conditions the schoolhouses and learning that once represented paradise itself began to fill his every thought. The young boy's desperation and his ingenuity are conveyed both by the fraud he perpetrated in order to get himself into his first schoolhouse, and by the energy and determination he displayed in getting himself into the next.

When a schoolhouse finally opened in his town, young Booker found himself in a tight spot. As his family was strapped for funds, he was granted permission to attend school on the condition that he rise early and work in the salt furnace until nine o'clock. The school, however, was some distance from the furnace and class started promptly at nine. How could he balance duty and desire? An old and thorny problem, but the young boy worked it out, literally by altering time. He adjusted the hands of the clock that regulated the workday in the furnace, moving them from half-past eight up to nine. Never mind that his solution inconvenienced a hundred or more workmen. "This I found myself doing morning after morning," Washington recalls, "till the furnace 'boss' discovered that something was wrong, and locked the clock in a case."[18] But a little schooling whetted his appetite for more.

The first day of school, memorable for most any child, was especially so for

Washington. But the difficulties he overcame in order to get there were as nothing compared to the difficulties he faced once he arrived. Two, in particular, were instructive:

> In the first place, I found that all of the other children wore hats or caps on their heads, and I had neither hat nor cap. In fact, I do not remember that up to the time of going to school I had ever worn any kind of covering upon my head, nor do I recall that either I or anybody else had even thought anything about the need of covering for my head. But, of course, when I saw how all the other boys were dressed, I began to feel quite uncomfortable. . . .
>
> My second difficulty was with regard to my name, or rather *a* name. From the time when I could remember anything, I had been called simply "Booker." Before going to school it had never occurred to me that it was needful or appropriate to have an additional name. When I heard the school-roll called, I noticed that all of the children had at least two names, and some of them indulged in what seemed to me the extravagance of having three. I was in deep perplexity, because I knew that the teacher would demand of me at least two names, and I had only one.[19]

Washington's mother helped him out of the first difficulty:

> She explained to me that she had no money with which to buy a "store hat," which was a rather new institution at that time among the members of my race and was considered quite the thing for young and old to own, but that she would find a way to help me out. . . . She accordingly got two pieces of "homespun" (jeans) and sewed them together, and I was soon the proud possessor of my first cap.[20]

Washington solved the second dilemma himself: "By the time the occasion came for the enrolling of my name, an idea occurred to me which I thought would make me equal to the situation; and so, when the teacher asked me what my full name was, I calmly told him 'Booker Washington,' as if I had been called by that name all my life."[21]

Washington, the autobiographer, leaves no doubt about the lesson he learned (or that we too should learn) from the incident with the hat. It was his first lesson in self-regard, in the difference between taking his bearings from himself and taking them from others. "I have always felt proud," he writes, " . . . that my mother had strength of character enough not to be led into the temptation of seeming to be that which she was not—of trying to impress my schoolmates and others with the fact that she was able to buy me a 'store hat' when she was not."[22]

Though he doesn't spell it out, it is also easy to ascertain the lesson Washington learned from his self-naming. Evidently, the roll call forced the young boy, probably for the first time, to confront his own namelessness and rootlessness as a problem. Sensing that it might be extremely difficult to take his bearings from himself so long as he lacked all self-identity, he created an identity for himself. He thus took his first crucial step toward self-assertion, and hence, toward freedom and independence. In addition, though he very likely did so unknowingly, by taking the name that he did, Washington laid claim to his American heritage, the heritage he had hitherto been denied, the very heritage that would justify his claim to be somebody. As author, then, of his own American identity, it is no wonder that in thinking back over these matters, Washington as autobiographer claims that he was thereafter able to act as if he had been called by the name "Booker Washington" all his life.

Washington's eagerness to continue his schooling grew even greater when he moved from his job in the salt furnaces to a job in the coal mines, work that was more arduous and also more dreadful. Inspiration came when he accidentally overheard a conversation in the coal mine:

> In the darkness of the mine I noiselessly crept as close as I could to the two men who were talking. I heard one tell the other that not only was the school established for the members of my race, but that opportunities were provided by which poor but worthy students could work out all or part of the cost of board, and at the same time be taught some trade or industry.
>
> As they went on describing the school, it seemed to me that it must be the greatest place on earth, and not even Heaven presented more attractions for me at that time than did the Hampton Normal and Agricultural Institute in Virginia, about which these men were talking. I resolved at once to go to that school, although I had no idea where it was, or how many miles away, or how I was going to reach it; I remembered only that I was on fire constantly with one ambition, and that was to go to Hampton. This thought was with me day and night.[23]

Young Booker, age (roughly) eleven, thereafter riveted his full attention on getting to Hampton. But well before he got there he was prepared to receive its lessons, as a result of what he learned in the "school" of Viola Ruffner, the wife of General Lewis Ruffner, the owner of the salt furnace and coal mines. Washington's continued dread of the mines and his dreams of Hampton led him to volunteer for her employ, despite what he knew of her intimidating reputation. Under her tutelage, his early lessons in self-regard and self-assertion were developed and deepened, and he acquired the habits he needed for self-governance and success.

Mrs. Viola Ruffner was a displaced "Yankee," every inch the daughter of the land of steady habits. Herself industrious, fastidious, orderly, clean, punctual, honest, and frank, she insisted on the same in those who served her. "Nothing must be sloven or slipshod; every door, every fence, must be kept in repair."[24] Her respect for people was a function of her respect only for their work. Thus, few servants had remained with her for more than two or three weeks. "I had heard so much about Mrs. Ruffner's severity," Washington recalls, "that I was almost afraid to see her, and trembled when I went into her presence."[25]

Young Washington stayed with Mrs. Ruffner for about a year and a half, long enough to learn her lessons, lessons "as valuable to me," hindsight now assures the autobiographer, "as any education I have ever gotten anywhere since." Finding that she could trust him, Mrs. Ruffner did so absolutely. And, gradually, from fearing her, Washington "learned to look upon her as one of my best friends."[26] Their friendship, though based on utility, was built upon the highest ground: mutual respect. Under the careful scrutiny of Mrs. Ruffner's critical eye, Washington learned to appreciate the importance of doing a job thoroughly and systematically, no matter how small or how large. He saw for himself the connection between competent work and self-esteem. Even more important, he soon learned as well the close connection between competent work and self-fulfillment.

Notwithstanding his success at Mrs. Ruffner's, Washington did not give up the idea of going to the Hampton Institute. In the fall of 1872, now about age thirteen, he made an effort to get there. Endowed with little more than drive and resilience, and no doubt helped by a good dose of luck, he managed to complete the five hundred mile journey all by himself. But it was his application of Mrs. Ruffner's highest of high standards to the task of sweeping a classroom that gained him admission:

> As soon as possible after reaching the grounds of the Hampton Institute, I presented myself before the head teacher for assignment to a class. Having been so long without proper food, a bath, and change of clothing, I did not, of course, make a very favourable impression upon her, and I could see at once that there were doubts in her mind about the wisdom of admitting me as a student. . . . For some time she did not refuse to admit me, neither did she decide in my favour, and I continued to linger about her, and to impress her in all the ways I could with my worthiness. . . .
>
> After some hours had passed, the head teacher said to me: "The adjoining recitation-room needs sweeping. Take the broom and sweep it."
>
> I swept the recitation-room three times. Then I got a dusting-cloth and I dusted it four times. All the woodwork around the walls, every bench, table, and desk, I went over four times with my dusting-cloth. Besides, every piece of furniture had been moved and every closet and corner in the room had been thoroughly cleaned. . . . When I was through, I reported to the head teacher. . . . a "Yankee" woman who knew just where to look for dirt. She went into the room and inspected the floor and closets; then she took her handkerchief and rubbed it on the woodwork about the walls, and over the table and benches. When she was unable to find one bit of dirt on the floor, or a particle of dust on any of the furniture, she quietly remarked, "I guess you will do to enter this institution."[27]

Admitted to Hampton, Washington became, by his own reckoning, "one of the happiest souls on earth."[28]

Washington's demonstrated ability and eagerness to do the most menial job thoroughly and efficiently did more than gain him admission to Hampton. These qualities also paved his way through. His performance so impressed the head teacher who had administered the "exam" that she promptly offered him a job as janitor, and he, in turn, so enthusiastically performed his janitorial duties that he made his services indispensable to the well-working of the school. Washington's success at Hampton paved the way for his call to Tuskegee, and thus, eventually, for his own social and political prominence, and for the happiness and success of the hundreds of students who passed through its halls.

For readers of the autobiography, Washington's story of his successful sweeping functions not only to record the pivotal episode in his life. As one of the most moving and inspiring stories in the book, it stirs the souls of its readers.

Even today, with Washington himself in obscurity, this story is told over and over. Yet, by detaching this story from the larger picture of Washington's life, the people who tell it have missed the crucial lesson: the gift of inspiration is the crucial link between helping oneself and helping others. Washington's school sought to embody and spread the lessons of Washington's life. It offered inspiration and the support needed for others to emancipate themselves from their own despair and self-pity. Inspired by the story, we are ready to join Washington's campaign. We move from self-help to helping others.

Washington's Teaching: Helping Others to Help Themselves

As Washington sat down to write his autobiography, his school was, as usual, very much on his mind. "Much of what I have said," he explains, "has been written on board trains, or at hotels or railroad stations while I have been waiting for trains, or during the moments that I could spare from my work while at Tuskegee."[29] But a quick glance at the autobiography, as a whole, indicates that Tuskegee was the lens through which he looked into his past, and hence, understood his life.

Tuskegee is the explicit subject of the last two-thirds of his narrative, and, we realize in retrospect, the implicit subject of the first third as well. After his arrival at Tuskegee, Washington depicts all of his loves and hates, his pleasures and pains, and his deeds and speeches as intimately connected to its founding and establishment (Chapters VII through XI), and then to its enlargement and perpetuation (Chapters XII through XVII). Each of Washington's three wives— Fannie Smith, Olivia Davidson, and Margaret James Murray—lived and, we infer from his narrative, also died for Tuskegee. Each of Washington's three children—Portia, Booker Jr., and Davidson—earns a place in the narrative as he or she either participates in Tuskegee's activities or benefits from its programs.

Only once does Washington even hint that he might have had a private life apart from his work at Tuskegee: "the time when I get the most solid rest and recreation," he writes, "is when I can be at Tuskegee, and, after our evening meal is over, sit down, as is our custom, with my wife and . . . my three children, and read a story, or each take turns in telling a story."[30] Yet even this diversion is not simply recreational. For it is reported at the end of his chapter on "the secret of success in public speaking," after he has emphasized that the secret of success in public speaking is a well-chosen story:

> If in an audience of a thousand people there is one person who is not in sympathy with my views, or is inclined to be doubtful, cold, or critical, I can pick him out. When I have found him I usually go straight at him, and it is a great satisfaction to watch the process of his thawing out. I find that the most effective medicine for such individuals is administered at first in the form of a story.[31]

Washington's allegedly solid rest and recreation seems but another name for field research, another way of serving Tuskegee. In fact, Washington's written life story, viewed as a whole, makes it difficult to escape the conclusion that it, too, is just one more way of serving Tuskegee. But this should come as no surprise. For the Tuskegee program systematically institutionalized Washington's own journey up from slavery. According to his own narrative, Washington's Tuskegee was, quite literally, Washington's life. By reconstructing his life story in this way, Washington emphasizes the fact that Tuskegee is not only his top priority but that it (or something like it) should become ours as well.

In May 1881, Washington was invited to take charge of what was intended to be a "normal school," that is, a teacher-training school, for black men and women in the little town of Tuskegee, Alabama. From the outset he thought that if the school was to be for blacks, it ought also to be built up and run by blacks. But Tuskegee was situated in the heart of the South, which until sixteen years earlier had been zealously devoted to slavery and had proscribed all books and learning for blacks. Thus, notwithstanding the official support of some of the white people in Tuskegee both for the founding of the school and for him as its leader,[32] Washington anticipated difficult times ahead. He knew, as he says, "the presumption was against us."[33] But he hadn't fully anticipated how difficult the circumstances would be. "Before going to Tuskegee," he writes, "I had expected to find there a building and all the necessary apparatus ready for me to begin teaching. To my disappointment, I found nothing of the kind."[34] Neither had he foreseen exactly with whom his battles would have to be fought and over what sort of issues.

Washington reached Tuskegee early in June and spent the next month searching for accommodations for the school and traveling through Alabama, "examining into the actual life of the people," and trying to drum up interest in his school. Traveling as he did, with mule and cart through back country roads, and eating and sleeping with the people in their cabins, he "had the advantage of seeing the real, everyday life of the people," and learning, first hand, just what sort of education could and would make a difference.[35] Around every bend, he found himself coming face to face with his old boyhood self—many liberated ex-slaves, but very few free men and women.

There were cabins equipped with "showy clocks," sewing machines, and organs, but none of their inhabitants knew how to tell time, work the machines, or play the instruments. There were many people eager and willing to study, but they thought study meant "big books" and "high-sounding" subjects like Latin and Greek, cube root, or banking and discount. Few of these would-be classicists could read or write competently in English; few of the would-be mathematicians or bankers had mastered the multiplication tables. There were many people who wanted to be in school but "as they could remain only for two or three months, they wanted to enter a high class and get a diploma the first year if possible."[36] Everywhere he went he met people who were ill fed, ill clothed, and without any elementary knowledge of personal hygiene. Everywhere he went he met people who regarded school as a way of avoiding work, especially work with their hands. To live by their wits was the common goal.

DuBois once quipped that Washington "learned so thoroughly the speech and thought of triumphant commercialism and the ideals of material prosperity that he pictures as the height of absurdity a black boy studying a French grammar in the midst of weeds and dirt. One wonders how Socrates or St. Francis of Assisi would receive this!"[37] The example is, indeed, Washington's, but the reasoning surely is not. Washington saw as the "height of absurdity" not the black boy's study of French grammar as such, but rather the vast disjunction between the interests and the abilities, the ambitions and the readiness, the hopes and the reality of the "hundreds of hungry, earnest souls" he met. He paid particular attention to the material needs of the people he met (and would later teach), but he was himself no materialist.

In developing Tuskegee, Washington took his bearings from the "real life needs" of his students.[38] Their immediate material needs came first: they needed something to eat, so they learned to clear and farm the land; they needed a place to sleep, so they learned to build beds and houses; they needed to earn a living after they left, so they were trained in practical and marketable skills. Necessity and logic dictated not only what was taught but also the order of Tuskegee's development. But this is only half the story. His month on the road in the Alabama countryside had warned him against too constricted a view of necessity. The "real life needs" of his students were, as his own had been, as much personal as they were economic, as much spiritual as they were physical. Thus, while he kept one eye on developing Tuskegee's buildings and grounds and on sharpening the practical skills of his students, he kept his other on cultivating their personal habits and attitudes (literally, their habits and attitudes regarding their persons).

Although education for work was the core curriculum, students were also taught the care of their bodies and their belongings. They were taught how to bathe, how to care for their teeth, how to look after their clothing, how to eat properly and well, how to care for their rooms. These habits and abilities, Washington believed, were even more important than industrial skills for producing self-regard and self-respect, and for enabling self-governance. Personal self-esteem, more than even material well-being, was Washington's, and hence Tuskegee's, overriding goal. Nowhere is this more evident than in what Washington, following the example of his mentor at Hampton, General Samuel C. Armstrong, called Tuskegee's creed or "gospel," "the gospel of the tooth-brush." Closely examined, it not only bespeaks the heart of the master's fundamental teaching. It also makes clear why living well includes giving well, why caring rightly about oneself requires caring well for others.

The Gospel of Tuskegee

No student was permitted to remain at Tuskegee who did not keep and use a toothbrush. Indeed, after the school's first few years, Tuskegee's emphasis on the toothbrush had become so widely known that students would sometimes arrive with nothing except a toothbrush, convinced that it alone would suffice to make a good impression. "I remember," Washington writes, that one morning, not long ago, I went with the lady principal on her usual morning tour of the girls' rooms. We found one room that contained three girls who had recently arrived at the school. When I asked them if they had tooth-brushes, one of the girls replied, pointing to a brush: "Yes, sir. That is our brush. We bought it together, yesterday."[39]

Under Tuskegee's program of self-discipline and self-care, "It did not take them long to learn a different lesson."[40]

Washington was apparently very serious about the importance of this seemingly minor matter. Twice he connects the toothbrush with the growth and development of civilization itself. Early in his narrative, he writes, "In all my teaching I have watched carefully the influence of the tooth-brush, and I am convinced that there are few single *agencies of civilization* that are more far-reaching."[41] Later, he repeats and extends his observation:

> It has been interesting to note the effect that the use of the tooth-brush has had in bringing about a higher degree of civilization among the students. With few exceptions, I have noticed that, if we can get a student to the point where, when the first or second tooth-brush disappears, he of his own motion buys another, I have not been disappointed in the future of that individual.[42]

Washington does not spell out why the toothbrush is "good news." He regarded the matter as self-evident.

We, however, are likely to laugh at Washington's reverence for the toothbrush. For us, the toothbrush is merely a tool for cleaning our teeth, and brushing, a merely ritual procedure. Brushing our teeth becomes habitual in childhood; once we are adults we just do it. We do not usually regard ourselves as better, or more noble or just, for having brushed. We do it mindlessly and out of routine. Hardly anyone thinks a lot either about brushing or about teeth, except, of course, when our teeth begin to bother us.[43] Yet a little reflection shows the deeper significance of this seemingly trivial ritual.

The neglect of the brush shows itself most immediately in the condition of the teeth. In the short run, the teeth will show signs of what they lately chewed. In the long run, they will decay. "A carious tooth," as the proverb says, "is like an enemy in the mouth," causing difficulties in chewing, swallowing, speaking, and thinking, and producing objectionable odors that imperil social intercourse.

The use of the toothbrush expresses our interest in conserving our health and in safeguarding our appearance. Because no one else can do it for us, tooth brushing manifests our responsibility for ourselves and consideration of others. When we open our mouths to speak to others, we take care not to give offense, refusing to compel others to participate in the aftermath of our incomplete digestion. The toothbrush, then, is an instrument of both self-help and sociability, and its regular use is a sign of our self-respect, self-control, and self-governance, as well as our sense of shame and our concern for others. The well-ordered mouth bespeaks the well-ordered person.

If civilization means, in the first instance, the cultivation of oneself and one's relation to others, then Washington's high regard for the civilizing power of the toothbrush makes sense. For the toothbrush is, in a deep sense, a teacher of how to live: it teaches self-respect through self-governance and, hence, encourages responsibility; it teaches self-help through habituated regular use and, hence, encourages reliability; it links self-concern with concern for appearance and reputation, and encourages consideration of and for others. To say, then, that the toothbrush is "gospel" at Tuskegee means that, at Tuskegee, internalizing system and order, cultivating responsibility and reliability, and fostering dignity and pride come first. A mouth full of brushed teeth is, to be sure, far from freedom and fulfillment, far from openhanded philanthropy. But it symbolizes and embodies the attitudes and habits of life—the disposition—most conducive to their realization.

Washington chose the Fourth of July (1881), as the date for the official opening of Tuskegee. With this reminder of our country's self-declared independence, Washington pointed to his highest hope and purpose: to transform newly freed black men and women into free and independent, self-reliant and self-governing individuals, capable and ready to serve and contribute to their community. Washington's Tuskegee was, first and foremost, a school for human freedom. Work, material wealth, and worldly success were looked upon not as ends in themselves, but as the necessary means for obtaining and perpetuating dignified independence.

The expectations and hopes of the would-be students who flocked to Tuskegee when it first opened were often very different from what Washington had in mind. Yet, as Washington writes with thinly veiled delight, "They were all willing to learn the right thing as soon as it was shown them what was right."[44] Washington was determined to build with them a solid and firm foundation in book learning and in the habits of life. Many came to appreciate and esteem his way, and, more important, to find their own way in life, as human beings and as public spirited citizens, thanks to his guidance. During his thirty-four years at its helm, Tuskegee grew from thirty students to more than fifteen hundred, from a dilapidated shanty plus a one-room church to more than one hundred substantial buildings, from a faculty of one to a faculty of close to two hundred. Its initial small group of backers grew into a nationwide network of supporters. Washington's students cast down their buckets where they were. The waters they tapped by doing so were deep, nourishing, liberating, empowering, and self-sustaining.

Washington and Us

Today's Tuskegee is no longer Washington's Tuskegee. Indeed, notwithstanding Washington's own long and productive tenure, the seeds for change were planted, even growing, well before his departure. Neither the students nor the faculty at Tuskegee were long immune to the social and political changes taking place in the black community. By 1900, as noted earlier, Washington was himself well aware of mounting opposition. Yet, he stood firm. Was he foolish or farsighted? Stubborn or wise? More important, are Washington's teachings really useful today?

It is easy to see why someone might answer, "No." Washington's largely rural America is not our America. Washington knew nothing of the conditions of life in contemporary American cities, nothing of the great variety of the new temptations that now abound. Washington's world and its job market were far less complex than ours; work has changed, keeps changing, and the rapidity of technological advance often makes education centered on work obsolete by the time it is complete. Thus, Washington's much touted core curriculum is both narrow and somewhat simplistic, and the jobs for which he trained his students in agriculture, mechanics, commerce, and domestic service are anachronistic. Washington believed in hard work and "bootstrapping." He often repeated the dictum (attested to by his own life experience), "The individual who can do something that the world wants done will, in the end, make his way regardless of race."[45] But history has shown such methods to be far from foolproof and such dicta naive. Washington was optimistic and hopeful, as another of his often repeated dictum attests: "there is something in human nature which always makes an individual recognize and reward merit."[46] Yet today, pessimism and cynicism seem to be standard fare, and for understandable reasons. All this is true.

But it is not the whole of the truth or even the most important part of it. Washington's life story amply demonstrates that no matter how much times have changed, the fundamental human challenge has not. Washington's autobiography makes clear that he was himself no stranger to danger and fear, temptation and sorrow, racism and oppression, and not even to despair. He was born, recall, in the "midst of the most miserable, desolate, and discouraging surroundings,"[47] a slave among slaves on a Virginia plantation, and his rise was neither easy nor automatic. Washington's life story also makes clear that he was no fool or innocent. He knew that work, no matter how needed or well done, could go unrewarded. He knew that work didn't always pay, literally or figuratively. He knew as well as we the urgency and importance of satisfying material needs and of changing desperate circumstances. But he knew, and better than we, that human needs or wants would grow, even as they were satisfied, and indeed, often as a result of being satisfied. He knew that however much one changes one's circumstances, one still has to take oneself along. Failure to improve oneself internally defeats efforts to improve one's lot. This was Washington's fundamental insight.

Washington understood that slavery was, to begin with, institutional, but that it succeeded so well and for so long, lingering well beyond emancipation, because it took hold of people from within. It deformed their attitudes toward others and the world and, most especially, toward themselves, precisely by rubbing their noses in their own neediness and humiliation. The way up from slavery for Washington and, he thought, for everyone, was necessarily and fundamentally personal and individual, not social or political. It required casting down one's bucket where one was, taking stock of who one was, and measuring the gap between where one was and where one wanted to be. It required acquiring or consciously re-acquiring habits. It required replacing the old toothbrush and starting again—learning system and order, learning to be reliable and responsible, learning dignity and pride in oneself.

If the desire for self-respect or personal dignity is an abiding longing of the human soul, Washington's teaching is surely still useful to us and most especially inasmuch as we aspire to be philanthropic citizens. For though his way up from slavery is essentially personal and individual, and though it fosters self-regard, it neither condones nor encourages a life that is self-centered or self-involved. Quite the contrary. The achievement of independent personhood that Washington both demonstrates and advocates requires caring about and concerning oneself with others. Living well goes hand in hand with giving well.

Precisely because it begins with self-knowledge and encourages the love of one's better self, philanthropy so guided aims, likewise, at the development of the better self of others. It neither valorizes victimhood nor dignifies immiseration. It does not foment or appeal to the guilt of would-be benefactors, nor does it seek to promote generosity under duress. It refuses to maim the spirits of the downtrodden by ratifying their self-proclaimed or assigned inferior position, by exacerbating their sense of indebtedness, or by pretending that victims as victims are or ever can be true heroes. On the contrary, it lifts their spirits by encouraging them to lift their sights. It emphasizes the importance of seeing oneself as an active agent, a prime source of one's own well-being, responsible for oneself and one's conduct, regardless of one's station in life, regardless of one's life circumstances. In every endeavor, no matter how menial or prestigious, it tries to develop the desire, the need, and the know-how to lift up oneself. It holds benefactors and beneficiaries equally to the same high standard, valorizing in both self-respect, self-reliance, and self-command: in a word, their human freedom and dignity.[48]

Such are the teachings of Washington's life story and the standards he would set for would-be philanthropists. Still, one might rightly ask, are these teachings ultimately of any real use to us? Can we really hope to achieve his goals? Here, too, Washington was one step ahead of us. Indeed, offering hope and inspiring the effort to act on it may well be the chief sign of his own true philanthropy and, though even less visible than his other gifts, his most important benefaction. He extends this offering by telling his story in the first person, that is, as an autobiography.

In conveying how he achieved self-esteem and self-definition, Washington, like many autobiographers, looks closely at his own particular beginnings but also moves beyond them. Without telling us that he is doing so, he thereby leads us, his readers, to think about and to appreciate his message even before we hear it. In the very act of reading, we are led to a concern for the importance of attaining individual distinction—both to be distinctive and to make a difference. We are summoned to think about what genuine individuality really means, what it requires, why it is important both for oneself and one's community, and what might be necessary to assure its survival. But the thoughtfulness thus evoked is, by no means, merely abstract.

In the very act of writing, Washington, like all autobiographers, tacitly asserts his independence and self-sufficiency. Literally, he becomes his own author, defining who and what he is. But because Washington actually started life as a slave—from the point of view of social definition, literally, a "nobody"—because he rose to become an important somebody, he is for us, from the outset, more than a mere literary hero. Further, because he takes us inside, emphasizing not only how he lived but also how he felt, exposing his joys and sorrows as well as his strengths and vulnerabilities, reading Washington's autobiography we realize that his rise from nobody to somebody can speak to anybody, including ourselves. Moreover, we also recognize, again from the outset, that his circumstances were far worse than those most of us will ever have to endure. Thus, reading his story engenders, in each of us, not only self-respect but also ammunition against despair. We are inspired to hope—to believe—that we too can achieve the independent individuality he prompts us to reflect upon and esteem, as well as the desire and knowledge to help others gain it as well.

At one point, Washington remarks on the unselfishness of his own teachers at Hampton Institute: "It was hard for me to understand how any individuals could bring themselves to the point where they could be so happy in working for others. Before the end of the year, I think I began learning that those who are happiest are those who do the most for others. This lesson I have tried to carry with me ever since."[49] By presenting this teaching in the form of his own autobiography, Washington has assured that his ability to help others help themselves has continued long after his death. For by reading Washington's narrative thoughtfully, we, his readers and beneficiaries, can answer his invitation to carry on his efforts and to find our own happiness in helping others do the same.

Booker T. Washington claimed that experience had convinced him that "the thing to do, when one feels sure that he had said or done the right thing, and is condemned, is to stand still and keep quiet. If he is right, time will show it."[50] Has not time shown that Washington was right? Isn't it about time for us to go back to Washington?

Notes

1. Booker T. Washington, *Up from Slavery* (Penguin Classics: New York, 1986), p. 229.

2. Few things show this more clearly than some of the complications that have arisen as a result of the wonderful response to 9/11. See, for example, David Smith's brief overview of our collective efforts to do good after September 11

in his introduction to this volume. Consider too the stalled efforts to significantly increase the ranks of Americorps (the government-funded corps of young volunteers), despite the outpouring of citizen interest, thanks to arguments in Congress about, among other things, whether and when to pay volunteers, however minimally.

3. Herbert Storing rightly observed that "the ranks of the [black] 'protest' movement [that evolved in the twentieth century] were . . . largely formed in opposition to Washington and . . . that movement, for all its variety of forms and objectives, still finds its definition in that original protest." Herbert J. Storing, "The School of Slavery: A Reconsideration of Booker T. Washington," in *100 Years of Emancipation*, ed. Robert A. Goldwin (Chicago: Rand McNally Company, 1966), p. 49. This remarkable article, written in 1963, appears as valid today as it was when it was written. Another article that reviews the opposition to Washington, though not through a political lens, is James M. Cox, "Autobiography and Washington," *Sewanee Review* 85 (1977): 235–61.

4. W. E. B. DuBois, "The Evolution of Negro Leadership," *The Dial* 31 (July 16, 1901): 54.

5. Washington, *Up from Slavery*, p. 219.

6. Additional grounds for doing so, perhaps more convincing than those offered here, can be found in the following, more recent, studies of Washington: Louis R. Harlan, *Booker T. Washington: The Making of a Black Leader, 1856–1901* (New York: Oxford University Press, 1972), and *Booker T. Washington, The Wizard of Tuskegee, 1901–1915* (New York: Oxford University Press, 1983). In his masterful two-volume biography of Washington, Harlan makes quite clear that Washington's seeming optimism and simplicity may well have been calculated, and that despite his seeming lack of method, he was a master of strategy. See too Houston A. Baker, Jr., *Turning South Again: Re-thinking Modernism/Re-reading Booker T.* (Durham, N.C.: Duke University Press, 2001). Though, for some, Baker's Washington is likely to fuel the criticism of his naiveté, Baker's own return to the study of the man surely testifies to the enduring importance of the figure he cut.

7. Washington, *Up from Slavery*, p. 245.

8. Ibid.

9. Ibid., p. 246.

10. Ibid., p. 1.

11. Ibid., p. 2.

12. Ibid., p. 9.

13. Ibid., p. 6.

14. Ibid.

15. Ibid., p. 7.

16. Ibid., p. 10.

17. Ibid., p. 26.

18. Ibid., p. 32.

19. Ibid., pp. 32–34.

20. Ibid., p. 33.

21. Ibid., p. 34. Washington's addendum here accounts for his full name: "Later in my life I found that my mother had given me the name of 'Booker Taliaferro' soon after I was born, but in some way that part of my name seemed to

disappear and for a long while was forgotten, but as soon as I found out about it I revived it, and made my full name 'Booker Taliaferro Washington.'" Ibid., p. 35.

22. Ibid., p. 33.
23. Ibid., pp. 42–43.
24. Ibid., p. 44.
25. Ibid., p. 43.
26. Ibid., p. 44.
27. Ibid., pp. 51–53.
28. Ibid., p. 53.
29. Ibid., Preface.
30. Ibid., p. 264.
31. Ibid., p. 243.
32. Tuskegee was a product of black and white Southern initiative. In 1881, Lewis Adams, a mechanic and ex-slave, and George Campbell, a banker, merchant, and former slave-owner, both of Tuskegee, Alabama, secured a charter from the Alabama State Legislature to start a normal school for blacks. General Armstrong, Washington's mentor at the Hampton Institute, had recommended Washington for the job, and though they agreed to hire him, the men who made the request, Washington writes, "seemed to take it for granted that no coloured man suitable for the position could be secured, and they were expecting the General to recommend a white man for the place." Ibid., pp. 106–107.
33. Ibid., p. 145.
34. Ibid., p. 108.
35. Ibid., pp. 111, 112.
36. Ibid., p. 124.
37. DuBois, "The Evolution of Negro Leadership," p. 54.
38. Though many of the practices and, especially, the language used to describe the practices were borrowed from Washington's alma mater, the Hampton Institute, the principles, as will become evident, derive directly from Washington's own experience.
39. Washington, *Up from Slavery,* p. 175.
40. Ibid.
41. Ibid., p. 75; emphasis added.
42. Ibid., p. 175.
43. Following Washington's lead, I abstract here from the evident concern for teeth that is connected to the interest in beautification, namely, orthodontia.
44. Ibid., p. 123.
45. Ibid., p. 155.
46. Ibid., p. 154.
47. Ibid., p. 1.
48. Were Washington alive today, he would very likely subscribe to what we now call "virtue ethics" as the core of philanthropic activity, in respect to both benefactor and beneficiary. For the view he tacitly upholds is that neither can take part in the philanthropic exchange in a nondestructive way without themselves instantiating the self-same virtues—self-knowledge, self-command, and so on. I owe this suggestion to Philip Turner, a co-author of this volume, but Washington's teaching in this regard specifically invites closer reflection on essays by two of my other co-authors, those by David Craig and Paul Schervish.

Though Washington would probably acknowledge the importance of Craig's contention that the best motivation for giving is making a better life possible for another person, would he endorse it? Though Washington's way of thinking about the philanthropic landscape may seem, at first glance, far from Schervish's, isn't Washington, too, looking to develop the "moral citizenship of care"? Doesn't he too regard the identification that each side of the philanthropic divide must have with the other as crucial? If so, might self-help, as the root to better giving, have far wider implications than even I have drawn out?

49. Ibid., p. 66.
50. Ibid., p. 232.

2 Common Work: Jane Addams on Citizenship and Philanthropy

Paul Pribbenow

A Story

Imagine this scene:

It is 1895 in Chicago and a young businessman, who has inherited considerable wealth, learns from family friends of the work being done in one of Chicago's most blighted neighborhoods by a group of women and men who live together in an institution known as Hull-House.

The young man, taught from a youthful age to be concerned about the poor and to be generous with his wealth, contacts the head of Hull-House, a thirty-five-year-old woman named Jane Addams, and says that he wishes to send a check to support her work.

In response, Miss Addams replies that, though she appreciates his interest in the work of Hull-House, she would like for him to come to the neighborhood to talk with others about what his gift might accomplish.

When the young man alights from his carriage on Halsted Street, he witnesses firsthand the squalid conditions in the streets and tenements. When he enters Hull-House he is greeted by youngsters at play in the kindergarten class and is ushered into the comfortable living room, where a small group of men and women has gathered.

In the next hour or so, our young man engages in conversation with Miss Addams, along with several residents of the neighborhood—with Italian and Greek immigrants seeking to make their way in a new country; with a few residents of Hull-House, men and women like Julia Lathrop and Ellen Gates Starr, who live and work in the neighborhood and throughout the city; and with two sociology professors from the University of Chicago, who are working closely with Hull-House to craft plans to make the neighborhood a healthier place to live.

Before he departs Hull-House that afternoon, the young man has gained a keener sense of the needs of the neighborhood, he has participated in conversations about potential responses to those needs, and his philanthropic intention to support the work of Hull-House has become not simply a distant sense of "doing good" for those in need, but an engaged act of mutual support for the human condition.

In subsequent years, the young man participates regularly in Hull-House book discussions, grows to be an advocate for child labor legislation (even urging some of his family friends to be more mindful of how their own businesses inappropriately employ children), and becomes a member of the board of Hull-House. His philanthropic support increases as he gets more and more engaged in the work of Hull-House.

The Moral of the Story

The story of how Jane Addams encouraged a more "humane" approach to philanthropy[1] in her work during the late nineteenth and early twentieth centuries at Hull-House, on Chicago's west side, offers a parable for our contemporary efforts to reimagine the work of philanthropy as a public practice[2]—work we do together, in and through institutions, on behalf of public causes.

This is philanthropy as common work.[3] The story illustrates appropriate and mutual roles within philanthropic organizations for donors, recipients, volunteers, experts, and others, as the valuable work that philanthropy supports is pursued. Why turn to Jane Addams on this topic?

Jane Addams was a remarkable actor in the history of our country. She lived and worked at the end of the nineteenth and the beginning of the twentieth centuries, when significant changes were underway in all aspects of social life: the economy, education, urban development, politics, and the world order among them.[4] She was a dialogue partner with a pantheon of distinguished thinkers and actors: John Dewey, W. E. B. DuBois, Leo Tolstoy, Theodore Roosevelt, and countless other citizens of the world. She, however, chose a particular path for her life in the world, a path embodied in her work at Hull-House. Some have called her America's "only saint" and she certainly is recognized as a world leader; witness the Nobel Peace Prize she received in 1931. But Jane Addams chose as her primary platform her work in the neighborhood around Hull-House. She believed deeply in the social context of human relations and she lived out her faith at Hull-House.

There are many similarities between Jane Addams and Booker T. Washington, whose life is similarly held up for examination on this topic by my colleague Amy A. Kass in her essay. Both Addams and Washington believed in meeting needs where they are found. They both had a sense of optimism that guided their lives and work. Washington, though, is classically American in his concern primarily for the individual, while Addams is focused on the social. Their differing priorities, of course, are the tension at the heart of our American democracy.

How Jane Addams came to understand philanthropy as common work is a story of personal character and civic virtue. It is a story that unfolded over many years in a young woman's life. It is also an instructive story for those of us who care about philanthropy in the twenty-first century.

Consider how fragmented our philanthropic efforts have become. There are real chasms today between donors and recipients, between philanthropic organizations and the wider public, between professional fundraisers and other staff members in the organizations they serve, and so on.[5] Our parable and the story of Jane Addams teach us how to overcome these chasms, to find ways to pursue philanthropy as common work, work that properly belongs to all citizens.

This reimagining of the work of philanthropy in the twenty-first century seems more relevant and urgent than ever. Robert Payton has suggested that philanthropy is a "tradition in jeopardy,"[6] diminished by public misunderstanding and an increasing emphasis on the "business of fundraising." Though there is no denying that philanthropy has become more and more professionalized in our society (on both the giving and receiving side of the equation), the question is whether there are images, metaphors, and concepts that might help us to reframe our understanding and practice of what Payton calls a "mother-tradition" of our democracy.[7]

The parable of philanthropy as common work is one potential source of an image of renewal for philanthropy in the twenty-first century. To make my case, I will tell a more expansive story about Jane Addams and how she came to embrace this common work. I begin with the building blocks of the citizen that Jane Addams became—a brief biography of her vocation as a citizen. With that civic biography in mind, I then explore three themes in Jane Addams's social ethic, the foundation for her criticism of the standard philanthropic practices of her day. These themes illustrate not only the very concrete nature of her perspectives on "humane philanthropy," but also remind us that her perspectives are grounded in a vision of a strong democracy, inhabited by responsible citizens and responsive organizations.

I then will focus my conclusion by describing the implications of this "humane" approach to philanthropy for our own time, suggesting that several lessons may be learned both for philanthropic organizations and for the profession of philanthropic fund raising, two institutions (but by no means the only institutions) integral to the work of philanthropy in the twenty-first century.

The Vocation of Citizen Jane: The Building Blocks of a Civic Life

Jane Addams was born in 1860 in Cedarville, a small town in north central Illinois. Her father, John, owned a mill and was active in state politics. He was a contemporary of Abraham Lincoln, and was the central influence on his daughter. Jane's mother, Sarah, died when Jane was two years old. Her stepmother, Anna, introduced Jane to music, the arts, and literature. Jane was a studious young girl, often sickly, but also curious about the world in which she lived and not shy about exploring the rural countryside with her many brothers, sisters, and stepbrothers.

Most of us know Jane Addams as the founder in 1889 (along with Ellen Gates Starr), of Hull-House, a settlement house on Chicago's west side. To understand why Jane Addams founded Hull-House, we must first understand the citizen she was becoming and the social ethic that she came to value as the basis for her work as a citizen.

I am particularly interested in the notion of *vocation*, defined by theologian Frederick Buechner as that place where our deepest gladness meets the world's deepest need.[8] Four "moments" in the first thirty years of Addams's life seem relevant as she came to understand her vocation: these moments are pertinent to the gladness she found as a citizen meeting needs in our democracy.

The Eyes of a Child

In her autobiography, *Twenty Years at Hull-House,* Addams recounts an incident that occurred when she was perhaps seven years old, when she visited the small city of Freeport, Illinois, near Cedarville, with her father on a business trip. She writes:

> On that day I had my first sight of the poverty which implies squalor, and felt the curious distinction between the ruddy poverty of the country and that which even a small city presents in its shabbiest streets. I remember launching at my father the pertinent inquiry why people lived in such horrid little houses so close together.[9]

With the eyes of a child—and with "that curious sense of responsibility for carrying on the world's affairs which little children often exhibit"[10]—Addams sees and names the inequity that she would fight against throughout her life. At the same time, however, she illustrates through her "pertinent inquiry" the actions of a citizen who seeks both to understand unfair distinctions between peoples and to resolve to make the world fairer.

Seeking the Heroic

Jane Addams devotes an entire chapter in *Twenty Years at Hull-House* to a man she never met and who died when she was but four years old—Abraham Lincoln.[11] There is, however, a clear connection between young Jane's visit to Freeport, where she first recognized an unjust class system in America, and her great love for the life and legacy of Abraham Lincoln, her father's colleague and friend.

Lincoln is one of the great heroes of Jane Addams's life. "Is it not Abraham Lincoln," she writes, "who has cleared the title to our democracy? He made plain, once for all, that democratic government, associated as it is with all the mistakes and shortcomings of the common people, still remains the most valuable contribution America has made to the moral life of the world."[12]

In *Becoming A Citizen: Jane Addams and the Rise of Democracy, 1860–1898,*[13] historian Louise W. Knight describes the influence of Rockford Female Seminary professor Caroline Potter on Addams's understanding of the heroic. A professor of history and literature, Potter understood her primary duty as the teaching of character, "that force that . . . shaped history and supplied the central theme in the study of Western civilization."[14] She therefore lifted up in her courses the persons of character, those heroic individuals worthy of admiration.

Jane Addams came to understand her life and work as the pursuit of the heroic. In her graduation essay at Rockford Female Seminary, Addams writes of Cassandra, tragic heroine of Greek myth, and challenged her classmates to find in the example of the heroic Cassandra the resolve to understand their own calling in the world.[15] Addams foreshadows her own "heroic" aspirations when she claims that "The actual justice must be established in the world by trained intelligence; by broadened sympathies toward the individual man and woman who crosses one path, only an intuitive mind has a grasp comprehensive enough to embrace the opposing facts and forces."[16] Cassandra's story would not be in vain, Addams argues, if the "intuitive" minds of educated women in the nineteenth century were used to face "social ills and social problems as tenderly and intuitively as she can now care for and understand a crippled factory child."[17]

Socialized Education

The experiences and heroes of young Jane Addams's life gave a foundation to the education she received at Rockford Female Seminary. It was an education guided by a fairly rigorous and classical liberal arts curriculum, but more than that, it took place in an institution, "a community led by women that encouraged young women to have ambition. . . . "[18] The school was, in other words, a "dangerous place" for Jane Addams because it raised her expectations for the late nineteenth-century world in which she would live after graduation.

In addition to the strong influence of Caroline Potter, Jane Addams also formed lifelong bonds with classmates and other faculty members. She honed her oratorical skills. She struggled with institutional pressures to respond to the evangelical appeal so prevalent at Rockford, where it was assumed that women were best suited for Christian missionary work. Though Addams remained unconverted while at Rockford (she later was baptized in the Presbyterian Church), she did admit to succumbing to the "beauty of holiness" while reading the Greek testament with her professor each Sunday morning.[19] We might also surmise that Addams took up some of the missionary zeal of the college as she pursued her work at Hull-House.

Perhaps the most important factor of Addams's own education for her later life was her growing belief that education is the basis of strong democracy. In the final chapter of *Twenty Years at Hull-House*, Addams argues that "the educational activities of a Settlement . . . are but differing manifestations of the attempt to socialize democracy, as is the very existence of the Settlement itself."[20] In other words, education (understood in its broadest sense) is at the heart of the civic biography. "[T]hose 'best results of civilization' upon which depend the finer and freer aspects of living must be incorporated into our common life and have free mobility through all elements of society if we would have our democracy endure."[21]

The World Calls

Now grown and graduated from college, Jane Addams set off into the world still looking for aspects of her vocation that would lead her to a civic life. What would she do to make sense of her early life experiences, her heroic aspirations, and her education? She first traveled to Philadelphia to attend medical college. Illness, however, forced her to drop out. Her father died in the summer of 1881, leaving her confused and without an anchor in her life.

Two trips to Europe—in 1883 and 1887—helped to integrate the evolving aspects of Addams's civic biography. She spent nearly two years in her first trip (a fairly common duration for a young woman of her social class) involved in intensive academic study and reflection. She continued to learn, to read, and to be challenged by the great thinkers of human history—but she continued to worry about the utility of her life.[22] What difference would it all make, she asked?

At the end of the second trip to Europe, Addams and her companion, Ellen Gates Starr, visited London, where Addams studied women's trade unions, socialism, and activism. Visiting Toynbee Hall in London's east end, she first learned of the settlement house movement. Founded and led by Canon Samuel Barnett and his wife, Henrietta, Toynbee Hall became Addams's graduate education.[23] The "settlement" had both physical and social forms. Physically, it was a building in a working-class neighborhood where recent college graduates would "settle," living with their neighbors. Socially, it was a community center where people of all classes would find common ground, as well as opportunities for education, recreation and conversation.[24]

The mission of Toynbee Hall was grounded in a belief in the possibility of human transformation through human relations.[25] Idealistic, yes—but ideals were at the heart of Jane Addams's civic biography. The settlement philosophy was guided by the eyes of the child, the heroes who inspire, an education that sets a path of expectation and aspiration, and finally a world that calls for activism and social reform in a particular place, at a particular time, for particular people. Call it applied idealism, but the settlement philosophy became for Jane Addams the integrating theory for her work as a citizen. She summarizes it best in her essay, "The Subjective Necessity for Social Settlements":

> We have in America a fast-growing number of cultivated young people who have no recognized outlet for their active faculties. They hear constantly of the great social maladjustment, but no way is provided for them to change it. . . . Our young people feel nervously the need of putting theory into action, and respond quickly to the Settlement form of activity.[26]

Jane Addams herself seized the opportunity to put theory into action when she founded Hull-House in Chicago in 1889. Citizen Jane thus found the path for her civic life—and the world has never been the same.

The Responsibilities of Being Human:
The Foundations of a Social Ethic

It is no coincidence that Hull-House was founded in the same year (1889) that industrialist Andrew Carnegie wrote his famous essay, *The Gospel of Wealth*. The growing concern about the urban poor and the needs of an increasingly industrialized society in the late nineteenth century led Carnegie to argue that the wealthy had an obligation to act as "trustees of the poor," to develop an ethic of the responsible use of their fortunes.

For Jane Addams, however, herself the daughter of a relatively wealthy family —and looking for ways to respond to the same social circumstances—Carnegie's views contrasted with her sense that what was required of citizens in a democracy was not the redistribution of wealth through philanthropic acts but direct interaction with each other, and a seeking to understand each other's burdens and working together to respond to social issues. Addams also posited an ethics of responsibility, but her responsibility was grounded in her argument that what we must offer each other is our empathy and attention, not simply the riches we accumulate. Knight has suggested that Addams was more concerned about the "responsibilities of being human" than she was about the "responsibilities of wealth."[27]

At Hull-House, Jane Addams found concrete expression of her social ethics. The tenets of her ethic help us understand her notion of "humane philanthropy."

Citizenship and Philanthropy

Jane Addams came to her work at Hull-House with an enigmatic upbringing. As the daughter of a wealthy family, she had the means to be philanthropic in the traditional sense of her times. At the same time, however (as we have seen), there is good evidence that even at an early age, Addams was concerned about the plight of the less fortunate and also struggled with understanding her role as a woman of means who wanted to help others.[28]

There is considerable research on how Jane Addams reshaped public understanding of the role of women in late nineteenth- and early twentieth-century America.[29] Suffice it to say that for Addams, the issues surrounding the role of women in society are part of a larger philosophical framework in which she attempted to frame a balance between individual motivations and responsibilities and common ends and purposes. Addams was interested in "human fellowship"[30] and she interpreted much of the social and political life of her day in light of her concern that all citizens be able to play effective roles in democracy.

This sense of citizenship and our common humanity meant that, for Addams, philanthropy—properly understood—was the work of citizenship. Philanthropy was public work, meeting the needs of all citizens of a democracy. In this sense, the work of Addams and her colleagues at Hull-House surely was philanthropic in the broadest meaning of the concept—namely, loving humankind.[31]

All citizens had both needs *and* something to offer others, Addams argued, and Hull-House sought to be an institution in which all might both receive and give. Clearly the poor had very real needs. The neighborhood around Hull-House presented concrete, pressing issues about health, safety, and opportunity.[32] The poor, though, also offered Addams and others lessons of "uniform kindness and courtesy."[33] At the same time, there were working people living in the neighborhood who also had stakes in the well-being of the community. These residents perhaps had the resources to make ends meet, but they still had the need to better themselves and their environment. In return, these working people—usually recent immigrants—taught others about their cultural traditions and practices, enriching the neighborhood. The wealthy who—like our young businessman—sought to make a difference in the Hull-House neighborhood also had Addams's respect—not because of their wealth, but because of their common struggle to make sense of their lives in the world. There is nothing in Addams's writings that express anger or resentment about the wealth of others.[34] In fact, Addams shows great interest in the wealthy as people whose motivations may be puzzling and sad (e.g., George Pullman as described in Addams's essay, "A Modern Lear"),[35] but who deserve an opportunity to find a role in the common humanity she so valued.

For Addams, the practice of philanthropy—loving humankind—then becomes the work of citizenship. And there is no more important work.

Citizenship as Mutuality of Interests

Perhaps the clearest statement of Addams's social ethic appears in the introduction to her *Democracy and Social Ethics*:

> We are learning that a standard of social ethics is not attained by traveling a sequestered byway, but by mixing on the thronged and common road where all must turn out for another, and at least see the size of one another's burdens.[36]

In an essay entitled "A Modern Lear," Addams applies her standard of social ethics specifically to what she calls the "liberal philanthropy" of her day. Here she analyzes the Pullman Company strike of 1894 and concludes as follows: "Modern philanthropists need to remind themselves of the old definition of greatness: that it consists in the possession of the larger share of the common human qualities and experience, not in the acquirements of peculiarities and excessive virtues."[37]

The comparison of George Pullman, owner of the Pullman Company, to Shakespeare's King Lear remains instructive today. Pullman had created a company town on Chicago's southeast side. The workers lived in company-owned houses and made their purchases at the company store. When the workers decided to strike, Pullman was outraged at their ingratitude for his largesse. Like Lear, whose anger was aimed at his daughters for their lack of appreciation of his generosity, Pullman simply could not understand how his workers could want more than he was "giving" them.

For Addams, the claim upon Pullman—as for all citizens of a democracy—focused primarily on overcoming social and economic class differences. In *Twenty Years at Hull-House,* she notes, "Hull-House was soberly opened on the theory that the dependence of classes on each other is reciprocal; and that as the social relation is essentially a reciprocal relation, it gives a form of expression that has peculiar value."[38]

The implications of this belief in the mutual dependence of the classes is a critique of the power imbalance that normally ensues when those of wealth deem it appropriate to share their wealth with those in need. Addams comments on this issue in her essay "The Objective Value of a Social Settlement": "I am always sorry to have Hull House regarded as a philanthropy, although it doubtless has philanthropic tendencies, and has several distinct charitable departments."[39] Her point is that philanthropy, as understood in her own time, often conflated the needs of the poor with a moral judgment about the recipients of charity. She says, instead, that what Hull-House was organized to provide was recognition and stimulation of the aspirations of the neighborhood residents, with the means of attaining them to be put at their disposal.[40] Humane philanthropy thus helps to build and sustain the web of mutual interests, the work of common purpose, rather than perpetuating the class differences and power imbalances that characterize philanthropy in the industrial age.

The Work of Organizations

Given her strong commitment to the mutuality of interests and to the work of citizenship in a democracy, it is no surprise that Addams sought in her work at Hull-House to create an organization that provided opportunities through its various programs and activities for all citizens to interact in pursuit of common goals and a healthier democracy.

As Addams writes in *Twenty Years at Hull-House:*

> The one thing to be dreaded in the Settlement is that it lose its flexibility, its power of quick adaptation, its readiness to change its methods as its environment demands. It must be open to conviction and must have a deep and abiding sense of tolerance. . . . It must be grounded in a philosophy whose foundation is on the solidarity of the human race, a philosophy that will not waver when the race happens to be represented by a drunken woman or an idiot boy.[41]

The point is that authentic philanthropic organizations must be organized according to the values espoused (in this case, human solidarity). These organizations must be accountable for their activities in light of those values and the wider environment. And they must be inclusive, always adapting to meet the needs of all they serve, no matter how difficult that may be. The work of Hull-House, well documented as it is in Addams's writings and those of countless biographers and observers, offers a compelling illustration of how the work of authentic organizations is genuinely philanthropic, seeking to "love humankind." Such work is not always successful—witness the various projects that Addams admits failed to accomplish their purposes[42]—but the organization is nonetheless accountable for its activities in pursuit of human solidarity and a stronger democracy.

What Our Parable Means for Philanthropic Organizations and the Fundraising Profession

To take seriously the moral of our parable for our work in philanthropy is not to be nostalgic or sentimental about a supposed better time and place; rather, it is to see whether or not we can make sense of the principles of Jane Addams's civic biography, social ethic, and work at Hull-House for our contemporary circumstances. I suggest that there are at least six implications of our parable for the common work of philanthropy in the twenty-first century—three implications each for philanthropic organizations and the fundraising profession.

I have chosen to focus my conclusions on these two institutions in the contemporary work of philanthropy because I believe that philanthropic organizations and the fundraising profession are situated as crucial aspects that encourage a vision of philanthropy as common work in the twenty-first century. There are, of course, other important roles in the work of philanthropy—individual and organizational donors, volunteers, professional associations, and so forth—but I believe that the facilitating role of philanthropic organizations and the fundraising profession deserve special attention.

Implications for Philanthropic Organizations

The diversity of organizational missions and programs—along with geographic, demographic, and scale differences—sometimes makes it difficult to draw firm conclusions that are relevant to all organizations involved in the philanthropic sector in our country. It is possible, however, to define three simple ideas that are common to the work of all philanthropic organizations:

- Philanthropic organizations are governed by a *public service mission*
- Philanthropic organizations are *accountable to a variety of publics* for the efficacy of their mission-based work
- Philanthropic organizations have *a moral purpose* as they serve public interests and goods

In light of these defining characteristics, the implications of a vision of "humane philanthropy" for such organizations include:

Philanthropy is a core value of the mission of all philanthropic organizations.

Addams criticized the more narrow understanding of what she called "liberal philanthropy" and suggested instead that genuine philanthropy describes the work of citizenship in a democracy. Nonprofit organizations must embrace the fact that they are, by definition, philanthropic institutions (legally, financially in most cases, and morally) and that the practice of philanthropy belongs to all members of the organizational community. Without philanthropy as a core value of their missions, nonprofit organizations fail to honor the public trust they enjoy and must uphold as fellow citizens of a democracy.

Positioning philanthropy as a core value of organizational mission has concrete implications for the ways in which organizations function. For example, an institution's strategic planning process that names philanthropy as a core value for an organization will challenge its board and staff to think strategically about how philanthropy is integrated into all aspects of the organization's work. The results of such planning might include relocating the fundraising office to a more visible and central location; involving a wider group of organizational staff in building philanthropic relationships (e.g., including faculty members in a college or social workers in a counseling agency); and establishing a more proactive communications program that seeks to build relationships by engaging and informing constituents about how philanthropy transforms organizational work.

Philanthropy as common work implies aggressive public accountability.

The fact that philanthropic activity is common work (an obligation of all organizational constituencies and publics) means that the organization "owes" its various publics honest, candid, and regular reports on what it does well (and not so well). Addams argued for the need of all citizens to be offered the tools and opportunities to play a role in society—and then she demanded that they be responsible and accountable for how well they played their roles.

I have argued elsewhere that too many philanthropic organizations wait for accountability to be imposed by funding sources or regulatory agencies.[43] Instead, philanthropic organizations must pursue accountability, gathering evidence and sharing findings with all relevant constituencies as part of transparent efforts to build trust and accountability for the work done on behalf of public goods and interests. For example, at one institution we developed a newsletter that was sent to all organizational constituents after each meeting of the board of directors; the newsletter informed them of how the board was fulfilling its governance responsibilities on behalf of the organization's various publics.

> Philanthropic organizations must link the values of their missions with their day-to-day business and management practices.

In other words, philanthropy as common work means that the well-being of staff and volunteers, the good stewardship of organizational resources, the fair and responsible implementation of policies and procedures, and so on are as important as the pursuit of particular programs. Organizations must have integrity—the right and moral fit between mission and institutional practices.

The vices and virtues of organizational life are known to all of us who have devoted our lives to working in institutions. Philanthropic organizations have a special burden to pay close attention to the fit between the values as stated in organizational mission and the ways in which we do our work on a daily basis. For example, the strategic plan and mission for my organization claims that we seek to create a civil and responsive organization. The fit between that part of our mission and how we treat each other as we work together is a concrete illustration of how philanthropy helps to ensure organizational integrity.

Implications for the Philanthropic Fundraising Profession

The remarkable growth of the fundraising profession in America during the past thirty years parallels an increasing reliance on these professionals to manage the philanthropic work of organizations.[44] The "professionalization" of fundraising—as important as it is to increasing technical sophistication and success—sometimes leads to a skewing of the appropriate roles of all participants in the common work of philanthropy.

The vision of philanthropy as common work challenges the fundraising profession to see its work not as a substitute for the responsibilities of various participants in a philanthropic community but as facilitators of philanthropic work. There are three specific implications for the fundraising profession:

> Philanthropic fundraisers must recognize and embrace their public roles.

Philanthropic fundraisers who help society pursue philanthropy as common work must both provide responsible service to the nonprofit organizations that employ them and to the publics whose trust is at the core of philanthropic activity. These public roles might include modeling volunteer service, pro bono professional assistance, and a willingness to advocate for philanthropy in their communities. Jane Addams herself offers a role model of the philanthropic leader who devoted herself to a particular institution while also participating broadly in organizations and causes that promoted public goods.

This claim has clear implications for the loyalties of professional fundraisers. Imagine a situation in which a fundraiser is working with a prospective donor to her organization. In the course of the relationship, it becomes clear to the fundraiser that the donor cares more deeply for the work of another local philanthropic organization. What duty does the fundraiser have to help counsel the donor to direct her personal philanthropy to causes and organizations of greatest meaning and import to her life? What about her loyalty to the organization that pays her salary? These are important questions raised by imagining the fundraiser's role in relation to the public practice of philanthropy.

> Philanthropic fundraisers must endeavor within their organizations to model philanthropy as common work.

Fundraisers must advocate for programs and policies that focus on donor interests, that challenge all organizational constituencies to participate in philanthropy (and facilitate such participation), and that are fully accountable to organizational publics. In other words, philanthropic fundraisers must be facilitators and teachers of responsible citizenship in the organizations they serve. The residents of Hull-House were first and foremost teachers in the various activities they planned and managed.[45]

Fundraisers are uniquely situated to help make philanthropy a daily practice within organizations. In a talk to a group of college faculty members, I once described my vision of philanthropy as common work. After my presentation, a chemistry professor remarked that in all his years of work at the college, no one had ever suggested that he could participate in the work of philanthropy as anything other than as a "leech" (his language!). My challenge was clear. I needed to create appropriate ways for the faculty member to participate in philanthropic work for the college—perhaps meeting with prospective donors to discuss his work, helping to shape proposals to foundations, and reviewing language about chemistry that appeared in college publications. This is an example of philanthropy as common work.

> Philanthropic fundraisers must seek to illustrate through their individual and corporate activities a model of professional activity that is publicly accountable.

Philanthropic fundraisers have the remarkable privilege to be present when others make moral decisions about supporting causes they care deeply about. This privilege carries with it the obligation to be self-critical, to pursue personal and organizational integrity, to keep confidences, and to keep the social relationships that philanthropy creates in proper perspective and balance. This is common work and fundraisers must be its conscience.

Philanthropic fundraisers clearly are situated to care for the gifts that are given to an organization. There are many technical aspects to these duties, but there also is a vocational aspect to that work—it is the work of stewardship, of caring for gifts that belong to someone else. As the fundraising profession evolves, the example that Jane Addams and her work at Hull-House illustrates for us is that the work of philanthropy—stewarding gifts of time, personal resources, institutional integrity and mission, and public trust—is a daily responsibility that demands both a vision and the personal skills and values to make that vision a reality. In the end, perhaps it is the personal example of Jane Addams that is most crucial to my argument. It was her vocation to be a citizen of our democracy, and she embodied in all that she did a sense of stewardship for the gifts and the work that sought to make humane philanthropy and healthy democracy a reality.

The life and work of Jane Addams and our parable of philanthropy as common work challenge all of us who care about the practice of philanthropy in the twenty-first century to examine the abiding links between individual responsibility, common purpose, and the well-being of our democracy. How does our deep gladness meet the world's deep needs in the work of citizenship and philanthropy? I believe that as we answer that provocative question—as Jane Addams did more than a hundred years ago—we will find both the means and the resolve to reimagine the public practice of philanthropy and the crucial roles we all play in the work we share.

Notes

1. Louise W. Knight, "Jane Addams's Views on the Responsibilities of Wealth," in *The Responsibilities of Wealth*, ed. Dwight Burlingame (Bloomington: Indiana University Press, 1992), pp. 118–19. It is important to note that Addams herself used the word *philanthropy* sparingly—and usually in a pejorative way. She railed against the liberal philanthropy of her day that, she believed, perpetuated the gaps between people. I am going to use philanthropy in a way that I think is true to Addams's vision of citizenship, though I recognize it is not the language she would have used.

2. The concept of "public practices" is described in Robert Bellah and William Sullivan's "Professions and the Common Good: Vocation/Profession/Career," in *Religion and Intellectual Life*, Spring 1987, pp. 7–20. Bellah and Sullivan define public practices as the activities that help a national community to define itself, affirm its common end, and promote its life (p. 16). They point to education, justice, and health as examples of public practices around which the work of professions is given meaning. See Paul Pribbenow, "Pursuing Accountability: Organizational Integrity, the Advancement Profession, and Public Service," *The CASE International Journal of Educational Advancement*, February 2001, pp. 197–208, for a fuller description of how the public practice of philanthropy grounds the work of the fundraising profession. I recognize that the language of "practices" can be interpreted to presuppose a certain historical-boundedness to those who learn and live out the practices. I want to argue that the aspirations of the public to affirm its common ends and promote its

life, though certainly not universal and immutable, can be described in at least "interim" and "evolving" terms, enough to warrant our abiding public discussions about goods we might hold in common. The idea of a public philosophy provides both a theoretical and practical framework for understanding how these public conversations might occur. See William Sullivan, *Reconstructing Public Philosophy* (Berkeley: University of California Press, 1986), for a fuller discussion of public philosophy.

3.   See essay by David Craig in this volume. Though Craig has chosen to introduce the language of "giver" and "taker" to more clearly distinguish the appropriate roles for individuals in philanthropic communities devoted to visions of the good life (and to overcome the misperceptions caused by contemporary philanthropic language), I think there is strong resonance between Addams's vision of citizenship and philanthropy—what I am calling "philanthropy as common work" and Craig's notion of recovering the agency of individuals in the philanthropic project.

4.   Jean Bethke Elshtain, *Jane Addams and the Dream of American Democracy* (New York: Basic Books, 2002), p. xxii.

5.   Witness, for example, the recent Illinois lawsuit *Madigan* vs. *Telemarketing Associates,* which pitted various philanthropic organizations (via *amicus* briefs) against each other over an issue that focused on the first amendment rights of donors versus those of philanthropic organizations.

6.   Robert W. Payton, "A Tradition in Jeopardy," *Philanthropy and the Nonprofit Sector in a Changing America,* ed. Charles Clotfelter and Thomas Ehrlich (Bloomington and Indianapolis: Indiana University Press, 1999), pp. 495–97.

7.   Ibid., p. 485.

8.   Frederick Buechner, *The Hungering Dark* (New York: Harper Collins, 1969), pp. 31–32.

9.   Jane Addams, *Twenty Years at Hull-House* (New York: Penguin Putnam, 1961), p. 2.

10.   Ibid., p. 3.

11.   Ibid., pp. 15ff.

12.   Ibid., p. 27.

13.   Louise W. Knight, *Becoming a Citizen: Jane Addams and the Rise of Democracy, 1860–1898* (Chicago: University of Chicago Press, forthcoming 2005).

14.   Ibid., 4:7.

15.   Mary Lynn McCress Bryan, Barbara Bair, and Maree De Angury, *The Selected Papers of Jane Addams,* vol. 1: *Preparing to Lead, 1860–1881* (Urbana and Chicago: University of Illinois Press, 2003), pp. 428–30.

16.   Ibid., p. 429.

17.   Ibid.

18.   Knight, *Becoming a Citizen,* 4:1.

19.   Addams, *Twenty Years,* p. 33.

20.   Ibid., p. 295.

21.   Ibid.

22.   Marilyn Fischer, *On Addams* (Toronto: Thomason Wadsworth, 2004), pp. 3–4.

23.   Knight, *Becoming a Citizen,* 7:7.

24.   Ibid., 7:19.

25.   Ibid., 7:20–21, 24–25.

26.   Addams, *Twenty Years,* pp. 79–80.

27. Knight, "Jane Addams's Views," p. 118.
28. Bryan, et al., *The Selected Papers*, pp. 318–19; Elshtain, *Jane Addams and the Dream of Democracy*, pp. 156–57.
29. Gioia Diliberto, *A Useful Woman: The Early Life of Jane Addams* (New York: A Lisa Drew Book/Scribner, 1999), pp. 16–18.
30. Addams, *Twenty Years*, p. 17.
31. For an interesting extension of this notion of moral citizenship and philanthropy, see Paul Schervish's essay in this volume.
32. Addams, *Twenty Years*, pp. 103ff.
33. Ibid., p. 73.
34. Knight, "Addams's Views," pp. 126–27.
35. Jean Bethke Elshtain, ed., *The Jane Addams Reader* (New York: Basic Books, 2001), pp. 163ff.
36. Addams, *Democracy and Social Ethics* (Urbana and Chicago: University of Illinois Press, 2002), p. 7.
37. Elshtain, *The Jane Addams Reader*, p. 172.
38. Addams, *Twenty Years*, p. 59.
39. Jane Addams, "The Objective Value of a Social Settlement," in *Philanthropy and Social Progress*, by Jane Addams, Bernard Bosanquet, Franklin H. Giddings, J. O. S. Huntington, and Robert A. Woods (Montclair, N.J.: Patterson Smith, 1970), p. 55.
40. Ibid., p. 55.
41. Addams, *Twenty Years*, pp. 83–85.
42. Ibid., pp. 89–90.
43. Pribbenow, "Pursuing Accountability."
44. The Association of Fundraising Professionals (AFP), the largest professional association for philanthropic fundraisers, has seen its membership increase fivefold since 1985.
45. Addams, *Twenty Years*, pp. 279ff.

Part Two: Deciding Whom to Help

3   The Give and Take of Philanthropy

David M. Craig

Along with religion, sex, and politics, we might add *giving* to the list of topics that many people avoid in everyday conversation. I am not thinking of the secrecy needed to surprise loved ones with gifts at special occasions. I am thinking of the reluctance that many people seem to have about discussing their philanthropy with other people. There are various motivations for giving, of course, and perhaps the people who talk most freely about their philanthropy give primarily to reinforce their social standing. This kind of talking about philanthropy is not what I mean when I say that we need to engage in more public conversations about giving.

In the United States, at least, we can draw an imperfect but instructive contrast between conspicuous consumption and inconspicuous philanthropy. Americans are often equally comfortable showing off and talking about their purchases of consumer goods. Discussing the use of money for purposes of consumption is relatively easy because it involves little more than stating personal preferences. Conversations about consumption presuppose room for disagreements over trivial differences in tastes. When we move to discussing the use of money, time, and talent for philanthropic purposes, however, we declare our commitments. As if articulating those commitments for ourselves were not difficult enough, discussing philanthropy with other people subjects our commitments to their scrutiny and judgment.[1]

I propose that our difficulties in talking about philanthropy have a great deal to do with the broader challenge of articulating a robust understanding of the good life. I do not mean the term *good life* as it is sometimes used today, signifying the life of leisure and consumption sold by advertisers. Again, philanthropy concerns more than personal tastes; otherwise, the subject would be much easier to discuss. I mean the *good life* in Aristotle's sense of it. For him, the good life consists in the pursuit of that set of ends and goods that together constitute human flourishing. In his *Nicomachean Ethics*, he describes the virtues—that is, the cultivated traits and habits that dispose a person toward excellence—that he deems necessary if one is to be able to live such a life and to be recognized by others as living well. As he conceives the good life, it is normative in the sense that specific ends, goods, and virtues are necessarily of value because they comprise the best kind of life for a human being.

My thesis in this essay is that people give on the basis of their vision of a good life. They value some set of activities and goals and they see that the pursuit of these activities and goals requires the existence of societal conditions and the development of personal capacities. Perhaps now we can see why discussing one's philanthropy can be so difficult. It is hard enough to clarify how one arranges the various components of a good life for oneself. It is far more challenging to state out loud why other people's lives would be bettered through the gifts that one chooses to make on the basis of one's own vision of such a life.

In this essay I urge givers to articulate their conception of a good life more clearly and to assess their giving in that light. I also offer assistance in meeting these daunting tasks. In the first part of the essay, I address the question, why do people give? I develop my argument that people's giving is motivated by visions of the "good life." In the second part of the essay, I model a way of applying this concept to philanthropy to help givers clarify their goals and set priorities in deciding where to give. I borrow from Martha Nussbaum's recent attempt to recast Aristotle's conception of the good life in terms of the "central capabilities" of a good human life. In the concluding part of the essay, I turn to the issue of how givers should relate to those who receive their gifts. I propose a shift in terminology here. I view the parties in a philanthropic relationship as *giver* and *taker*, not *giver* and *recipient*. Admittedly the new vocabulary is morally troubling because of the pejorative connotations of *taker*. It captures, however, the importance of agency in my way of thinking about philanthropy. The goal of philanthropy should be to develop other people as they seek to pursue their own vision of a good life. The active term *taker* conveys this sense of agency in a way that the word *recipient* does not. The term *taker* is also helpful for understanding the word *giver*. To be a giver, one must have taken a great deal from other people in many ways. Indeed, one of the most important reasons to be a giver is the recognition that we take turns as takers, too. Although I develop this argument at the end of the essay, my discussions of why and where people should give are directly related to it.

Why Give?

Not all giving is inconspicuous, of course. Gifts of talent and time tend to be public in a way that gifts of money need not be. Investing talent or time engages a person in a philanthropic effort, usually with other people. This public expression of a person through direct involvement in specific activities and goals is central to the approach I am advocating. Although money does not require a direct involvement in the same way, gifts of money can be made in a public way, too. The rite of passing the plate is a visual performance of an act of worship, a shared commitment to a community and a not so subtle nudge to pay one's dues. Gifts to establish named foundations and institutions are clearer examples of what we might call conspicuous philanthropy, at least as judged by the headlines that they command.

Interestingly enough, it is this conspicuous philanthropy that marks the highest form of giving for Aristotle. In his account of the virtues required for the good life, he describes two that center on giving gifts to others: liberality and magnanimity. Magnanimity has pride of place for him, and the "magnificent" or "magnanimous man" is that well-off male citizen who gives great gifts in a public manner.[2] The word *public* has two meanings here. The magnanimous gift is public in the sense of contributing to the good of the community.[3] This emphasis on the public good is often cited as the principal motivation for or object of philanthropy.[4] The magnanimous gift should also be public, however, in a way that borders on showiness, a declaration of one's position and attainments and, thus, a display of one's capacity to do good for others on a grand scale.[5] The many historical examples of men *and* women whose monetary gifts created named institutions and foundations in the United States reflect a similar mixture of seeking to do good in order to be seen by others as living well.

I claim that this connection between doing good and being seen as living well is integral to much philanthropic giving. It is noteworthy, therefore, that the desire to be recognized for one's gifts is often criticized on religious and moral grounds. Authorities in both Judaism and Christianity praise the anonymous gift over such public displays.[6] In these faiths, the only recognition that finally counts is God's, though these traditions are replete with scriptural, Talmudic and theological elaboration about what exactly is most pleasing to God when giving to others. The influence of these two religions on the West helps explain why the apparent mixing of altruistic and egoistic motives in philanthropy raises moral hackles.

Aristotle's approach, which makes the attainment of excellence the goal of human action, does not separate altruism and egoism by refusing praise for such deeds. Nevertheless, he still offers a way of distinguishing gifts that deserve recognition from gifts that do not. He appeals to a conception of the good life that involves as a central part of it contributing to the good of other people. Those contributions can have two objects: they can enhance the *general conditions* for or other *people's capacities* for the pursuit of the good life. Both considerations will be central to my discussion of where one chooses to give. More importantly for now, we can see that Aristotle supports the argument that philanthropic gifts should serve others before oneself. But he challenges the notion that people should give out of a vague desire to improve the public good with no concern for how their gifts relate to everything they care most deeply about in their own lives.

Clearly anonymous giving does occur, perhaps most often where a religious virtue of humility is put at a premium, though preserving community and protecting individual dignity are other important reasons for giving anonymously, too.[7] What is rarer than anonymous giving and almost inconceivable to me is giving that entirely removes from consideration the giver's own vision, however vague, of what makes for a good life. While I acknowledge the variety of motivations for giving, I can now restate my thesis more fully. In my judgment, the chief *moral* motivation for philanthropy is not some general desire to enhance the public good, but a more personal desire to make a better life available to another person. The giver's vision of this better life for other people is inextricably bound up with his or her own understanding of the content, shape, and goals of the good life, in Aristotle's robust sense of the term.

In short, I propose that some notion of the good life does and should function as the lens through which givers make their giving decisions. This approach to thinking about giving cuts through some of the contradictions between idealized portraits of philanthropy and actual giving behavior.

As already emphasized, this approach admits praise as a just reward for doing good. The desire to be seen as a "good person" in one's own or others' eyes need not taint philanthropic motivations. To the contrary, publicly recognizing people's gifts can provide worthy examples that others might imitate. Not only are givers' motivations answerable to their conception of the good life, however. Their philanthropic aims may also seek to form other people's lives in the image of their own. Taken together, this deeply personal element in philanthropic motivations and aims helps account for a key feature of giving in the United States today. Susan Ostrander and Paul Schervish observe that "consumption philanthropy"—which they define as "contributions to churches, schools, cultural institutions and professional organizations, from which givers and their families benefit directly"—is the "largest single category of philanthropy" in this country.[8] If I am right that giving decisions typically answer to one's vision of the good life, then this fact should be not surprising. One's sense of what is necessary to such a life will lead one to support those organizations that sustain key parts of the good life as one sees it—not only for oneself, but for others, too.

A further point follows from this observation, though it puts consumption philanthropy in a more critical light as I intend to do in this essay. The readiness to give to organizations that share one's commitments and that enhance the pursuit of the good life as one sees it highlights significant obstacles to the approach I am advocating. The problems can be illustrated by using Aristotle once again. As noted, he reserves special praise for the "magnanimous man." This great respect reflects the direct correspondence that Aristotle charts between having cultivated the virtues necessary to the good life and being able to know, as a result, what is good for the community. The magnanimous man warrants honor and imitation because, in exemplifying the good life through his actions and his judgments of what to give to others, he grasps and displays both his own and the community's good.

Aristotle makes two assumptions that are untenable in a pluralistic, democratic society. He presumes that there can be a single, authoritative conception of the good life, and he accords the authority for determining its contents to the wise who, in his view, are a select group of men.[9] Imagine Bill Gates as the magnanimous man and everyone taking moral cues from him. The uniform conception of the good and the good life that Aristotle presupposes falters in light of the diverse views that people hold in this country and elsewhere. In addition, the hierarchical structure of his good society adds yet another concern. Given these problems, I focus not on Aristotle's conception of *the* good life, but on people's visions of *a* good life. I borrow selectively from him, therefore, abstracting his concerns with human development and the contents of good lives from the historical practices and hierarchical society that shaped his understanding of both. Two likely objections confront my strategy.

First, for Aristotle, not everyone is capable of the good life. Women, artisans, slaves, and aliens are excluded, and few men attain its full flowering. So, by claiming that people should give on the basis of their vision of a good life, am I simply providing cover for the wealthy and other powerful people? If givers rightly support the organizations and causes that sustain a good life as they see it, then must recipients simply accept these "wise" efforts for their own good?

I use the language of *giver* and *taker* partly to undercut the power and paternalism implicit in such a structure of philanthropic relationships. There is a moral distance between givers and takers, I argue in the final section of this essay, and respecting this distance means that takers' visions of good lives count, too. In discussing the setting of philanthropic priorities elsewhere in the chapter, I also encourage givers to practice another kind of critical distancing. Givers cannot simply focus on the excellent activities and achievements they most admire today. They need to remember the many gifts of sustenance and assistance that they have taken in becoming able to develop the personal capacities and to enjoy the societal conditions required for such pursuits.

The second objection to my approach is more practical. In calling givers to clarify their visions of a good life, I may be asking too much.[10] One reason that people do not typically ask themselves, "What is my vision of a good life?" is that the answer is already built into their lives. Through personal histories, ties with family and friends, obligations to work and community, affiliations with a religious congregation or civic organization, people find themselves in certain activities and groups that have specific goals. People have good reasons to value the relationships and commitments that structure their lives, which partly explains why givers often support the nonprofit organizations and programs that either they or their friends, family, and colleagues know best.

The tendency to give through local or communal networks of associations and to rely on the value grid and broader ties of one's tradition is an important theme in several essays in this volume. John Langan emphasizes the Catholic principle of subsidiarity that favors addressing social needs at the least centralized level possible. Philip Turner argues that Christians in general are justified in putting their relationships with coreligionists first when the core commitments of their fellowship are placed in jeopardy. He adds that ignoring one's particular loyalties as a giver is unrealistic and likely to lead to half-hearted, ineffective, or even harmful philanthropy. Elliot Dorff richly details how discussions of ethical issues facing Jewish nonprofits proceed from the sources, norms, and values of a long-standing, though continually interpreted, practice of holiness. The motivations for and shape of *tsedakah* similarly reflect the ongoing efforts of Jews to understand and act on a common, if complex and contested, tradition.

My focus on individuals' visions of a good life may seem to set aside this broader context of people's religious or communal reasons for giving. That is not my aim. Although I do not discuss special relationships in this essay, the kinds of reflection about inherited commitments and priorities that Turner and Dorff discuss fit with my goal of encouraging public conversations about giving and good lives. The conversations I envision can and do take place within religious congregations, community foundations, corporate boards, and so on. Even where norms and values are broadly shared, as in a religious tradition, there will be considerable debate, and asking how one's vision of a good life relates to traditional teachings can be a mutually clarifying exercise. When conversations cross religious, cultural, political, economic, and gender lines, agreements may be harder to come by, but these broader conversations match Langan's call for solidarity, too. Clearly the efforts at personal reflection and public conversation that I am encouraging do not start from nowhere. They may also be very difficult to achieve. Indeed, how can givers even begin to articulate their different visions of good lives, let alone engage in discussion with other people?

Where to Give?

I turn now to Martha Nussbaum's use of the so-called "capabilities approach" to human development. Important for my purposes is her account of the "central capabilities" of a good human life. Two features of her approach are most helpful. First, like Aristotle she emphasizes the need to foster the *general conditions* for and *people's capacities* for the pursuit of the good life. Instead of discussing virtues, however, she focuses on developing people's "capabilities," that is, what they can do and be as people.[11] Second, she outlines what she calls a "thick" but "vague" conception of the human good. It is "thick" in that she aims to include what everyone would agree are the necessary component parts of a good human life. By describing these central capabilities in "vague" terms, however, she acknowledges that individuals and cultures will describe and rank them differently.[12] In my judgment, Nussbaum's list is a valuable aid to personal decisions and public conversations about where to give.

Let me emphasize why I am using Nussbaum's scheme of "central capabilities." I want givers to clarify their vision of a good life and its relationship to their giving. Simply knowing where to begin is hard. I offer Nussbaum's scheme as a starting point. Her scheme consists of ten interrelated capabilities, all of which she claims are necessary to a good human life. Despite her insistence on these ten central capabilities, she recognizes that the contents of a good life must be debated and detailed. She locates these deliberations in political debates, and she assigns governments the task of guaranteeing the conditions for people's development of their capabilities. Here she ignores the limits that critics would draw around her broad view of state activism. I will return to this point later. She also neglects the efforts of nonprofit organizations and the private giving that contributes to their work.[13]

How might Nussbaum's account of capabilities be used to think about giving? Due to its length, I cannot include her full description of these central capabilities. I summarize her ten categories to indicate the breadth of her account and its controversial aspects. This synopsis also highlights the fact that capabilities are interrelated—that they are all integral to a well-developed life. Indeed, part of what makes her list valuable as a starting point for reflection and discussion is that it prompts us to ask how the various component parts of her list support or conflict with each other. Nussbaum's "central capabilities" are as follows:

1. Life (centers on concerns about life expectancy and avoidable morbidity)
2. Bodily Health (includes shelter and nourishment, along with "reproductive health")
3. Bodily Integrity (involves freedom of movement and "sovereignty" over one's body in matters of assault, abuse, and consensual sexual conduct)
4. Senses, Imagination, and Thought (emphasizes education and culture and religious and expressive freedoms in being able to use one's mind and to experience meaning, beauty, and pleasure)
5. Emotions (focuses on fostering a rich and unstunted emotional life and, by extension, on sustaining relevant "forms of human association")
6. Practical Reason (means the ability to "form a conception of the good" and to direct one's life accordingly)
7. Affiliation (involves concern for and cooperation with people in friendship and work and in relationships of equal dignity with people who are distant due to geography, culture, "race, sex, sexual orientation, religion, caste, ethnicity or national origin")
8. Other Species (acknowledges interdependence with "animals, plants, and the world of nature")
9. Play (includes laughter and recreation)
10. Control over One's Environment (includes "political" control in the form of rights to political participation and "material" control in the form of property rights, backed by the opportunity for work so as to benefit from them)[14]

I do not share Nussbaum's confidence that everyone would agree to these basics as she outlines them. Her emphases on individual rights and bodily integrity and her lack of explicit attention to forms of association like the family are issues with which some would certainly disagree. I want to emphasize, therefore, that givers who find her list unsatisfactory should feel free to develop their own list of central capabilities. My approach does not require her list; I use it as one possible way of describing a good life as requiring developed capabilities.

Let me offer a personal anecdote to indicate why the language of capabilities is so valuable for thinking about philanthropy. Sometimes I feel that there is no limit to the worthy causes clamoring for contributions, and this impediment can be a barrier to my deciding to give in general. Despite this feeling, I have no compunctions about refusing every telephone request to support some group. A letter might get my response, I tell them, but not a phone appeal. Then although I try to remain calm, invariably my blood boils. I sense that my reaction is not simply due to the doggedness of these telemarketers in refusing to respect my wishes. By trying pitch after pitch, they restate their cause in order to fire my moral imagination, repeatedly demanding a response to the unspoken question, "Don't you care that other people need your support just to live their lives as you do?"

I place myself on the couch to invite readers to consider how philanthropic giving appeals to judgments about the worthiness of causes based on how well they serve other people's lives. Consider, by contrast, another sort of ethical appeal. Several years ago, the ethicist Peter Singer argued in *The New York Times Magazine* that for people with family incomes of $50,000 or more, it is a moral duty to a contribute at least 40 percent of their earnings to feed starving people overseas. He bases these figures on the utilitarian calculus of the greatest happiness of the greatest number. He weighs the pleasures purchased by spending this "extra" income on luxuries against the pains allowed by not sending the money to save the hungry.

It is noteworthy, however, that Singer opens his piece by comparing the refusal to forgo extras in order to feed the hungry to a scene from a Brazilian movie, *Central Station*. As he relates the scene, a woman buys a television set with part of the thousand dollars that she has received for delivering an orphan boy to people who, she later finds out, intend to kill him by harvesting his organs for sale. She must decide whether or not to take the television back so that she can return the money and save the boy.[15]

In recounting this vignette, Singer actually appeals to such capabilities as *life* and *bodily integrity,* contrasting their moral force with the woman's desire to enjoy a little *play* in her dreary existence.[16] This part of his argument, I contend, is far more likely to inspire reflective giving than the part of his argument that relies on the abstractions of utilitarian philosophy. When asked to give or when told about some gift, our vague notions about what comprises a good life—notions we might not have known we had—take on greater prominence, if not much clarity.

What follows is an effort to model a series of steps that givers can take to clarify what they see as the component parts of a good life and how this structured vision of a good life relates to their giving goals. I chart four main steps in this process, culminating with some general guidelines about setting giving priorities. I also encourage givers to explore where they draw the lines between government and nonprofit efforts in the task of developing people's capabilities. Knowing one's sense of the division of labor between these two sectors helps determine one's priorities and responsibilities as a giver. Although I use Nussbaum's list and my own examples, givers should not feel limited by either. The approach will be effective only if givers look to their own histories and concerns. Finally, while I model these steps as an individual, the approach works just as well as an aid to discussions and debates among groups of givers, from congregations to corporate boards.

Detailing Goals

Since many givers have a track record, a good first step is to chart one's giving history. How much talent, time, and money has one given to which types of organizations? In analyzing past giving and in planning future giving, givers should characterize these "types" according to the capabilities that each organization develops. On Nussbaum's scheme, for example, support for an art museum would seem to be directed toward cultivating the *senses, imagination,* and *thought.* Identifying the relevant capability is only the first step. More important is considering how exactly giving to this organization might enhance that capability. A gift to an art museum presumes that displaying works of art for other people's enjoyment, study, and inspiration is educational. In making significant works of culture available to the general public, these institutions insist that "the people" all share a rich artistic history, one not reserved for an elite. Exposure to a sampling of the history and variety of artistic expression deepens people's explorations of beauty, hope, suffering, place, etc., in their own and in others' lives. It can also spur creative initiative in museum visitors who were previously unaware of their own artistic sympathies or gifts.

Note that I have already begun to detail how I envision an art museum's contribution to a specific capability. Having that capability in view frees up those details. If I did not have a scheme of capabilities before me, I would find it far more difficult to describe the purposes that I ascribe to these institutions. Here we see the efficacy of a "thick" but "vague" list. It is thick enough to focus my attention on the specific aims that I might seek in helping to develop other people's capabilities. It is vague enough to invite my own reflective efforts in describing these aims in detail.

This combination of thickness and vagueness has a further benefit. Other people will specify the contributions of art museums differently as they decide what really counts for them in cultivating the *senses, imagination,* and *thought.* Consider, for instance, the dual emphasis on free expression and religious meaning in Nussbaum's description of this capability. There will continue to be disagreements about controversial exhibitions of artworks that parody religious symbols. Instead of simply stopping conversation and giving in these cases, however, I suggest that these controversies might now move toward a bit more clarity, though I hardly expect them to vanish.

While I believe that specifying lines of disagreement is usually a productive process, what is most important at this stage is that givers start by detailing their goals. I have used the example of an art museum. The same process of identifying the capabilities served by the other organizations one supports and describing those capabilities in one's own terms can be undertaken for all of one's giving. Having clarified one's goals at the level of distinct capabilities, one will be better positioned to begin deciding where best to direct one's gifts. Which organizations support the goals one has detailed, and which of those organizations target their resources most effectively? Maybe different nonprofits match one's philanthropic purposes better than do groups on one's current giving list.

Coordinating Efforts

This initial example simplifies the exercise of clarifying philanthropic goals. Gifts to art museums can target multiple capabilities, not just one. Despite the stultifying atmosphere of some of these institutions, they are places of *affiliation* and *play,* potentially at least. Art museums might be encouraged to support the capability of *affiliation* by exhibiting more works by people from unfamiliar cultures. Similarly, photography exhibits that blend formal technique with sympathetic renderings of silent suffering or dignifying portraits of dishonored differences can also invite a broadened sense of relationship with distant others. Combining the goal of educating the *senses, imagination,* and *thought* with the goal of cultivating *affiliation* (and possibly *play* as well) reinforces the need for programs that introduce school-age children to art, contributing to cultural literacy and cross-cultural understanding simultaneously.

Here we shift from the level of distinct capabilities to the interconnections among them. Indeed, a full scheme of capabilities is valuable in helping to move givers from *ad hoc* donations to a more coordinated approach. The first step is to consider how this coordination in support of related capabilities might happen within a single organization. The arts outreach program that teaches schoolchildren about cultural differences is a good example. In addition, givers should consider how different organizations might coordinate efforts. Museum outreach is likely to be more successful if students have already gained an interest in art through classes in the schools. Here we encounter the shifting line between private giving and public funding, but the issue of coordination on behalf of human development is more complex than simply combining public and private efforts. Nonprofits have their own coordination to do, and givers need to be aware of this challenge.

Consider, for example, the complex mission of shelters for women and children who are escaping from domestic violence. These shelters provide space and protection, two "general conditions" required for a good life. These general conditions are important, however, because they allow people to develop and exercise a wide range of capabilities.

Nussbaum's scheme is particularly instructive for thinking about the interactions among capabilities in this case. She defines domestic violence as a denial of *bodily integrity* and names "adequate shelter" a part of *bodily health.* Thus, her focus on capabilities highlights just how much work these women and the shelter's staff may have to do. Providing space and protection meets only the first need. To help abuse victims recover a full sense of health and safety in their lives, or, perhaps, become capable of experiencing these "states of being" for the first time, these shelters must foster other capabilities, too. A good example is exercising *control over one's environment,* though the material and political control that Nussbaum celebrates might appear hopelessly out of reach in such circumstances. Indeed, traumatic experiences of violence can jeopardize nearly all of one's capabilities. As a result, assistance with *emotions* and training in *practical reason* are also essential to the difficult transformations that these women may have to endure.

No doubt the challenge of coordination affects service providers most directly. Even so, givers should consider the need for integrated strategies to see if the groups they support are able to serve all of the requisite capabilities. If not, there may be other groups that do, and it may be wise to redirect one's support toward them. Realistically, though, no one organization can develop a complete set of capabilities. There will often need to be broader coordination among various nonprofits. Here givers may be positioned to offer valuable perspective and guidance. While individual givers might be unable to sustain a broadly integrated approach—there are, after all, only so many hours one has to give—groups of givers, like religious congregations, can adopt a coordinated strategy. Whether through monetary allocations or volunteer networks, a group of givers can help integrate the work of different organizations. Along with supporting a shelter, the group might assist a program for young boys that models respectful behavior. Advocating on behalf of affordable housing for single-parent households could fit here, too. The more broadly coordinated the group's strategy is, the more the group can make the goal of improving general conditions for human development part of the narrower task of developing specific capabilities.

Once again, different individuals and groups of givers will view the interactions among capabilities in terms of their own visions of a good life. Their sense of the necessary general conditions will differ, too. Nussbaum's approach, for example, conceives individual agency in a way that makes marital and familial ties expendable if they prove harmful. Thus, she links the fostering of a rich emotional life to those "forms of human association that can be shown to be crucial" to its development.[17] The verdict is out for her on just what shape these associations should take. In the case of domestic violence, this is appropriate. Critics of Nussbaum's account might object, however, that the problems that battered women's shelters address are symptoms of the breakdown in families and the religious and community networks and pressures that once helped to sustain them.

My concern is not to wade into debates about the family. I simply want to note that this objection does not vitiate a capabilities approach. The objection does not deny the need to develop capabilities or the importance of individual agency. It reflects, instead, a disagreement about how to characterize the capability of *affiliation* and the general conditions of human flourishing. As such, the objection should prompt further reflection about how best to conceive capabilities, envision their interconnections, and describe the general conditions for a good life.

Anticipating Conflicts

The conflicts that arise from different descriptions and from different lists of capabilities are not the only conflicts to consider. Even if capabilities are often integrated with each other, there will be occasions when particular capabilities have to be privileged and tradeoffs must be made. Environmental causes highlight the need to examine such conflicts.

Of the ten capabilities on Nussbaum's list, the main one served by environmental groups is that of *other species*. Several conflicts are immediately apparent. If *life* includes preventing the "avoidable morbidity" that goes with malnutrition and if *bodily health* requires "adequate shelter," then developing these capabilities would seem to entail the need to farm agricultural lands more intensively and to press on into new territories for growing food and building homes. Both strategies destroy existing habitats, a condition necessary to cultivating a capability of living "with concern for and in relation to" a wide variety of other species.[18] Likewise, *material control over one's environment* underscores another conflict—the conflict between the need to respect private property rights and the need for public oversight of shared natural resources and common ecological threats.

Perhaps the capabilities approach reveals its limitations here. Arguably, the conflicts are so pronounced in this case because an anthropocentric focus on developing *human* capabilities is antithetical to environmental concerns. In my judgment, though, an approach that calls attention to conflicts has great value because it presses to the fore the difficult but necessary questions of what ends to seek and how best to arrange them. This approach also has the flexibility to make a concern for *other species* central to a good life by reshaping a host of other capabilities. A reverent wonder before the world's intricacy and beauty might be cultivated as vital to rightly tuned *emotions* and to a meaningful exercise of the *senses, imagination,* and *thought.* Even capabilities that conflict with *other species* can be brought into greater compatibility. Increased agricultural production is not the sole requirement for *life.* Concerns for *life, bodily health,* and *play* can all justify protecting water, air, land, and other resources. Similarly, if *political control of one's environment* includes ensuring a voice for the powerless, then the disadvantaged citizens who tend to live in the most degraded areas can speak up more effectively, both for themselves and for environmental health.

Clearly the issues raised by this example are complex, and they reach beyond the task of clarifying one's giving goals. Nevertheless, the exercise of anticipating conflicts among capabilities is a valuable step toward a more reflective practice of giving. Thus, if givers choose to support environmental groups, they should consider how attentive different groups are to such conflicts. Some organizations devote themselves entirely to regulatory advocacy and litigation, leaving no room for solutions that balance property rights with habitat protection. For some givers, this hard-nosed approach may be necessary to the fostering of a completely neglected capability. Other organizations join these legal actions with public education about nature's splendor. Still others promote farming and forestry practices that seek more "kindly use" of land both in this country and abroad.[19] The organizations' strategies are myriad, and givers should direct their support toward the groups that best match their own philanthropic aims. If not, their gifts may prove counterproductive to their goals.

Prioritizing Aims

So far I have discussed several types of organizations that benefit from philanthropy. There are many others that I have omitted. I have chosen these examples partly because they reflect some of my concerns. They also allow me to touch on each of the central capabilities on Nussbaum's list. In walking through the steps of detailing goals, coordinating efforts, and anticipating conflicts, I have concentrated on the fit between a giver's vision of a good life and the nonprofit organizations through which he or she might choose to give. The institutional mechanics of most philanthropy justifies this organizational focus. A further act of moral imagination is called for, however, because one's gifts are usually not meant to serve the nonprofit. The philanthropic concern should be the people the organization serves, at least if I am right that the chief moral motivation for giving is to make a better life available to others.

Here my approach can seem dizzyingly open-ended. There are countless people whose lives might be bettered and various ways to make this happen. One's gifts are not unlimited. Choices have to be made; priorities must be assigned.

In the literature on the ethics of giving, gifts are sometimes divided into categories of mercy and excellence.[20] Gifts for the sake of mercy alleviate people's suffering or meet their most basic needs. Gifts for the sake of excellence promote the advancement of knowledge, the improvement of public spaces, the achievements of artists and athletes, and so on. These goals take well-developed people and further their accomplishments, enhancing their own and others' lives.

While alleviating suffering and meeting basic needs might seem to be privileged outright on moral grounds, there are reasons to object to this judgment. Gifts for the sake of promoting excellence may contribute significantly to many people's lives. Supporting cutting-edge medical research can improve the general conditions for people's health. Or consider gifts to one's alma mater. As the Latin implies, these institutions nurture their graduates' values and goals. Gifts back to them reflect not simply a sense of gratitude, but also a desire to instill those values and goals into a continuous stream of like-minded people.[21] The Aristotelian insistence that training into a good life is requisite to knowing how to live well *and* knowing how to promote the community's good is, arguably, most clearly at work in alumni donations and volunteerism. Such gifts underscore the attractions of supporting nonprofits that promote one's vision of a good life and enable other people to attain the kinds of excellence that one values.

Given the close connection that I see between individuals' visions of a good life and their philanthropic goals, givers will have strong personal reasons to assign priority to gifts of excellence. If making a better life available to other people requires development of those people's capabilities, however, the issue is more complicated. A capabilities approach puts mercy and excellence on a continuum. As a concept, capabilities aim at excellence, but they begin with acts of mercy. In other words, a person's development requires considerable assistance from other people until it reaches a level where it can begin to build on itself. Nussbaum captures this point by observing that capabilities have minimal thresholds. Only after crossing these thresholds does a person find himself or herself in "conditions and circumstances in which a good human life may be chosen and lived."[22]

How does this consideration apply to giving? It reminds us that mercy is not simply a matter of staving off immediate needs. Ideally, gifts of mercy help people become capable of developing themselves.[23] If people can take charge of their lives only after they have crossed over these thresholds of capability, then this is a compelling reason to put gifts of mercy before gifts of excellence. But considering the range of capabilities on Nussbaum's list, where should such mercy be given first? We can begin to answer this question by asking how these categories might be ranked in order of importance.

One reason to assign high priority to a specific capability is how central it is to the full scheme of human capabilities. *Life* can be construed as a precondition for all of the goals, activities, and aspirations of a human life. *Bodily health* could be, too. Nussbaum names *practical reason* and *affiliation* her core capabilities because they make all of the others "human," that is, they are the capabilities of agents who can plan a life and relate to other people as an equal.[24] Depending on the giver's experience or vision of a good life, other capabilities might be seen as basic, too.

Here, then, is a first general guideline in setting one's giving priorities. The more basic a capability is to human development, the needier are the people who are deficient in it.[25] Even if capabilities can only be grouped in tiers of importance, this exercise can be valuable. It can help givers decide to ignore some capabilities, even if there are people who exist far below the minimal threshold in those areas. If we think back to Singer's use of the film *Central Station*, the moral force of that example arguably reflects the greater significance of *life* over *play*. This ranking of capabilities is by no means the only consideration in setting priorities, however.

As previously noted, people's capability deficiencies will often not be limited to one area. This observation justifies a second guideline in setting priorities. Where people are broadly deficient in their capabilities, their needs will also be relatively greater. This warrants not only providing more aid in these cases, but also considering where the aid has the most efficacy. Take, for instance, my discussion of environmental causes. I noted the importance of ensuring political voice for the powerless who live in degraded areas. In fact, efforts of this sort can lead to a host of changes if the voiceless are then able to advocate for changed conditions that better allow them to cultivate a full range of capabilities.

A third general guideline is that givers should understand where people's capabilities are not just underdeveloped, but also compromised. My example of a battered women's shelter is a case in point. Overcoming the trauma of domestic abuse involves more than developing a sense of *bodily integrity* and *affiliation* and a healthy balance between them. Domestic violence creates harmful patterns that also must be addressed. Such entrenched obstacles add a further reason to increase one's giving commitments.

A fourth general guideline is that givers should examine how these various instances of capability deficiency may result from prevailing social, economic and political conditions. Even if a certain capability is less basic or less central than the others, it may be so threatened that additional support is justified. A giver might be especially concerned to promote *play* in the form of jungle gyms or music festivals in some blighted neighborhood, even if he or she sees other capabilities as having more overall importance in people's lives. A corollary to this guideline is that greater priority should be granted where there is a clear lack of public funding and private giving. So, for example, proponents of educating the *senses, imagination* and *thought* through music and art might devote their volunteer efforts to an area of the public school curriculum so prone to the budget axe.

The first three guidelines, at least, seem likely to push givers away from "consumption philanthropy." A complete turn in that direction, however, is unrealistic given what I have said about the importance of one's vision of a good life to philanthropy. Nor do I think that a wholesale shift is desirable. My final guideline acknowledges that givers have good reasons to support organizations from which they benefit directly. Simply put, givers know that the groups they participate in help to sustain a good life as they see it. The guideline, though, is this: givers should still take steps to extend as widely as possible the benefits these groups make available. Gifts to a college or congregation are examples. The benefits of higher education can be spread through scholarship funds and the recruitment of needy students. Congregations can be encouraged to direct more of their annual budget toward charitable relief and social action, and to make their facilities available for public and civic events.

Animating these guidelines is the recognition that a good life consists not simply in what the giver values most in his or her present life. The fruits of one's development as a person require having taken many steps *and* having accepted many gifts in getting there. One risk of the approach I am advocating is that givers may overlook all that they have taken, concentrating instead on the achievements that they most admire right now. Perhaps the Aristotelian emphasis on human excellence is a liability here. Indeed, apart from the religious practices and teachings and the communal commitments and relationships that often stretch people beyond themselves, their families, and their peers, how can a capabilities approach justify not only the relative priority that I assign to gifts of mercy, but also a basic duty to give?

This essay has moved from a descriptive claim that people give to make a better life available to other people and onto a normative model and a set of priorities for giving well. As noted above, I fully accept that givers should be praised for their excellent acts, but justice is not one-sided. Giving is one of many activities that people can practice well, but not without having benefited from many other people's contributions to their own development, whether through direct support or through all of the efforts that sustain a common good. The praise due to givers who give well reflects, then, a recognition by others that this person is acknowledging and reciprocating for the benefits that have enabled him or her to pursue a well-developed life. In this sense, the "giving" of philanthropy is a fitting answer to all of the "taking" required for human development.

Justice entails giving others their due, but this due may be measured in terms of merit, need, or equal treatment. The first two criteria help show important connections between philanthropy and justice. If giving well *merits* praise, then judgments of givers' merit should be based, in part, on how well their gifts meet other people's *needs* as these people develop and exercise their capabilities. A full scheme of capabilities like Nussbaum's is a good reminder of the many needs that other people will have as they seek to lead good lives. Conversations with other people, including the potential takers of one's gifts, can help ensure that the priorities one sets as a giver reflect as complete a vision of a good life as possible.

Personal and Public Responsibilities

I have pressed the capabilities approach in a new direction. As noted before, Nussbaum charges governments with ensuring citizens the wherewithal to reach the minimal thresholds of human development. For her, the requisite deliberations are a matter of political debate. Maybe the difficulties and the potential divisiveness of the approach that I am advocating make the machinery of politics and the agencies of the state the only appropriate vehicles for choosing and providing the types of assistance that I envision. Arguably, individual givers do not have the expertise to answer the complex questions of need posed by these general guidelines. Perhaps givers should be free to support whatever groups and projects inspire them, without having to ponder how mercy and excellence relate to a good life.

Up to this point, I have set aside the relationship between public programs and private philanthropy. This division of labor must be addressed now because it is implicated in the task of setting giving priorities. Givers are tax-payers, too, and philanthropy operates alongside and often in conjunction with the state's efforts.

Consider one famous philanthropist's views on the proper division of labor between public funding and individual giving. The steel magnate Andrew Carnegie argued in his *Gospel of Wealth* that philanthropists should concern themselves with the aspiring human spirit alone. He supported libraries, cultural institutions, universities, research hospitals, public parks, pools, church buildings, and organs "to give those who desire to rise the aids by which they may rise." By contrast, gifts of mercy only deepen the plight of the "irreclaimably destitute, shiftless, and worthless." Governments, not individuals, are responsible for doling out mercy, understood by Carnegie to include meeting the immediate needs of the destitute and isolating them from the industrious.[26]

In the previous section, I noted that expecting givers consistently to privilege mercy over excellence runs counter to my thesis—that people give to make a better life available to others in view of the giver's own vision of a good life. Carnegie's rhetoric is shot through with appeals to the good life and the managerial virtues that make for a vigorous pursuit of excellence. But I challenge his single-minded devotion to excellence as another extreme invited by too sharp a distinction between mercy and excellence. Even as he derides the people who fail to provide for themselves, he does not deny that there is a certain shared responsibility for meeting their basic needs. He simply assigns this responsibility to governments. Of course such a "public" responsibility cannot be met without the political will and fiscal support of citizens.[27]

For this reason, individual givers should examine their giving priorities in light of their view of the proper role of the state in the task of developing capabilities. Is the state the only agent charged with this task, as Nussbaum suggests? Is the state responsible only for meeting basic human needs on a temporary basis, as Carnegie claims? Is the state perhaps better at assisting some capabilities than others? These are just some of the relevant questions, but the moral is clear. If philanthropy answers to a desire to make a better life available to other people, then one's personal responsibilities will be set in part by one's political commitments. If one has a broad view of the state's responsibility for human development, then one should promote such policies and the taxes to pay for them, while tailoring one's personal giving to other areas or to complementary programs. By contrast, if one has a minimalist view of the state's responsibility, then one's giving should be increased accordingly and directed more toward gifts of mercy.

This line of argument retains its force despite two likely objections—first, that increasing gifts of mercy only contributes to a culture of dependency and, second, that private enterprise, not private giving, is the proper means for advancing human development. Note that each of these objections makes the exercise of individual agency the goal. In this sense, the objections are still compatible with an emphasis on capabilities, even if they reflect a different vision of the necessary general conditions for developing them. No doubt Carnegie and today's proponents of such arguments are right to acknowledge that people respond to incentives and that people's choices bear on their levels of development. The more compelling these concerns with incentives and choice are to givers, the more the givers will reject the strategies and aims of some nonprofits as being harmful. But innovation in response to need, not denial in the face of that need, is then called for. This innovation can fruitfully start from reflection on the capabilities of a good human life, whether the list is Nussbaum's or a giver's own.

Competing Conceptions of the Good

We have entered contested political terrain. Such controversy is often assiduously avoided by those nonprofits that depend on gifts from all comers. I welcome such controversy, however, over shyness about discussing philanthropic giving. Stating one's giving goals overtly can help make philanthropy more democratic. Articulating these goals to other people will force philanthropy more into the realm of open discussion and debate. It will also serve to highlight the plural conceptions of good lives that motivate giving. Although there is the risk that culture wars over philanthropy might hamper important efforts by nonprofits, stronger engagement by givers might result, too.

Consider the current HIV/AIDS crisis in Africa and elsewhere. For most people, this crisis is too distant to contribute their talent and time. This obstacle to personal involvement removes the issue from many people's direct concerns, leaving public entities like the United Nations and national governments the primary sources of assistance and funding. My own view is that so large a crisis demands a structural response by public authorities and international organizations. I also strongly support "safe sex" education as part of that response. Resistance to this strategy comes both in the countries served and in the United States. U.S. government financial contributions have been limited partly by disputes over sexual ethics. Calls for "safe sex" and condom use, in particular, do not sit well with various religious groups' views about sexual responsibility and contraception.

Here we have a case of public policy facing a conflict between conceptions of the good and the visions of the good life that go with them. Politics in the United States struggles mightily with these sorts of disputes, often resorting to inaction. Unfortunately, the HIV/AIDS pandemic's devastating effects are indisputable, all the more so now that women who are the bulwark of rural life and the family in Africa make up 58 percent of the people infected.[28]

What, then, should be done, given the U.S. government's reluctance to finance such efforts?[29] While small-scale initiatives pose significant risks, the crisis is so acute that these initiatives are preferable to political paralysis. Indeed, for those who share my views of how best to respond, funding nonprofit and nongovernmental organizations that include "safe sex" education may be the only viable route to achieving what is called for by one's vision of a good life. For others who reject this approach, there remains the imperative to act in ways that conform to their sense of how best to promote human flourishing. Here clarity about the relationship between giving goals and a good life can increase philanthropic giving, even if the groups receiving the funds in this case may work at cross purposes at times.

Let me briefly relate this observation to the current debate about faith-based initiatives in the United States. Proponents of faith-based programs argue that faith is integral to the social services they provide. Without the vision of the good life that their particular faiths offer, little can be achieved for other people. I have deep misgivings about the constitutionality of extending public funds to religious groups that make their own faith integral to the services they provide. I oppose granting public funds to groups that do not follow federal anti-discrimination laws in their employment practices. Finally, I worry that offering "faith" is a poor substitute for developing people whose capabilities may be deeply compromised, including the drug and alcohol addicts, the homeless, the illiterate adults, the juvenile offenders and released convicts, who are currently served by faith-based service providers. I am not criticizing the religious concern shown by these groups, which is laudable. My worry has to do instead with the expectation that the "recipients" of this philanthropy must adopt the vision of the good life advanced by those helping them.

That said, this worry actually suggests one reason why faith-based initiatives might deserve a second look from critics. Where givers and takers share a common vision of the good life, there may be efficacy in a more culturally specific strategy that promotes a "thicker," communal sense of the shape and ordering of a full set of capabilities.[30] Governments cannot adopt so prescriptive an approach. Although the constitutional and legal issues should be resolved first, pilot projects along these lines might have merit, provided again that participants are free to choose these programs because, as participants, they either share or choose to adopt the "ultimate meaning of life" upheld by others in the group, along with the specifications of all of the other capabilities that these commitments entail. The "freedom" to choose a faith-based provider will be meaningful, however, only if there are fully accessible secular alternatives adequately funded by public money. Otherwise this country may return to the days when religious and community charities dominated the provision of many services but were unable, as David Hammack notes in this volume, "to begin to provide for all, or to meet the ideal standard of equal access for all to education, adequate work, health care, and the arts."[31]

How to Relate to Others?

For much of this essay, I have proceeded as if givers were the only people whose visions of a good life matter. Clarifying one's giving goals leads to thinking about how one's priorities relate to other people's capabilities. A further step follows because givers are not the only ones with particular ways of describing and arranging the components of a good life. As we move onto the question, "How should givers relate to those who receive their gifts?" the agency of both parties is vital.

Again I recommend new terms for characterizing philanthropic relationships. The words *benefactor* and *beneficiary* have fallen out of favor because they are archaic and hierarchical. Moreover, only one of the parties has independent agency. The benefactor literally "*does* well," while the beneficiary awaits the offering or "benefice." Granted, being a beneficiary implies some consent in accepting benefits, but the role is circumscribed, even if it is not fully passive. The language of *giver* and *recipient* sheds the feudalistic overtones but still bears traces of this role division. Simply put, the term *giver* shows its verb overtly; the word *recipient* answers to that action and only in a nominal way.

I propose replacing this pairing with the terms *giver* and *taker*. No doubt *taker* is morally loaded, suggesting a lack of gratitude, reciprocity, or contribution. When the takers of philanthropic gifts exhibit these faults, they may deserve criticism. I urge reserving judgment, though, and in concluding, I explain the ways that a language of giver and taker can aid personal reflection and public conversations about philanthropy.

First, the term *taker* is preferable to *recipient* because it emphasizes that agency is a goal of any better life that a giver might help make available to another person. Perhaps the taker of a philanthropic gift should be expected to show gratitude to the giver right away. What is more significant, ultimately, is that the taker uses the gift in a way that adds to his or her capabilities for choosing, planning, and pursuing a good life. If we adopt the longer-term perspective of a capabilities approach, it makes more sense to judge the fruits of a philanthropic gift and the moral acknowledgment of it when the taker is positioned to contribute to others and either does or does not reciprocate.

Consider gifts of excellence here. Such gifts are meant to be taken by independent and enterprising people. While givers to an art museum might put restrictions on their donations, they are finally trusting the curatorial staff to take their donation and use it well. Philanthropic support of basic science and artistic creativity are even clearer cases. The giver cannot achieve the desired excellences, so he or she supports others who can take these gifts and accomplish something of their own, a gift of new knowledge or artistry that will enrich more people's lives in turn. In other words, gifts of excellence demand takers, even if the givers also deserve letters of thanks and public recognition for having had a vision and then letting go.

A second implication of my proposed language follows. The term *taker* implies that it is better to conceive the gratitude, reciprocity, and contribution due for taking gifts as circular rather than transactional. Giving met by gratitude is not the sum total of a philanthropic relationship, nor, presumably, is it the giver's aim to gain the recipient's gratitude. Takers, for their part, need reasons for being grateful, and often the best reasons emerge later on, especially if the goal of giving is to *develop* other people's capabilities. By the time the taker is able to appreciate the significance of a past gift, the best response is likely to be contributions to new takers, not gratitude to the giver.

Let me offer an illustration from my time with the national teacher corps, Teach For America. As a recruiter for that organization, I hired mostly recent college graduates to teach in under-served urban and rural schools in the United States. I heard many candidates express their desire to "give back." Many of them had studied at expensive and prestigious universities. They recognized how much they had benefited from their own educations, and they wanted to reciprocate. But soon after these new teachers entered the classroom, their words sometimes revealed a myopic one-sidedness. A rigid commitment to giving back exactly what one has received is hard to sustain in challenging new circumstances. It also fails to allow for all that students bring from their own lives, no matter how young they are.

Giving and receiving are not enough by themselves. In the case of Teach For America, if "giving back" what "one received" proved the full measure of the teacher's goals, then the initial motivating gratitude was too transactional and insufficiently circular. Even though the gratitude was prompted by gifts from one set of givers and put to work in serving new recipients, there was too little forward motion. The teachers' aims stopped short in seeking to return the gifts received, suggesting that the teachers had received those gifts as a "recipient" and had not taken them on as a "taker." The more successful new teachers, by contrast, were those who saw themselves not as giving back what they had received, but rather as giving *and* taking. They gave it out to their students and took (some of) it from them, too, most notably, a broadened perspective on America.

Here we see a third reason why the term *taker* is illuminating. The line between givers and takers is a shifting one; people move between these roles continually. For the Teach For America recruits to have been successful candidates in the first place, they had to have taken a great deal from others. Consider their interactions with teachers and professors, the people who often modeled the commitment that the recruits wanted to take on for themselves. Anyone who has taught in a classroom knows that teachers take a great deal from students. Instructors also want their students to take what they learn in their own directions. I strongly suspect that the recruits who brought more of their own resources to bear in taking on their instructors' gifts for themselves were the ones who proved best equipped to engage in the give-and-take of their new classrooms.

A common element in the preceding examples is that a certain distance exists between giver and takers. This distance is the final reason for favoring the new vocabulary. The distance is moral, not spatial. In fact, the Teach For America case differs from most examples of giving because it is so immediate. While there may not be always an actual distance separating givers and takers, especially in cases of giving talent and time, there is often a "moral distance" at work. By this I mean that people bring different visions of a good life to philanthropy, both as givers and takers. Here we return to the issues of hierarchy and diversity that I introduced in discussing Aristotle. When givers aim to make a better life available to other people, there is the risk that they will impose their own vision of a good life on others in inappropriate ways. With gifts of excellence, the issue of hierarchy is less pertinent because of the independence granted to the takers of such gifts. Diversity, however, is very much at play. Indeed the takers' distinctive vision, goals, experiences, and talents are vital to these gifts' success.

Turning now to gifts of mercy, I claim that here, too, the moral distance between givers and takers should be respected. I anticipate more resistance to using the term *taker* in cases where gifts of mercy are concerned. These gifts are arguably different for two reasons. First, since basic needs are often the focus, givers may think they know the road that others are traveling because givers have followed the exact route. Yet people's understanding of basic needs and the requisite gifts will reflect the circumstances in which they took such gifts themselves and the purposes to which they have since put them. Likewise, other people's needs will reflect their circumstances and the ends that they seek in their vision of a good life, so gifts of mercy will frequently look different to the taker.

It will not always be possible, then, I claim, to identify other people's "true needs" as readily as is suggested by the model of philanthropy of care that Paul Schervish outlines in this volume. Indeed, my use of Nussbaum's full scheme of capabilities is meant in part as a check on givers' impositions of their visions of a good life on others. I share with Schervish the conviction that philanthropy very much involves one's self, but I also stress the distance between givers and takers. The more that his emphasis on the giver's sense of a shared "destiny" with takers entails an ongoing relationship dedicated to exploring the moral distances between them, the more likely I think it is that a giver's "identification" with others can lead to an understanding, or successful negotiation, of takers' actual needs.

The second reason to be more prescriptive with gifts of mercy, perhaps, is that they often go to people who have not yet reached the minimal thresholds needed to take charge of their lives. Admittedly, the term *recipient* may be more appropriate here. Sometimes philanthropy serves people who can only assume the passive role of accepting or rejecting the aid given, without taking it on for themselves as capable agents with their own histories, relationships, goals, and visions of a good life. To say that the word *recipient* may fit this one class of philanthropic relationships better, however, only underscores why *taker* is the preferable term in most cases. Even where people's capabilities are underdeveloped, too rigid a set of expectations will inhibit the agency ultimately sought. A capabilities approach to philanthropy calls for givers to err on the side of allowing leeway when it comes to where and how their gifts are taken by others. That is not to say that givers should never pass judgment on the fruits of their gifts, but I do counsel delay. If givers come to disagree with the ways their gifts have been taken, they can always halt their support then.

I want to return to a phrase I mentioned earlier. I noted the "give-and-take" that some Teach for America teachers experience in their classrooms. This phrase is instructive, but we need to move from the immediacy of this philanthropic relationship to the far-flung interactions of other kinds of philanthropy to imagine what the "give-and-take" of philanthropy might look like more generally. For readers familiar with Marcel Mauss's classic study of gift-giving societies, a useful contrast may be drawn here. Mauss canvasses early anthropological literature for archaic societies that exhibit a kind of circular reciprocity best described as a "give-and-give." No gift is ever free, he argues. Whenever one steps back to look at a society's "total system of gifts," there are always obligations to receive gifts and obligations to give back.[32]

To an extent, I see the "give-and-take" of philanthropy resembling Mauss's portrait of circular reciprocity. By taking gifts, one becomes obligated to give. More specifically, all of the taking required in developing one's capabilities calls for some giving in support of other people's development, too. The give-and-take I envision, however, also differs from Mauss's account. It is often the case, he notes, that gift-giving societies keep the same gifts in circulation. Some item continues to make the rounds without end, binding all of the members of the group into relations of mutuality that are often shadowed, he observes, by a stratified hierarchy of social status.

By contrast, I foresee the give-and-take of a philanthropy dedicated to developing human capabilities as changing the gifts that people give and unsettling the social divisions between them. If takers are granted agency and are allowed to take gifts in new directions, then the gifts they "give back" will be very different, having taken on the stamp of the concerns, commitments, and priorities that these takers-become-givers have developed in their lives. Here the original gift is not free in the sense of having no obligations attached, but should be sufficiently free to be taken in new directions. Givers should also be prepared to take something back other than the praise due for giving well. In the case of Teach For America, the most successful teachers gained a new perspective on the nation from their give-and-take with students. They did so because they were committed to giving well, and so they remained open to and worked to cross over the moral distance that separated them and their students. As a result, they learned to see different visions of good lives along with some of the "common bads" in the United States that prevent students in low-income areas from benefiting fully from the common good.[33]

In sum, I advocate adopting the term *taker* because it underscores the agency that is the goal in developing people's capabilities. It also reminds us of the moral distances between people in many philanthropic relationships. While these distances should be respected, one of the best reasons for doing so is that an actual "give-and-take"—an engaged, reflective public discussion of philanthropy—might arise. Thus, in acknowledging the goal of agency and the existence of moral distances in philanthropy, the term *taker* underscores how valuable it is to discuss giving with other people.

The conversations I am calling for include debates among givers and between givers and takers, too. Both can make philanthropy better serve civil society. We recognize the nonprofit sector's role in sustaining the voluntary associations of civil society. Discussions of giving can further those contributions. The clearer that givers become in their purposes through discussing their goals with fellow givers, the stronger the collaborative ties between these givers can grow. But civil society builds not simply from shared commitments to common ends. It thrives on deliberation, debate, and even division over these matters, the kinds of engaged, reflective exchanges between different visions of a good life that Nussbaum's "thick" but "vague" scheme invites. Here conversations between givers and takers can prove especially vital. Just imagine if philanthropy involved not only giving and receiving, but an actual give-and-take across societal boundaries that all too often look more like the gulf between benefactor and beneficiary than a dynamic relationship of givers and takers.

Notes

I thank the authors in this volume, the members of the Religious Studies Department at Indiana University-Purdue University Indianapolis and the 2002–2003 Jane Addams—Andrew Carnegie Fellows at the IU Center on Philanthropy for the comments that contributed to this essay. I am grateful, too, to Jocelyn Sisson for all of her help and advice throughout the project. I developed the initial idea while conducting research funded by a Summer Research Grant from the School of Liberal Arts at IUPUI. A grant from the Center on Philanthropy's IU Faculty Research Fund supported my writing. My thanks to both funders.

1. I thank Robert Lynn for a conversation we had about people's reluctance to discuss giving and also for his careful reading of this essay. For interesting reflections on the incongruence between people's ease in discussing consumer goods and people's difficulties in discussing how their spending of money relates to the guiding values of their lives, see Robert Wuthnow, *Poor Richard's Principle: Recovering the American Dream through the Moral Dimension of Work, Business, and Money* (Princeton, N.J.: Princeton University Press, 1996), Chapter 6.

2. David Ross translates this virtue as *magnificence* in Aristotle, *The Nicomachean Ethics*, trans. David Ross (Oxford: Oxford University Press, 1980), pp. 40–41, 85ff. Other translators use *munificence*, but the term *magnanimity* conveys both the magnitude of these gifts and the aim of contributing to a larger good. I follow Alasdair MacIntyre here: *After Virtue*, 2nd ed. (Notre Dame: University of Notre Dame Press, 1984), p. 159.

3. Aristotle's examples of magnanimity include gifts to fund religious offerings, buildings, and sacrifices, public feasts, city decorations, theater productions and other public works of art. These purposes are narrower than those of the philanthropic gifts I discuss in this essay. Aristotle, *The Nicomachean Ethics*, pp. 87–88.

4. Robert L. Payton, *Philanthropy: Voluntary Action for the Public Good* (New York: American Council on Education/Macmillan Publishing, 1988).

5. I say that the magnanimous gift "borders on showiness" to distinguish the virtue of magnanimity from the vice of vulgarity. Vulgarity involves a "lack of taste . . . which [does] not go to excess in the amount spent on right objects, but by showy expenditure in the wrong circumstances and the wrong man-

ner." The magnanimous man does not "spend [his vast] sums" out of vanity, but for "honour's sake." Aristotle, *The Nicomachean Ethics*, p. 86.

6. Two oft-quoted sources that praise anonymous gifts are Maimonides's eight degrees of charity and the Sermon on the Mount (Matthew 6:2–4).

7. The anonymous giving praised by Maimonides probably reflects other concerns than humility. Given the religious persecution that Maimonides faced, he and the other Jews in his community had only each other to rely on for their needs. While that closeness made unity a necessity, it increased the likely harm caused by publicizing people's dependence on other people's gifts. Here anonymity helps preserve independence and dignity. Anonymity also protects givers from being deluged by requests for support. Maintaining such distances between givers and takers remains important in larger communities, too. I thank Elliot Dorff and Robert Lynn for their observations on this point.

8. Susan A. Ostrander and Paul G. Schervish, "Giving and Getting: Philanthropy as a Social Relation," in *Critical Issues in American Philanthropy*, ed. John Van Til et al. (San Francisco: Jossey-Bass, 1990), pp. 77–78.

9. For Aristotle, a person's magnanimity has to be recognized by other people. As a result, the members of the community, who are fit to pass judgment, can refuse praise for certain gifts. I thank David Hammack for pointing out this built-in limitation on hierarchy in Aristotle's ethics.

10. Thanks to Michael Reinke, former Executive Director, United Way of Monroe County, Indiana, for helping me appreciate the best reasons for giving to the nonprofit organizations supported by the people one knows.

11. Amartya Sen, the recent Nobel laureate in economics, formulated the idea of "capabilities" as an alternative to the two standard measures of the quality of life, "income" and "utility." Instead of asking how many goods individuals can buy or how much satisfaction they can get from these goods, Sen asks, what are people themselves capable of "being" and "doing"? In other words, his "capabilities approach" focuses on developing people, or what is now called "human development." For Sen's most accessible book on the capabilities approach, see *Development as Freedom* (New York: Anchor Books, 1999). Sen rehearses his criticisms of the income and utility approaches to the standard of living on pp. 19–25, 56–63. Nussbaum's approach differs from Sen's in important ways. She details those differences in *Women and Human Development: The Capabilities Approach* (Cambridge: Cambridge University Press, 2000), pp. 11–15.

12. Nussbaum discusses her "thick vague conception of the good" in a series of writings spanning more than a decade. She explains why her approach is "thick" and "vague" and how she arrives at her universalist account of capabilities in "Aristotelian Social Democracy," in *Liberalism and the Good*, ed. R. Bruce Douglass, Gerald M. Mara, and Henry S. Richardson (New York: Routledge, 1990), pp. 217ff. In this article she also gives her initial list of "basic human functional capabilities," p. 225. Her most recent list of the "*central human functional capabilities*" comes from *Women and Human Development*, pp. 78–80. I call them "central capabilities" to reflect her more recent vocabulary and to omit some of the cumbersome terminology.

13. Nussbaum charges governments with ensuring that every one of their citizens is "capable of functioning well"; "Aristotelian Social Democracy," p. 211. This narrow focus on government is surprising considering that one of her fa-

vorite examples is a nongovernmental organization in India called the Self-Employed Women's Association bank and union. *Women and Human Development,* pp. 15ff.

14. Nussbaum, *Women and Human Development,* pp. 78–80.

15. Peter Singer, "The Singer Solution to World Poverty," *The New York Times Magazine,* 5 Sept. 1999, pp. 60ff.

16. For the sake of clarity, I italicize Nussbaum's ten central capabilities when I refer to them.

17. Nussbaum declares a *"principle of each person's capability,"* underscoring her emphasis on individual agency. She is aware, however, of the vital role that family and community relations play in upholding views of the good life and fostering people's capabilities. *Women and Human Development,* pp. 79, 245–46.

18. Ibid., pp. 78, 80.

19. I borrow the phrase "kindly use" from Wendell Berry. In the 1970s, he used this phrase to criticize the historical tendency of environmental groups to make the preservation of "unspoiled" places their primary mission. One result of this "vacation" mentality is that people stopped using these areas and so stopped being caretakers of the land. This argument has helped me think through these issues differently. Berry, *The Unsettling of America: Culture and Agriculture* (San Francisco: Sierra Club Books, 1977), pp. 27–31.

20. For a discussion that builds from a distinction between mercy, or caring "for the being of others," and excellence, or fostering the "well-being" of others, see William F. May, "Introduction," in *The Ethics of Giving and Receiving: Am I My Foolish Brother's Keeper?,* ed. William F. May and A. Lewis Soens, Jr. (Dallas: Maguire Center for Ethics and Public Responsibility/ Southern Methodist University Press, 2000), pp. xvii–xix.

21. I thank Jonathan Freiman for the observation that gifts to an alma mater have a different intent than either mercy or excellence *per se.*

22. Nussbaum, "Aristotelian Social Democracy," p. 209.

23. I thank Jennifer Herdt for comments about the mercy–excellence distinction that clarified my thinking.

24. Nussbaum, "Aristotelian Social Democracy," p. 226.

25. Givers will want to consider the possible reasons behind people's deficiencies in their capabilities and the degree to which these deficiencies reflect personal failures that have to be accounted for. For a discussion of this issue that draws from Christian ethics, see Harlan Beckley, "Capability as Opportunity: How Amartya Sen Revises Equal Opportunity," *Journal of Religious Ethics* 30, no. 1 (Spring 2002): 107–35.

26. Andrew Carnegie, *The Gospel of Wealth* (Indianapolis: Indiana University Center on Philanthropy, 1993), pp. 14ff, 9, 13.

27. It is intriguing at a time when the inheritance tax is being called the "death penalty" to note that Andrew Carnegie advocated progressive inheritance taxes. His use of the term "death *duties*" underscores the moral significance he attached to funding public obligations. See *The Gospel of Wealth,* p. 6 (my italics).

28. Kofi Annan, "In Africa, AIDS Has a Woman's Face," *New York Times,* 29 Dec. 2002, sec. 4, p. 9.

29. I wrote this sentence before President George W. Bush proposed a new

HIV/AIDS initiative in Africa. At the time of submitting the final version of this essay, the details of that proposal remain to be worked out, but the emerging policy appears to be abstinence-centered.

30.   I thank Greg Bonds and George Rush, two African Methodist Episcopal ministers and two students of mine, for pointing out the potential communal efficacy of faith-based initiatives.

31.   See David Hammock's essay in this volume.

32.   There are other connections that might be drawn between my essay and Marcel Mauss's rich study of *The Gift*. The most important is the honor gained by givers. Although I argue that praise is justly earned for giving well, I do not discuss how giving upholds status in society, as Mauss explores at considerable length. The translator of Mauss's *The Gift* actually uses the phrase "*system of total services,*" but I follow Mary Douglas's foreword in using the phrase "total system of giving." See Marcel Mauss, *The Gift: The Form and Reason for Exchange in Archaic Societies,* trans. W. D. Halls, with a foreword by Mary Douglas (New York and London: W. W. Norton, 1990), pp. 5–6, viii. I thank Phillip Turner for prompting me to add this allusion to Mauss, contributing to the good suggestions he made to my revisions of this essay.

33.   David Hollenbach names the "suburban–urban" divide in public funding for schools as one of the "common bads" in the United States today. The many benefits that flow to suburban schoolchildren are common goods, but under the current system of funding, these benefits can come at the expense of urban and rural schoolchildren. David Hollenbach, S.J., *The Common Good and Christian Ethics* (Cambridge: Cambridge University Press, 2002), p. 42.

4 Focused Fairness in Philanthropy

Patricia H. Werhane

It is justice, not charity, that is wanting in the world.[1]

—Mary Wollstonecraft

Goodness means . . . responding well to what people expect, need, or are interested in; fairness means responding equally well to everyone, without discrimination.[2]

—World Health Organization

Philanthropy can be defined as "a desire to help [hu]mankind, especially as shown by gifts to charitable or humanitarian institutions; benevolence."[3] Yet the giving of time, effort, and money is not a simple task. In a society with scarce resources, it is difficult at best to respond to needs, and to respond in ways that are fair to all those in need. Mary Wollstonecraft argues that while many of us are generous, our targets of philanthropic giving are often misplaced. We often give to charities that are of interest or that are newsworthy without thinking about which groups of people are most in need, which can benefit best with our dollars or services, and how best to distribute these benefits, assuming that they are not unlimited. We also often give to those who are suffering, without considering whether or not those funds would be better spent giving to those who, with funding, will improve their life opportunities and then perhaps in turn help others who are in need. In this chapter, I shall deal with these issues. I shall claim that while philanthropy is often identified with goodness, we need to take into account the idea of distributive fairness as well. We need to consider how and to whom we give as well as the mere act of giving. While it is impossible, with scarce resources, to respond, and respond equally or well to all demands for philanthropy, taking into account what I shall call "focused fairness" gives philanthropists guidelines that prevent waste and help to spread gifts wisely and with the most benefits to those who are the recipients of such generosity.

I shall begin with a case. Janet Jones is a new member on the board of the AIDS Service Agency (ASA), a private community agency devoted to counseling, education, and outreach to HIV-infected individuals and their families. In addition to education programs, ASA serves about two hundred families of HIV-infected individuals in a five-county area, but the caseload is projected to double over the next five years to almost four hundred. Janet joined the board because she was interested in HIV (her brother had died of AIDS in the early 1990s) and because she wanted to contribute to a worthwhile venture. Having not been informed of the financial situation of the organization in advance, she was shocked to discover that the agency was in debt, it was spending its endowment, and it appeared to have no solutions to its financial difficulties, despite various popular fundraising events and an annual giving program.

Many of the financial difficulties centered around Smith House. Smith House is a single-family home with a capacity for six residents, established for HIV-infected homeless people who have nowhere else to turn. Harry Smith, who raised $50,000 for its endowment, founded Smith House about fifteen years ago, and each year the residence receives about $25,000 in support from the U.S. Department of Housing and Urban Development (HUD). There is one full-time social worker devoted to Smith House, but no overnight resident staff nor any additional counseling services. Smith House is run by the AIDS Service Agency. Presently there are three residents at the House.

When Smith House was established, those who were infected with HIV had almost no life expectancy, and all who came to Smith House came there to die. Recently, however, after the death (from natural causes) of Harry Smith, the HIV scenario has changed, and most of those infected who follow the strict regime of drug therapy can expect to live for seven to ten years or even longer. Because of this development, the lifestyles of the Smith House inhabitants have been affected as well. While drug use is forbidden at Smith, almost all its inhabitants are still using, and some are selling crack or other drugs. In the evenings, when there is no supervision, neighbors have repeatedly reported drug-related activities, and the local police have been at the House several times. The police have threatened to close Smith House if the drug trafficking continues.

HUD and endowment funding do not raise enough funds to cover the costs of running Smith House, and every year it costs ASA between $20,000 and 25,000 in additional expenditures to keep the house open and running. As a result, since taking over Smith House from its independent board five years ago, ASA has run a deficit. If this persists without a further influx of donations or foundation support, ASA will use up its endowment and in two years it will have to close its doors.

How should Janet evaluate ASA and Smith House? Some board members argue that Smith House should indeed be closed. It is too costly to run, qualified residents cannot be found, and the money could be usefully directed to ASA's education and outreach activities, and could assist many more people than the number of those in residence at Smith. Besides, if ASA goes bankrupt, other social services in the area are ill equipped to engage in the services ASA offers, both in education and outreach.

Others on the board who helped found Smith House find that position heartless. What will happen to the HIV-infected homeless if Smith closes down? There is a drastic shortage of housing for the poor in this affluent area, and these folks are usually turned down for subsidized housing because of their past records of drug use.

A month ago, Janet was asked to speak to the regional Society of Obstetrics and Gynecology. At that meeting, she ran into a young gynecologist whose father had endowed the lectureship. As they spoke, she learned that this physician spends about a third of his time in Nigeria training surgeons to treat a condition known as obstetric fistula.

An obstetric fistula is a hole that develops between a woman's vagina and her bladder or rectum as a result of trauma sustained during childbirth. If labor becomes obstructed, a woman's baby will not fit through her birth canal because her pelvis is too small or the baby is too large. In parts of the world that lack obstetric care, pregnant women may labor for days without relief. The baby's head becomes wedged tightly in the mother's pelvis, cutting off the blood supply to the soft tissues of her bladder, rectum, and vagina. After several days, the baby dies. If the mother survives, her injured pelvic tissues rot away, creating a fistula. Women with fistulas have absolutely no control over their urine or bowels. They are always wet. They stink of urine and feces. They are cast out by their families and are divorced by their husbands; yet the vast majority of these women are less than twenty years old. Estimates suggest there are 400,000 women with this condition in Nigeria alone, and millions more throughout the developing world.

The Worldwide Fund for Mothers Injured in Childbirth (WFMIC), an agency formed by the gynecologist, helps provide surgery for women afflicted with fistulas. The total cost of surgery and recovery is less than $200 per patient. The Fund trains doctors and nurses to treat them surgically, as well as to provide for their care; supports research on the causes, prevalence, and social consequences of this condition; and serves as an advocate for fistula victims worldwide. The Fund is currently raising $4 million to build and operate a free-standing fistula center in Plateau State, Nigeria, dedicated to research, patient care, and the social, physical, and spiritual rehabilitation of women devastated by the stigmatizing childbirth injuries.[4]

Recently, in her spare time, Janet has also become involved with a reading program that was initially funded in large part by Head Start. Volunteers spend one or two afternoons each week helping students who are having reading difficulties. While these efforts have not always produced positive results, on average, these students do better in the classroom, and a few have gone on to do well in secondary school and college. With budget cuts in her state, and the tightening of federal funds, the program must receive private funding if it is to continue.

Should Janet, who is able to contribute about $10,000 a year to charities and can devote a few days a month of her time and talents, donate funds to the WFMIC? Should she focus her charitable giving there rather than at ASA? Or should she help to fund the ongoing reading initiative? A dollar to WFMIC would do so much to help women in need, providing much more per capita than a dollar to ASA. And she would not be supporting drug users who threaten the viability and well-being of Smith House and the agency. On the other hand, Janet, who volunteers at ASA, knows most of the families on ASA's caseload.

Over half live below the poverty level, many are part of the uninsured working poor, and ASA is often their lifeline for rent support, food, and other necessities. These families require counseling services that other agencies in the area do not provide. Janet has never been in Nigeria; nor does she know anyone from that country. She will not be able to work directly with the organization or see the effects of her contribution. In contrast, the reading program creates opportunities for local young people to improve their skills and do better in school.

This case raises a number of questions with which I shall deal in this chapter. What criteria should individuals, foundations, and other philanthropic organizations use to evaluate their contributions and their giving policies? Are there limits to altruism? Is just "doing good" or helping those we know without taking into account distributive costs and benefits morally justifiable? With limited funds available, is it fair to support or enable two or three homeless people when an agency contributing unique social services is at risk? Is it better to relieve suffering or to provide positive opportunities for the less fortunate? Is the World Health Organization's definition of justice as "responding equally well to everyone, without discrimination" a useful criterion for philanthropic judgments, or should philanthropists take other factors into account? Is it morally questionable to take into account familiarity with recipients when practicing philanthropy? What about Janet's interests, talents, and emotional commitments? She is part of a community to which she feels certain social obligations, and she identifies with AIDS patients. Should those commitments factor into her decision making? Or should one use some more disinterested principle when practicing philanthropy? Is being fair *and* charitable an impossible goal?

Philanthropy, Altruism, and Self-Interest

As Janet wrestles with these challenges, one of her worries is whether her choice of giving will be based on her personal interests or feelings, rather than on which group is most in need. Should she take a more disinterested perspective on her giving? Philanthropy is sometimes identified with altruism, "a concern for the well-being of persons other than oneself where the concern is not in the service of one's own interest or a benefit to oneself."[5] If this is true, then few, if any, of us, are altruists. Most of us are incapable of pure selflessness, that is, of divorcing all self-interests from our allegedly philanthropic or benevolent motives, actions, and even moral judgments. Interestingly, there are good philosophical arguments to support the contention that one can be self-interested *and* altruistic.

There is a large body of philosophical literature that identifies moral action with concern for others. These concerns are sometimes defined as disinterested (non-self-related), agent-neutral, or impartial. Some theorists even exclude self-interested activities as morally relevant. Despite this predilection to exclude self-interest from morality, beginning at least as early as Joseph Butler, the alleged dichotomy between self-interest and altruism and the exclusion of self-interested activities from morality were challenged.[6] Following Butler's line of reasoning, in the *Theory of Moral Sentiments* Adam Smith makes two sets of argument that challenge the sharp distinction between self-interest and altruism. Smith begins the *Theory of Moral Sentiments* by stating that

> How selfish soever man may be supposed, there are evidently some principles in his nature, which interest him in the fortune of others, and render their happiness necessary to him, though he derives nothing from it except the pleasure of seeing it.[7]

Smith then argues that most of us exhibit a mix of passions, from which we derive our interests in ourselves and in others.[8] Out of these passions and interests, we distinguish virtues, those character traits we admire or conclude we should admire. Significantly for the arguments in this paper, Smith contends that a prudent person who has command of herself and acts in moderation is a virtuous person, and indeed, someone who neglects the self in pursuit of helping others is, according to Smith, not as virtuous as the person who exhibits prudence as well as benevolence and justice. The egoistic person who is interested only in herself is not necessarily selfish, greedy, or exhibiting avarice, but could be merely prudent and disinterested in others. Moreover, one can be self-interestedly concerned for others as the objects of one's interests, and thus may be philanthropic, without necessarily being self-sacrificingly altruistic. Thus self-interest is not identified with egoism. One can be philanthropic without being selflessly altruistic, and, indeed, Smith thinks that pure selflessness is almost impossible to achieve.[9]

However, Smith recognizes that benevolence, and thus acts of philanthropy, are often focused, parochial concerns for those we know or whose problems we are familiar with. In fact, Smith argues, only God can be perfectly benevolent or purely selflessly altruistic.[10] Thus we need to qualify benevolence with justice. The just person is one who is concerned with fairness and fair treatment of everyone, including strangers. While the just person may have no self-interests in strangers, her interest and passion for fairness will at the very least have "consciousness of ill-desert."[11]

Despite commentaries to the contrary, Smith is clear in his belief that human beings are mutually dependent social beings and can survive only through helping each other.[12] At the same time, he does not defend an absolute duty to beneficence, arguing that "Society may subsist, though not in the most comfortable state, without beneficence; but the prevalence of injustice must utterly destroy it."[13] A society without benevolence and kindness, while unpleasant, could survive, but without principles of justice or fair play it would fail. While it is "uncomfortable" and socially questionable to be ungenerous, unkind, and not to come to the aid of others, it is not always wrong not to be generous or kind.[14] What Smith recognizes, rightly, is the fallibility of human nature, and our often misguided, biased attempts at benevolence or philanthropy. He is not claiming that one has no duties to be philanthropic, since benevolence is a virtue. Rather, because we are imperfect fallible beings, we make mistakes in giving, often giving to those we know rather than to strangers, and sometimes misdirecting our gifts. Smith, then, raises a cautionary flag that being kind or generous is not enough, in itself, for individuals to achieve positive social outcomes without the groundwork of fairness or principles of justice.

Duties of Benevolence, Beneficence and Philanthropy[15]

Smith's conclusions can be helpful to Janet as she sorts out her interests and then tries to focus those interests so that she will distribute her gifts fairly to organizations she cares about. But she wonders whether we have *duties* to be philanthropic, as she was brought up to believe. To think through that question, she turns to the work of the eighteenth-century philosopher Immanuel Kant, famous for grounding his moral philosophy in the notion of duty. According to Kant, each of us has perfect duties always to treat oneself and other human beings as ends—that is with respect and dignity.[16] Indeed, Kant argues that it is always wrong and indeed irrational not to do so. It follows that it does not matter to whom one is benevolent and philanthropic, and what outcomes result in the last analysis if the goodness of an act is evaluated, so long as those sorts of behaviors and gifts are done out of the right motive—out of a sense of duty, with recipients treated with dignity and respect.[17]

Kant writes that respect for human beings as ends "compels us to regard one another as 'fellow-men—that is, rational beings with needs, united by nature in one dwelling place for the purpose of helping one another.'"[18] The duty to provide mutual aid does not require that we help everyone all the time, and indeed one cannot extend mutual aid beyond one's capacities because that would undermine self-dignity. But this conclusion does not imply a milder misanthropic argument that we do have such duties. Indeed, according to Kant, these duties are such that "we may refrain from helping only if such action would place our own rational activity (or life) in jeopardy."[19]

A Kantian analysis supports Janet's belief in respect for individual autonomy, clear limitations for self-sacrifice, duties to benevolence and mutual aid, and thus philanthropy. But Kant himself was less concerned with how one determines who needs and deserves aid, and how, in a scarcity society, that aid should be distributed. It is one's moral duty to *aid,* not to clarify to whom, and that is the primary moral concern. This is because, according to Kant, morality has to do with what I can control, my own choices and actions. Since I cannot control the results of my actions (because of social interactions that interfere with their perfect execution), the results are not the purview of morality.

Why We Need Evaluative Distributive Principles for Philanthropy

Kant presents Janet (and the readers) with three moral principles: duties to respect autonomy, duties not to harm, and duties to aid. Smith introduces a fourth: duties to be fair. What is more troublesome is the Kantian conclusion that acts of beneficence or mutual aid are moral duties, *whoever* the recipient may be, so that distributive principles are not necessary to measure and judge the goodness or evil of results despite the possible positive or negative outcomes of such aid. Janet is worried about this. As Smith recognizes, the act of giving is not enough to guarantee that the money or talents will be used wisely or well. Some distributive principle or principles are necessary in evaluating acts of benevolence. For a number of reasons, these principles are particularly important for philanthropy. Not every person or institution is equally needy or equally deserving of our kindness or generosity. Our sympathy for the plight of others does not necessarily require that we come to their assistance when they are capable of handling their own situations. Both Smith and Kant would concur that our duties to provide aid are not justifiable when what we are able to do does not help or even exacerbates the problem. A respect for persons as ends does not always require positive altruistic acts. Indeed, in some cases simply leaving people alone better serves the duty of respect.

While this last conclusion sounds like a good excuse *not* to be philanthropic, Janet will not be deterred by that conclusion. But she needs some more support for rejecting that idea, and she needs to figure out how to implement the duty to be fair in practical terms.

Let us suppose that each of us is perfectly altruistic, benevolent, and always treats others fairly. Let us also suppose that there are infinite resources available both to end human suffering and to provide equal opportunities for everyone. Still, the perfect altruist must take into account social conditions, value differences, and other contextual elements in her judgments. Thus it appears that a purely Kantian perspective on our duties to beneficence is unsatisfactory. This is not an easy calculation, and it depends on the good will and actions of others, not all of which are predicable or coinciding with one's own, and on how we define "well-being." At least part of that determination has to take into account the considered preferences of those we are trying to help, what they take to be basic needs, which social goods they might consider as enhancing their well-being, and the core values they share in their particular society or sub-culture. But these are contextual matters, even when one focuses on basic needs. Janet learned this lesson at ASA when her evaluation of the situation at Smith House clashed with value judgments of other board members who found that Smith House's activities were worthwhile.

For example, during the Afghan War, the United States dropped food packages into Afghanistan. Giving the government the benefit of the doubt, let us assume that this action was meant to be altruistic and a good-faith idea. Peanut butter, strawberry jam, and even moist towelettes were included in many of the packages, but these substances were unfamiliar to the Afghans and their diet. Accommodating Muslim customs, no pork products were sent, but some form of a rice consistency power bar was included. This seemed like a good idea, except that people in Afghanistan had never seen a power bar, and were fearful that it was lethal. Many of the product labels were in English, despite the fact that the literacy rate is quite low in Afghanistan. The packages were airdropped. This, too, seemed like a practical idea, since the war was going on and people were hungry. Unfortunately, many of the packages were yellow, the same color as bombs.[20] The lesson is obvious. Context, culture, mores, and what is valued and disvalued in a context and culture must be part of any philanthropic equation. And this is not merely because the hundreds of thousands of dollars spent on Afghan food drops could have better been spent on those whose needs we can actually predict. It is that there may have been harm created by the food drop itself, even if it was conducted out of a duty to benevolence.

Janet might conclude that the sentiment of benevolence is a good one, and that acting from that sentiment or from a duty to beneficence is usually admirable if one keeps in mind respect for autonomy and the duties to engage in fair evaluations and not incur harms. But still, what we have is a form of naïve philanthropy because, as C. Dyke argues, there are vices connected with altruism, just as there are vices connected with selfishness. I have outlined one—the failure to take into account considered preferences, contextual background, and traditions of recipients of philanthropy. Interpersonal comparisons of need are necessarily flawed, even when one makes comparisons in the same community.

Dyke outlines another reason, which, when made explicit, should help Janet. Acts that involve paternalism or coercion at least outside one's family are often questionable, and many so-called good acts are paternalistic if the benefactor imagines she knows what is "good," or "good for someone." Such acts violate respect for autonomy and are often insulting. Here is a third reason. When we move outside our own community, what we imagine as shared values may not be considered in the same way as in our society. Even within our communities, not everyone has the same value system. Value coercion, while best exemplified in apocryphal stories about missionaries,[21] occurs in more subtler ways when benefactors talk about what values others should espouse or what interests and preferences they should have. The Food Stamp program in our country is one such example: cigarettes and alcohol are not allowed to be purchased with food stamps. So Janet's interests in the Nigerian project are tainted by her lack of knowledge of the culture, traditions, and the work of the WFMIC.

While the value of autonomy (the value of independence and freedom of choice versus paternalism) and respect for persons (treating all persons as if they are of equal value whether or not they are capable of making choices) are ordinarily taken as goods, how one evaluates these two makes a difference in how we determine acts of philanthropy. Avoiding parochialism (in not recognizing cultural differences), paternalism, and values coercion prioritizes the value of human autonomy. Note, however, that we might want to call these *prima facie* priorities. When people are truly in dire need or are in abject suffering, sometimes paternalistic or even coercive acts of philanthropy are necessary just to bring people up to a level where the notion of autonomy and a sense of value difference make sense. Thus the U.S. food program in Somalia, a failure in most respects, was instigated for those reasons, and they were good motives. Janet's interest in women with obstetric fistula demonstrated her concern about reducing the personal and social suffering of these people within their own culture. Helping them is not necessarily a form of interference, but rather an attempt to level their playing field so that they will be on equal ground with other women in their society.

The Challenges of "Well-Being," Fairness, and Distribution

Janet faces a number of other issues. She recognizes a duty to benevolence and understands how to qualify that duty, while taking into account her own interests and well-being, the dangers of parochialism, and the need to consider the historical and cultural contexts in which her possible recipients operate. The question of benevolence versus justice in Wollstonecraft's statement and the World Health Organization quotation with which I began this essay focuses on distributive issues for Janet. At a minimum, justice requires fair play across the board, and requires "responding equally well to everyone, without discrimination." Questions then arise, including "Are we to give preference to the principle of producing as much happiness [or reducing as much suffering] as possible, or to the principle of spreading it [our largesse] as widely as possible?"[22] The issue is twofold. We often argue that it is better to focus one's altruistic or philanthropic efforts on one cause, increasing the effect or improving the conditions of one set of individuals or one set of problems, rather than distributing our philanthropy to all who are in need of help. But even if we can decide that issue satisfactorily, and even if we can avoid many of the vices or pitfalls of giving, with a scarcity of funds we must also decide whether it is best to reduce suffering or provide equal opportunities for improving well-being. This, of course, is part of Janet's dilemma. Should she give money to a reading program or to reduce the suffering of Nigerian women?

R. Corkey tries to resolve this dilemma by arguing that given the choice and scarcity of funds, it is better, all things considered, to give opportunities to those who can demonstrate that special opportunities (e.g., better education) will enable these people to make exceptional societal contributions to the common good.[23] The reasoning is that these people, when granted unequal opportunities, will improve the social good more than they would if an equal distribution of opportunities or a focus on reducing suffering were offered.

Bracketing the obvious naïveté of imagining that those with better opportunities will, in most cases, use them to improve societal well being, this proviso raises another issue. When choosing to provide opportunities for the talented and able, what should be done about those who suffer and simply need relief? The goal to reduce suffering is, obviously, a legitimate purpose of philanthropy, and for some is its primary purpose. Indeed, as Corkey recognizes, helping those who are suffering, even if those people cannot contribute positively to the improvement of society, is defensible on the grounds that "[t]he good-will expressed and evoked by such philanthropy, the diminution of misery thereby effected, and the general satisfaction brought to all who think about such things, would, in reality, make a substantial contribution to the common good that would compensate for the apparently unrequited cost of these services."[24]

That argument, however, while *possibly* justified on traditional utilitarian grounds, illustrates two problems. In the world of philanthropy where funding is scarce, is it better, all things considered, to reduce suffering or to improve opportunities? I shall return to this issue below. It also raises a question of privilege. While one may gain enormous self-satisfaction out of helping those in need, and while Smith is right that many of us are actually interested in being benevolent or philanthropic, there is a "slippery slope of privilege" (or vice) that might sneak in. It is true that much of philanthropy comes from self-interested motives, that is, self-satisfaction for helping others. There is nothing wrong with that. At the same time, however, self-satisfaction might turn into smugness or worse. The privilege of largesse, like Brooke Astor's pearls, cannot always be disguised.[25]

Returning to Janet's challenge of whether the focus of philanthropy should be to reduce suffering or to improve opportunities, the issue, baldly stated as I have done, is much more complex, and here again context and knowledge of background conditions are critical components in decision-making processes. Although starvation was abated, the United States failed miserably to reduce long-term suffering in Somalia. We knew little about the context, we had not reviewed carefully the unique cultural, political, and historical background conditions underlying that country's malaise, nor did we have the skills to improve that situation. Similarly, in many countries such as the Sudan, food aid programs, while relieving immediate starvation (and that is a good thing!) only temporarily solve endemic problems of war, drought, poor agricultural methods, and poverty. Altruistic acts are not always perfectly good even if they are done from completely unselfish nonpolitical motives, and some may actually harm. Thus the program at Smith House, while done with good intentions, may be merely enabling drug users to continue their habits.

Focused Fairness

To summarize, because any individual's or organization's resources are scarce, careful distribution is critical. At the same time, simply distributing funding and talents equally across all those in need is both impossible and immoral, because it does not help those most in need or most able to improve themselves if given support and aid. Therefore, we need a principle of fairness to evaluate philanthropic activities, and we need distributive criteria for that form of giving. The principle we will develop is what we shall call "focused fairness."

Philanthropists and philanthropic organizations are always faced with the difficult dilemma of choosing whether to reduce suffering or improve opportunities. This dilemma cannot be solved definitively. But in addition to knowing the social fabric of the potential recipients, some distributive sorting principles are helpful for evaluating the alternatives; these factors should be useful for Janet. First, one has to evaluate the worth of the project. Is there genuine need or opportunity, and what resources are necessary to make headway in alleviating that need? Can these people help themselves? Is there a possibility for a long-term solution or is this project merely a temporary solution? Who is going to carry out the philanthropic effort? Are those in charge qualified and capable of handling what is demanded? Is there evidence to support the use of philanthropic resources to create opportunities that might improve a particular society or group of people over the long term?

We often do and should look for justifications by engaging in some sort of utilitarian calculus when making decisions to give. Indeed, this is exactly part of the analysis that most foundations and large benefactors engage in when selecting their recipients. Our gifts should not merely be for those deserving or those in need, and given with respect (the Kantian proviso), but it is also not uncharitable to use another utilitarian qualification: that of achieving more help to more needy per-dollar than other alternatives can provide. For example, giving to a well-run charity is ordinarily more useful and, I would argue, more ethical, than giving to one that squanders its resources, all things considered. But the "all things considered" qualification must be specified. A well-run charity that raises money for a richly endowed private school or university might not be as deserving or needy as, say, a disorganized soup kitchen in a run-down neighborhood. One has to measure the need of the recipients and the satisfaction of that need per dollar given. We must do a bottom-line calculus, and indeed, with the scarcity of philanthropy dollars, this is morally necessary.

How, then, do we come out in practicing principles of distributive justice in philanthropy? In the practice of philanthropy, even large foundations are necessarily focused on a subset of those in need or who qualify for improved opportunities. But that does not preclude taking into account distributive criteria, now concentrated on the subset under consideration. Nor does this preclude evaluating past, present, and future philanthropic principles or practices in these terms. Distributing almost anything is messy. We make mistakes, and it is impossible always "to respond equally well to *everyone*, without discrimination." However, we can formulate some provisional principles of focused fairness that help in evaluating philanthropic acts.

The temptation is to appeal to Rawls's second principle of justice in formulating such distributive guidelines. In *A Theory of Justice*, Rawls outlines the basic distributive principle underlying his theory of justice. "All social primary goods—liberty and opportunity, income and wealth, and the bases of self-respect—are to be distributed equally unless an unequal distribution of any of all of these goods is to the advantage of the least favored."[26] Rawls spells out his second principle, the distributive principle of justice, as follows.

Social and economic inequalities are to be arranged so that they are both: (a) to the greatest benefit of the least advantaged, consistent with the just savings principle, and (b) attached to offices and positions open to all under conditions of fair equality of opportunity.[27]

Rawls' principles are developed to be applied to basic institutions, and they are perhaps less applicable if thought to be the only distributive criterion in philanthropy. This is because there is no guarantee, due to human frailties, that philanthropic activities that are intended to be to the advantage of the worst off will turn out to be so. Part of the thrust of some philanthropic efforts is not merely to bring the disadvantaged up to par, but also to offer opportunities or programs that will, in the long term, have some overall effect either in preventing further deterioration or in improving some aspect of societal well-being. Such programs may improve the worst off, but again, there is no guarantee that this is true for every case.

Given this discussion of distributive justice in philanthropy and taking into account the Kantian proviso of treating every person as an end and with respect as a human being, we might redefine the enterprise of philanthropic giving as the ideal of "focused fairness." Respect for individuals and their autonomy, however contextually defined, and avoidance of paternalism or coercion lead to the criteria affecting the kind and mode of distribution of gifts. Focused fairness requires that philanthropists take into account cultural differences, local traditions, and considered preferences of the pool of possible recipients. We might, then, start our definition of focused distributive justice as "a fair and equitable distribution of benefits and burdens, taking into consideration what is deserved, (needed), or due"[28] in the pool of individuals, agencies, or foundations under consideration to receive philanthropy. The "pool" usually refers a defined class of individuals or agencies, is thus limited in that regard, and is often linked to the interests of the donor or mission of the philanthropic organization. The pool itself is also a provisionally delineated group, always subject to revision and additions. The "fair selection" includes the qualification of equal opportunity—treating each person in the pool as an equal, but not equally, since to treat every person equally would unfairly benefit those who are not in need and overburden those who are. For example, the AIDS service organization that Janet became involved with considers in their pool all the HIV-infected and their families in the five-county area it serves. It considers each family equally and provides counseling for every family, but it gives aid only to those families in need.

Third, in working toward "fair" distribution, the individuals, agencies, and foundations with limited funds have to set priorities. The AIDS Service Agency prioritizes its use of funds, first to the most needy, then to all families with HIV, and finally to educational outreach. In times of severe financial difficulties, ASA spends its funds first on the HIV families who have financial as well as psychological needs. But this triage is not without its ethical issues. Bracketing the Smith House dilemma, should ASA spend its limited funds helping HIV-infected families or is its money better spent in educational and prevention programs that might, in the future, prevent further infections? There is obviously no definitive answer to that question, but it is a constant nagging dilemma for organizations with limited funds. One could imagine another AIDS service organization that concentrated on education and/or prevention as its first priorities, with equal justification.

One solution for agencies and foundations is to define their mission narrowly. For example, the foundations from which ASA obtains funds are by and large focused in funding certain aspects of ASA: some on education, others on disease, still others on housing, and others on those in need of financial assistance. ASA could define its mission narrowly as assisting the HIV-infected and their families, just as the WFMIC defines its mission narrowly to work only on obstetric fistula, and only in Nigeria. This readaptation of mission does not solve overall problems, for example, AIDS education and prevention, but for agencies with very limited funds, it sometimes prevents the distribution of resources so thinly as to preclude making a difference.

A fourth qualification for fair selection and distribution is that of measuring the efficiency and effectiveness of delivery mechanisms and use of funds. This is an important criterion of distributive fairness, since misuse or inefficient use of funds prevents their application elsewhere.

These qualifications that outline a provisional theory of focused fairness will not produce perfect results that are fair to everyone. Each philanthropic endeavor entails a series of triages delineating the population to be served, defining the mission and thus determining how that population is to be served: responding to needs and suffering, or improving opportunities and long-term social benefits, and allocating scarce funds. Each of these choices entails moral risks: the risks of paternalism, imperialism, misjudgments of needs and opportunities, and suboptimization of benefits. Still, without good efforts in philanthropy, society would be in dire straits indeed.

Conclusion

I have argued the following:

1. We are naturally mutually dependent social beings and thus have duties to provide mutual aid and beneficence.
2. To varying degrees, each of us is interested in others as well as in ourselves. We are both benevolent and self-interested. It is, at best, difficult to be purely selflessly altruistic, but this is no excuse for misanthropy nor a justification for normative egoism (the position that we ought, always, to act only with our self-interests as the object of our activities.) Thus,
3. To be philanthropic does not preclude self-interest. It make sense to argue that some are genuinely interested in the well-being of others without having to make the second assumption, that benevolence and philanthropy always entail divorcing that interest from oneself. Indeed, interest in others often accounts for generosity rather than the converse.
4. Duties to beneficence are different from the duties to be fair, but no less important. However,
5. Acts of philanthropy are not perfectly good acts without qualification. Paternalism, coercion, value differences, religion, culture, and variations in rankings of social goods all affect the considered preferences of the possible recipients of philanthropy. Even the term *autonomy* is peculiarly Western and that needs to be taken into account.

6. Still, respect for autonomy, contextually defined, is a critical element in acts of altruism and/or philanthropy in most cases, except in situations of dire need, where any exercise of autonomy is precluded by the experience of suffering.
7. Evaluative principles of distribution are critical in philanthropy. These should take into account:
   a. Contextually impartial selection procedures.
   b. The criterion of treating every person in the pool of philanthropic outreach as an equal, but not equally.
   c. Well-researched data about context, background conditions, social, religious, and cultural traditions, value differences, and even differing definitions of autonomy.
   d. Local knowledge.
   e. Scarcity of philanthropic resources.
   f. Projected estimates of the short-term and long-term effectiveness of the gift or the agency receiving the gift in bringing about reduction of suffering or some positive contribution to the well-being of the recipients in question, or the creation of improvement for some recipients that will in turn contribute to the social good, still contextually defined.

Returning to Janet and in response to the questions raised in the beginning of the chapter, Janet can make an argument that enabling (if not abetting) continued drug use in Smith House is not treating those inhabitants with respect, and is wasting agency money better spent on more needy clients. But unfortunately she cannot make a case, on more utilitarian grounds, that $200 "buys more results" in a Nigerian hospital than at the AIDS service organization. Such a calculus might go as follows:

- Need: There is more need in Nigeria for aid to suffering individuals, and fewer resources than in Janet's community.
- Prudence: Money per person goes farther in Nigeria.
- Merit: Based on need and potential to generate more philanthropy, one could imagine matching grants for WFMIC.
- Distributive justice: Distributive equity seems to demand distribution of charity among those most in need.

Unfortunately, such a calculus neglects some key contextual elements. There is an extraordinary fiscal and political risk involved in investing in any project in Nigeria, a country famous for corruption and fraud. Janet knows much more about her local charities than about Nigerian politics and religious traditions, traditions that, if Nigerian practice repeats itself with any regularity, will interfere with attempts of WFMIC and its well-meaning physicians to address obstetrical problems. Context, information (or the lack thereof), local knowledge, and ability to predict the success of investments should play roles in decisions about philanthropic ventures. Prudence thus suggests that either Janet work closely with WFMIC, politicians, the health ministry, and local leaders in Nigeria, or focus her attention on local agencies for which she is better equipped to evaluate the projects.

However, we need not abandon the demand for focused fairness in philanthropy. Rather, even with the scarcity of resources, we can focus attention on the institutions and agencies that do the work of philanthropy to make sure that they are competent, efficient, and achieve the ends which they espouse, and that they respond with equity with the clients they serve. While no one person or agency can tackle all social issues nor always strike a perfectly equitable balance between reducing suffering and increasing unmet opportunities, justice requires that each of us, and the institutions we are involved with, aim at "focused fairness," a concept that addresses Wollstonecraft's cry for justice without neglecting duties to benevolence. In no instance should Janet practice naïve altruism or naïve philanthropy, simply giving, and expect an institution, person, or agency to do its work wisely. There are numerous pitfalls to such practices that preclude success, and it is morally irresponsible as well.

Postscript

In the end, having weighed all the arguments for her largesse, and given her interests, Janet decided to work with WFMIC, linking that foundation with other agencies and donor organizations that know Nigeria and have been successful there. But she did not make a contribution to the organization. At home she worked with ASA to divest itself of Smith House, finding housing and adequate counseling for its inhabitants, and managing the negative fallout from this decision. Then she helped ASA get its organization and funding in order, and helped it raise new monies so that it could increase its outreach activities in the region. After the divestiture of Smith House, Janet gave a large donation to ASA. She then donated a small portion of her money to the reading agency, which was more in need of volunteers than money. She helped that agency expand its volunteers, created teams that follow up on student progress and linked that initiative to social service agencies that help the families of these children in other ways.

Notes

1. Mary Wollstonecraft, *A Vindication of the Rights of Women* (New York: Alfred A. Knopf, 1792; 1992), p. 77.
2. World Health Organization, *World Health Report 2000*, p. 1.
3. Victoria Neufeldt, ed., *Webster's New World College Dictionary* (New York: Macmillan, 1977).
4. Worldwide Fund for Mothers Injured in Childbirth, 2000. See http://www.wfmic.org.

5. Lawrence Blum, "Altruism and Benevolence," in *Blackwell Encyclopedic Dictionary of Business Ethics*, ed. Patricia Werhane and R. E. Freeman (Oxford: Blackwell's, 1997), p. 19.

6. Joseph Butler, *Fifteen Sermons Preached at Rolls Chapel* (London: Thomas Tegg & Son, 1726), p. 183. Bishop Joseph Butler, (1692–1752), was an eighteenth-century bishop in the Church of England, but he is recognized as a prominent moral philosopher, particularly in his collection, *Fifteen Sermons Preached at Rolls Chapel*.

7. Adam Smith, *The Theory of Moral Sentiments*, ed. A. L. Macfie and D. D. Raphael (Oxford: Oxford University Press, 1790; 1976), I.i.1.1. Adam Smith (1723–1790) was a well-known eighteenth-century Scottish economist and moral philosopher, best known for his work on political economy, *The Wealth of Nations* (1776). But he is a serious moral philosopher as well, as evidenced in his earlier book, *The Theory of Moral Sentiments* (1759).

8. Smith derives this conclusion by arguing that each of us, as human beings, has three sets of distinguishing "natural" passions, which he calls the selfish passions, the social passions, and the unsocial passions. The selfish passions are the basis for our interests in and of the self. These include selfishness, when I am both the subject and the object of these passions. But egoism, selfishness, or self-love does not exhaust the description of the selfish passions. Also included are my self-interests in others as legitimate objects of personal sympathy and concern. These latter passions overlap with the social passions, the sources of altruism, benevolence, and justice, where there is concern for needs, interests, rights, or fair treatment of others, including treatment of strangers. The unsocial passions refer to envy, revenge, hate, and so on. Smith, *Theory*, I.i.

9. Patricia Werhane, *Adam Smith and His Legacy for Modern Capitalism* (New York: Oxford University Press, 1991).

10. Smith, *Theory*, VI.ii.3.6.

11. Ibid., II.ii.3.4.

12. Ibid., II.ii.3.1.

13. Ibid., II..ii.3.3.

14. Thus in the *Wealth of Nations* Smith argues that because in commerce one is often dealing with strangers, one does not have duties to beneficence, but one does have duties—indeed, perfect duties—to play fairly. Adam Smith, *The Wealth of Nations*, ed. R. H. Campbell and A. S. Skinner (Oxford: Oxford University Press, 1776; 1976).

15. Benevolence and beneficence are used more or less interchangeably. *Webster's New World College Dictionary* defines each as follows:

    benevolence: an inclination to do good; kindliness; a kindly, charitable act or gift; beneficence.
    beneficence: the fact or quality of being kind or doing good; charity, a charitable act or gift.
    philanthropy: a desire to help mankind, especially as shown by gifts to charitable or humanitarian institutions; benevolence.

16. This is the second formulation of Kant's famous Categorical Imperative. ("Act in such a way that you always treat humanity, whether in your own person or

in the person of any other, never simply as a means, but always at the same time as an end." Immanuel Kant, *Groundwork of the Metaphysics of Morals*, trans. H. J. Paton (New York: Harper and Row, 1785; 1964), p. 96.

17. Kant is then often interpreted as saying that an obligation to be philanthropic is an imperfect duty in the sense that it is not always wrong not to be kind, generous, and giving. According to this reading, Kant concludes that it is prudentially wise to help others since one may need such help oneself at some time or another, but not a perfect duty.

In a recent book, *The Practice of Moral Judgment*, Barbara Herman has questioned this reading of Kant and argues that one can derive a duty to beneficence from the Categorical Imperative. She begins with the first formulation of the CI ("Act only on that maxim through which you can at the same time will that it should become a universal law."); see Kant, *Groundwork*, p. 89. From that statement one could speculate that a misanthrope could allegedly formulate a universalizable maxim that "no one should ever help anyone." But such a maxim has flaws. It would mean that I could not help myself, a violation of the second formulation of the Categorical Imperative. Moreover, I could not reasonably expect help from others, nor would it be rational to help others, as those actions would violate the maxim. But both of these moves, since they are self-destructive and socially destructive, would, by Kant's logic, be irrational! Moreover, Herman argues, since the CI in all its formulations contains the underlying assumption that we live in communities and thus have duties to each other, the duty to mutual aid follows. See Barbara Herman, *The Practice of Moral Judgment* (Cambridge, Mass.: Harvard University Press, 1993), pp. 60–67.

18. Immanuel Kant, 121, quoted in Herman, *Practice*, p. 60.

19. Ibid., p. 67.

20. Alex Perry, "Inside the Battle at Qala-I-Jangi," *Time*, 158:25 (2001).

21. Many stories about missionaries tend to depict them, often wrongly, as "values Nazis."

22. R. Corkey, "Benevolence and Justice," *Philosophical Quarterly* 9 (1959): 152.

23. Ibid., p. 159.

24. Ibid., p. 160.

25. This generous philanthropist (she has given away $195 million) is famous for delivering her gifts in person, even to the very poor, in her chauffeur-driven limousine, always wearing a black dress and a strand of real and very large pearls. Alex Kuczynski, "Candles for a Darling of Society and Charity," *New York Times*, March 20, 2002, B1.

26. John Rawls, *A Theory of Justice* (Cambridge, Mass.: Harvard University Press, 1971), p. 303.

27. Ibid., p. 302.

28. National Commission for the Protection of Human Subjects of Biomedical and Behavioral Research, *Belmont Report: Ethical Principles and Guidelines for the Protection of Human Subjects of Research* (Washington, D.C.: Department of Health, Education, and Welfare, 1979), pp. 8–10.

Part Three: Issues for Religious Communities

5 Nonprofits and Morals: Jewish Perspectives and Methods for Resolving Some Commonly Occurring Moral Issues

Elliot N. Dorff

Nonprofit agencies that provide educational, religious, cultural, and social services face some of the same moral issues that for-profit companies do. For example, nonprofits must negotiate contracts with their employees, provide a morally, physically, and emotionally sound working environment, and evaluate employees' performance fairly and frequently. Nonprofits must also manage their budgets with accuracy and integrity, and they must find ways to market their services effectively but honestly. But some issues arise in nonprofit agencies that either do not occur at all in for-profit companies or appear in a significantly different form. Philanthropists rightly expect that the nonprofit institutions they support will operate in a morally sensitive and upright manner. Because a multitude of books on business ethics deal with the moral issues that both for-profit companies and nonprofit institutions face, in this paper I shall consider a Jewish approach to a few of the most common issues faced by nonprofit institutions uniquely in their form, degree, or kind.[1]

Why specifically a Jewish approach? Why not just a moral approach? The answer is embedded in the very word *religion*. The *lig* in the word *religion* comes from the same Latin root from which we get the English word *ligament*, which is connective tissue. The Latin root means connection, tie, or link. Religions, among other things, describe our ties to the members of our family, our community, the larger human community, the environment, and the transcendent (imaged in the Western faiths as God). Religions thereby give us a broad picture of who we are—as individuals and as communities—and who we should strive to be.

Secular philosophies like Western liberalism, communism, and existentialism also offer large pictures of who we are and ought to be, but while religions grow up within the context of a community that tries to live according to the religion's convictions, secular philosophies are usually created by one or several individuals who have no specific connection to a community. Sometimes nations later adopt secular philosophies, as demonstrated in the ways in which the United States, Canada, Australia, New Zealand, and the Western European countries operate on the basis of the principles of Western liberalism, and as China and the former Union of Soviet Socialist Republics embraced differing forms of communism, but many secular philosophies never come to achieve that communal expression or influence. Moreover, in sharp contrast to religious theories, most secular theories ignore the transcendent element of human experience or claim that it does not exist.

When Americans speak of secular ethics, they are really speaking of the views of Western liberalism, where individual autonomy is the key value. This concept is embodied in Jefferson's words in the Declaration of Independence: "We hold these truths to be self-evident: that all men are created equal, that they are endowed by their Creator with certain unalienable rights, and that among these are life, liberty, and the pursuit of happiness." In contrast, Jews standing at Mount Sinai stood there as a community, not a collection of individuals, and as a group they received not a single right but rather 613 commandments. There are many overlapping convictions in the American and Jewish ways of looking at the world, including, for example, a thoroughgoing commitment to law and a fundamental respect for the individual, but there are many differences as well. I compare the American, Christian, and Jewish perspectives on life in some detail elsewhere.[2]

Specific moral norms are rooted in these big pictures of who we are and who we ought to be. For example, whether we should see the poor as immorally lazy, as criminal (remember that debtors' prisons existed in England until the nineteenth century), as objects of pity, as people down on their luck, as people who need to be taken off the streets so as not to impede business, or as creations of God for whom we are duty-bound to care will, obviously, have an immense effect on the specific responses to poverty that we think are right and proper.

In this chapter, then, I am rooting my responses to the problems I consider in the Jewish tradition, both because that is my own tradition and the one I know best, and also because Judaism uses a legal methodology that may be unfamiliar to most non-Jews but that has some distinct advantages in resolving new moral problems. I discuss the ways in which religions in general and Judaism in particular affect morality, both negatively and positively, in my book, *Love Your Neighbor and Yourself: A Jewish Approach to Modern Personal Ethics.*[3] I also discuss at some length the various methodologies that Judaism uses to gain moral guidance and motivate moral behavior. Suffice it to say here that Judaism seeks to accomplish those moral tasks through all of the following: story (especially the Exodus–Sinai story); history (e.g., the moral lessons of the Holocaust); general values, proverbs, and moral theories (e.g., the biblical Book of Proverbs and the Mishnah's *Ethics of the Fathers*); creation of a community that teaches moral norms and expects moral behavior; prayer (e.g., prayers of confession); theology (e.g., the doctrines stating that we should imitate God and that we are created in the image of God); and laws.

Judaism puts a great deal of emphasis on the last of those, law, as a tool to discern moral norms and motivate moral action—more, I think, than most other traditions, but Islam and Confucianism come close to Judaism in this facet. Christians may find this emphasis on the use of law for moral purposes surprising, for classical Christian texts express a very negative view of law. The Gospels' depiction of the Pharisees as legalistic, especially in Matthew, sets the tone for seeing Jews as concerned only with details of rules and not with broader aims. Paul's description of law as leading people to sin and as the exact opposite of a life lived by the Spirit is another major source of Christians' negative views of the law.[4] Society may need laws as long as we live in Augustine's City of Man, but law is not, for Christian writers, the way to know what is right and good. Moreover, Enlightenment thinkers such as John Locke and their political heirs (e.g., Thomas Jefferson) were wary of law because they saw it abused to advance the interests of the aristocracy through patronage, and so they sought instead to formulate "self-evident truths" and moral principles that would presumably apply to all human beings and thus be above the venal machinations of human rulers and governments.

Both the importance of law within Judaism and the disparaging attitude toward it within Christianity and Enlightenment thought motivated me to focus on the role of law in Jewish morality in the Appendix of *Love Your Neighbor and Yourself.* Here is a list of some of the ways Jewish law aids in defining and motivating morality, ways that I discuss at length there:

1. Law defines and enforces minimal standards.
2. Law articulates and helps to actualize moral ideals.
3. Law provides a forum for weighing conflicting moral values and setting moral priorities.
4. Law gives moral norms a sense of the immediate and the real.
5. Law gives moral norms a good balance of continuity and flexibility.
6. Law serves as an educational tool for morality.
7. Law provides a way to make amends and repair moral damage.
8. Law helps to preserve the integrity of moral intentions.

Note that Jewish law, like American law, is largely based on judicial precedents, in contrast to Continental European law, which is based more heavily on codes of laws (the Napoleonic Code, the Prussian Code, etc.). Thus the kind of legal reasoning that produces the advantages listed above is, within Judaism, not systematic, with the goal of putting everything into a clear and universal order, but rather casuistic—that is, it contains discussions of the similarities and differences in both facts and principles between the current case and previous ones—with supple attention to the complexities of life. It is precisely such reasoning that I will be using in this essay.

One other methodological point is critical. Jewish individuals and groups apply all the resources that Judaism provides to specific moral problems *within the context of a community covenanted to God and to each other.* That concept applies at least as much to law as it does to the other Jewish sources of morality, for the Torah depicts God as commanding us to obey Jewish law. Representatives of

Judaism's Reform Movement historically have gone furthest in focusing on the role of autonomy in determining what Jewish law demands of an individual now; but in recent years even Reform leaders have emphasized that for individuals' decisions to be recognizably Jewish, Jews must learn the Jewish tradition and make their decisions in light of their covenant with the Jewish people and God.[5] Those Jews who take a more traditional and communal approach root their decisions even more strongly in Jewish traditional texts and in the Jewish community's covenant with God. Thus the contemporary awareness among scholars of literature, religion, and law of *the importance of the reader and his or her community* in choosing, interpreting, and applying texts very much characterizes the various contemporary Jewish approaches to gaining moral guidance from the Jewish tradition.[6]

This point has another implication. Nonprofit organizations are valued because they serve human needs, but they also gain importance as a way to give a community a sense of identity. In 1982, Jacob Neusner suggested that with all the differences among groups of Jews today, it is precisely acts of social action and charity (*tzedakah,* justice) that form the core of many Jews' identity as Jews.[7] For philanthropy to do that, however, it cannot be just "love of human beings," as the etymology of the word suggests; it must flow out of Judaism's much more particular and robust sense of *tzedakah,* in which Jews are *commanded* and *expected* to engage in such acts for a variety of theological, communal, and moral reasons, and are given specific directions for doing so.[8] Thus it is important to run Jewish nonprofit agencies with specific and conscious rooting in the Jewish tradition not only because of the Jewish tradition's distinctive lens on the world and its particular methodologies, but also so that such agencies can function to give Jews a sense of identity.

I leave it to non-Jews to determine whether their particular religious or philosophical lenses and methodologies would concur with my Jewish responses to the specific moral issues I will be discussing and whether they can learn from the casuistic method I will be using and/or its results. I trust, though, that much of what I have to say will indeed be helpful to those of other faiths and those of no faith, for people commonly think about how individual cases should be resolved, although perhaps not as thoroughly as I will in this essay, and Anglo-Americans are additionally used to such casuistic reasoning in their legal system. I also suspect that this essay will be helpful to my fellow Jews, for most Jews are not trained in the kind of moral reasoning that our tradition provides. At the same time, since the old joke is that where there are two Jews there are at least three opinions—and some question whether you actually need two Jews for that!—I would imagine that at least some of my Jewish coreligionists might interpret our tradition differently. So what follows is one rabbi's application of the Jewish tradition to common moral problems faced by nonprofit institutions, with the hope that this discussion will help all readers think through these issues.

These matters, like most in life, do not exist on a moral plane alone. As Professor Robert Katz has pointed out to me, one other important vantage point from which to view these problems is economic.[9] Sometimes a good economic policy can support our moral ends, and in those instances a nonprofit institution will do well to pay attention to such economic advice. On the other end of the spectrum, sometimes our moral convictions force us to act contrary to what would otherwise be a good economic approach, and then we need to be aware of the costs we are paying and why, and we also need to find ways to make it economically possible to live by our moral principles. Either way, economics is an important factor to consider in some of these issues, for nonprofit institutions must remain economically viable if they have any hope of accomplishing their mission.

The three topics I treat in this chapter—tainted money, preferential treatment for donors and volunteers, and synagogue dues and contributions—do not have any obvious or intended connection. I have chosen them for two reasons: they all demonstrate how a Jewish lens on who we are and ought to be and a Jewish methodology based largely but not exclusively on law can contribute to understanding the issues involved and to resolving them; and they all occur often in the operation of both Jewish and non-Jewish philanthropic agencies. In articulating how one rabbi would use his religious tradition to respond to these problems, I hope that readers will gain an appreciation of the critical role of both the content and methods of a tradition in deciding difficult moral cases, together with whatever concrete advice readers may glean from my own Jewish resolution of them.

The Tainted Gift

1. The Boesky case. In the first case, someone who is accused of violating the law makes a substantial contribution to a nonprofit institution. Should it accept the gift? While this happens to many nonprofit agencies, I will use the example of Ivan Boesky's pledge to the Jewish Theological Seminary of America in New York before he was indicted. He had paid part of his pledge before the indictment, and that money had been used to erect the institution's new library building.

The first aspect to note is that when the issue came before the Seminary faculty and board of directors, Mr. Boesky had been indicted but not convicted. Jewish law presumes the innocence of everyone even more than American law does. In American law, confessions in both civil and criminal matters amount to a conviction. According to the Talmud, while confessions regarding monetary matters "are like a hundred witnesses," in criminal matters "a person cannot make himself a wicked person."[10] Thus until and unless Mr. Boesky had been convicted, the Seminary had to presume his innocence.

To his credit, on the morning before he was indicted for violations of the laws governing the stock market, Mr. Boesky called Chancellor Gerson Cohen to alert him as to what would be happening and to ask that his family's name be removed from the building so as not to embarrass the Seminary further. What, though, should the Seminary do with the money that he had already contributed? The Seminary would clearly not tear down the building, but should it try to raise money from other people and then hand back the sum of money Mr. Boesky contributed? After all, the Torah forbids the Temple from accepting "the hire of a harlot or the pay of a dog [a male prostitute],"[11] and that statement formulates the general rule against accepting ill-gotten gain.

Some, influenced by that law, by the moral idealism of the Prophets, and by concern for the Seminary's moral reputation, argued that the institute should indeed find a way to return the money. Others, though, noted that in Jewish law, even the thief himself who uses wood he stole to build his house need not tear down the house but must only return the monetary value of the wood together with a specified fine.[12] Moreover, according to Maimonides, an important twelfth-century rabbi and codifier of Jewish law, someone who acquires something from a person without knowing that it was stolen need not return even the money it was worth if the form of the object had changed (in this case, it was no longer money but a building) and if the original owners despair of getting their property back (which, given the difficulties of determining exactly who loses what in insider trading, could be assumed).[13] The decision, then, was that even though Mr. Boesky had only been indicted at that point, the Seminary would not accept any more money from him, for, as Maimonides also says, "It is forbidden to acquire anything that is [even] assumed to be stolen,"[14] but the Seminary would leave matters as they stood with the money that had already been used for construction.

The way the Seminary came to this decision is methodologically instructive. Clearly, everyone involved in the discussion was trying to root the decision in the Jewish tradition. Why they wanted to do that varied with each person. Members of the faculty and board of directors understand Jewish law to be authoritative variously because it is, at least in some way, the will of God, the tradition of the Jewish people, one important element of what defines us as Jews, and/or a rich source of moral guidance. Even so, people differed in how to interpret and apply the law to this case, with some emphasizing the laws that exempt unknowing recipients of stolen property from any liability and others focusing on Maimonides's warning against accepting anything that even *appeared* tainted. Others were interested in what Jewish law had to say, but were even more motivated by the Prophets' call to moral idealism and by the important principle in Jewish law and tradition holding that one's actions should not desecrate the reputation of God and the Jewish people (*hillul ha-shem*) and should instead sanctify God's Name (*kiddush ha-shem*). The result the Seminary reached combined these approaches by differentiating between the money that had already been collected and used, which it would not return, and the remaining portion of Mr. Boesky's pledge that it would not accept even if he could pay it after the indictment. This choice clearly indicated a commitment to make a recognizably *Jewish* decision by calling on the relevant sources within the Jewish tradition while at the same time asserting the authority and responsibility articulated by the tradition for the judges in each generation to make a *judgment* as to how those sources should be applied to the case at hand.[15] In other words, it was neither a decision that rested solely on individuals' consciences nor one that used Jewish sources as if they provided a "cookbook" answer that one could just look up; it was, rather, a decision rooted in Jewish sources but requiring *judgment* as to how to interpret and apply them.

2. *The Milken case.* Another case of tainted money, but with different issues and implications, involved Michael Milken, Mr. Boesky's right-hand man, who likewise served time in a federal prison for stock fraud. Before his conviction, however, he and his brother had established a charitable foundation. That foundation donated $5,000,000 to establish a Jewish high school in Los Angeles on condition that it be named the Milken Jewish Community High School.

Three issues distinguish this case from the previous one. First, the money did not come directly from the one who had done wrong but from a foundation. Does the fact that the money was not the direct product of a crime but at least somewhat at arms' length from it matter?

The Talmud discusses such issues. When legitimately earned money is mixed in with ill-gotten gain, the Talmud says that we decide whether we may use such money on the basis of the source of the majority of the funds (*azli'nan b'tar rubbah b'issurah*).[16] In this case, Mr. Milken was fined substantially, and so the funds that even he contributed to the foundation were most likely legitimately his. Thus it is possible that even had he contributed his own money to the school directly, it would be permissible to accept the funds; surely when his money had been mixed in with assets of the foundation from other sources, his money had lost whatever taint it had had.

The second factor that distinguishes the Milken case from the Boesky incident concerns Milken's efforts to make amends. In addition to serving a prison sentence, Mr. Milken cooperated with prosecutors and was clearly remorseful. Jewish tradition puts great stock in the ability of people to make up for their misdeeds and return to the proper path and to the good graces of the community and of God. The process is called *teshuvah,* return; it is not just "repentance," where the Latin root means punishment, for the object of the Jewish procedure is to compensate victims and to do nothing less than change the character of the culprit so that he or she does not act that way again. As a result, the requirements of return are stringent. The culprit must (1) admit the wrongdoing, (2) express remorse, (3) confess publicly, (4) ask for forgiveness from the aggrieved party, (5) compensate the victims monetarily and in other appropriate ways (such as telling people that negative remarks made about the person were wrong), and (6) ultimately, when the same opportunity arises to violate the law, act differently.[17] (Christians might compare this procedure to the lessons of the Gospel story of the Prodigal Son.) Whenever possible, the culprit must make amends directly to the victim, but in Milken's case, it is hard, if not impossible, to identify which investors were hurt by his crimes, and so giving money to the public, either the government or public charities, is the best that could have been expected.

The community also has responsibilities in this process: It must encourage and reinforce efforts to "do *teshuvah,*" and except if disclosing the past sin is necessary for some practical reason, as, for example, in the process of deciding whether to hire the culprit for a specific job, once a person has completed the procedure, nobody may ever speak of the wrongdoing again.[18] In this, the Jewish tradition acknowledges both human fallibility and the need for restoration of a person's sense of self-worth and communal acceptance to prevent recidivism, and it also rewards people for making sincere efforts to make amends for their wrongdoing. In light of Mr. Milken's remorseful behavior in court and after his conviction, the gift, even if it was his alone, might legitimately be seen as part of his process of return, such that the community would have not only the right, but possibly even the duty, to accept it for the school. (This was not relevant in the Boesky case because the Seminary had to make its decision shortly after he was indicted and thus before he had an opportunity to go through the process of return.)

Some, of course, would suspect Milken's motives: Was he merely trying to buy forgiveness? Even though the Jewish tradition is generally very realistic about people's actions and motivations, it would, I think, not doubt the sincerity of his *teshuvah*. First, it recognizes that motives are personal and hard for others to judge. For that matter, it is often hard for individuals themselves to know their true motives, for even when we have a primary motive for something we do, we often are moved by other concerns as well. So, for example, I may eat because I am hungry, but also because I am with other people who are eating; I paid for the meal; the food represents motherly love; and so on. Thus even if multiple motives, including some venal ones, moved Milken to go through the process of *teshuvah*, the fact that he did it is what counts. Conversely, no matter how much he expressed remorse, if he had not undertaken the concrete actions demanded by the process of *teshuvah*, the Jewish tradition would not believe him. Despite the understandable skepticism about Milken's motives, then, Judaism would consider his actions *teshuvah* for several reasons: (1) Actions are publicly verifiable while intentions are not; (2) good actions benefit others no matter what motivated them; and (3) even if less-than-admirable motives led to Milken's acts of restitution, the Talmud would prefer that he do the right thing even if it is for the wrong reason, for "in doing something not for its sake one will come to do it for its sake."[19] Thus Judaism does not require absolute moral purity in one's motives for remorse to be considered real; it takes a much more contextualized approach, which encourages sincerity in making amends but acknowledges that a culprit might have multiple motives, and in the end it requires that we grant forgiveness upon completion of the required reparative actions.

The third new factor in this case concerns the name of the school. What should we make of the condition that the school be named after the Milken family? Would naming it thus reward the sinner, an act that the Talmud specifically forbids?[20] Would the connection to Michael Milken sully the school's reputation forever?

Naming the school after the Milken family would not be rewarding a sinner, for the whole family was neither indicted nor convicted. The Torah explicitly forbids punishing one member of a family for the sins of another.[21] (In contrast, until 1830 English law recognized "corruption of blood" and "crimes of attaint," in which family members would suffer for the crimes of their ancestors or other family members, and so the founders of the United States saw the need specifically to prohibit such liability in Article 3, Section 3 of the Constitution.)

Moreover, even if the school had been named after Mr. Milken himself, since the gift came after he had been convicted and had served his sentence, the nomenclature could reasonably be seen as part of his own *teshuvah*. That is, the naming would be rewarding not a sinner, but one who was trying to expunge his sin through the process of return. Indeed, the Jewish tradition maintains that a person who has overcome sin is, in some ways, of stronger character and more to be admired than someone who has never been tempted to sin in that way in the first place. As Maimonides says,

> Do not imagine that one who has done *teshuvah* is far from the status of the righteous because of the transgressions and sins he has done. On the contrary, the repentant sinner is beloved and favored by the Creator as if he had never sinned. Moreover, his reward is great, for, after all, he has tasted the flavor of sin and separated himself from it and overcome his temptation for it. The Sages say: "In a place where those who have done *teshuvah* stand, there completely righteous people cannot stand";[22] that is, their status is greater than the status of those who have never sinned because they have overcome their temptation more than completely righteous people have.[23]

Whether the majority of Jews and non-Jews value return as much as the Jewish tradition does is, of course, an open question, and so those who recruit for the school and seek donations for it may be turned off by the name and its association with a former convict, but the Jewish tradition would have no such qualms. In the end, the school was created with the Milken funds and named as the family wished.

3. The Philip Morris case. This case involved legally less tainted money and therefore was, in some ways, harder to adjudicate. The situation also had somewhat different implications. It arose at the Jewish Family Service (JFS) of Los Angeles, where I am chair of the board of directors' ethics committee. The Philip Morris Company offered to donate $25,000 to one of the programs of JFS on condition that Philip Morris be allowed to publicize the fact that it had made this contribution. While tobacco companies have been convicted of hiding what they have known about the effects of smoking on health,[24] their earnings still remain legal. In that sense, this case differs from either of the former ones. At the same time, their tobacco products demonstrably cause harm to their users, even in small amounts (in contrast, say, to liquor). Moreover, one of the programs JFS runs is "L'Chaim!" a program cleverly named "To life!," the traditional toast, to help people overcome drug and alcohol abuse. Some of the board members consequently did not want JFS to be tied to a company that sells an addictive product. The verse from Deuteronomy (23:19) prohibiting the Temple from taking the hire of a harlot was invoked as evidence that we should avoid any involvement with the company.

There was another Jewish principle at play in these discussions. Leviticus

19:14 says, "Do not put a stumbling block before the blind." While the Torah probably meant the physically blind, the Rabbis extended this prohibition to apply to the intellectually and morally blind as well. Specifically, according to the Rabbinic expansion of the meaning of this verse, a Jew may not give misleading information about a business prospect to someone who does not know how to evaluate it, or directions to someone when the person asked does not really know how to get to the desired place.[25] Similarly, the Talmud asserts that one may not "put a stumbling block before the blind" by striking a grown child (who may then strike the parent back, thus violating the commands to honor and respect parents in Exodus 20:12 and Leviticus 19:3 and the specific prohibition of striking them in Exodus 21:15 or by offering alcohol to an alcoholic.[26] Would a JFS association with Philip Morris, then, be putting a stumbling block before the blind by giving the company advertising opportunities and perhaps even leading people to think that the agency endorses smoking?

Three issues were raised during discussions at the Ethics Committee and subsequently before the Executive Committee and the full board of directors. First, it was maintained that the Philip Morris Company is no longer simply a tobacco company; it now is a conglomerate that owns other companies that have nothing to do with tobacco. As a result, *if* the bulk of the conglomerate's money is not earned through the manufacture and sale of tobacco—a fact that we did not check—the same issue of mixed funds that arose in the Milken case might apply here.

The issue that occupied our fractious discussion more was brought up by one board member and major donor who earned his money through importing clothing. He asked how far we would go to investigate the sources of people's contributions. After all, we certainly do not want to endorse the sweat shops of the Far East, but does that mean that JFS should not accept this donor's own contributions? But then do we have a duty to check the source of every donor's income? That would clearly be an impossible standard to administer, even if it were deemed desirable to do so. In other words, in the broad network of relationships that have made us "a global village," it may now be rare to accept a gift that is completely morally pure; hence, the very language of moral "taint" may be too judgmental. As the board member put it, money may be filthy altogether, and even if some sources of money are filthier than others, as soon as you go beyond the standard of money criminally obtained it arguably becomes impossible in practice to sift morally good money from bad.

On the other hand, some companies on moral grounds divested their stock holdings in tobacco companies and in South Africa during the period of apartheid, but one has to be worried about making unfair judgments. Recently, for example, some universities have found themselves with petitions to divest their holdings in Israel to protest Israel's occupation of the West Bank, but then why not also divest holdings in all Arab countries, for they, after all, are not democratic and they discriminate against women and all religions but Islam? Thus "taking the high moral road" in such matters, while tempting, quickly leads to murky situations.

The third issue was privacy. Even for donors whose sources of income raise no moral problems whatsoever, we do not, as a matter of policy, allow companies to film our clients in programs that the donor sponsors. For that matter, JFS itself takes great precautions to preserve privacy and dignity when filming clients for advertising and fund raising for its own programs.

The issue of *teshuvah* was not seriously discussed because the company never presented its offer as part of an attempt to make up for past wrongdoing. If it had, we would have confronted an interesting question—namely, whether corporations can do *teshuvah*. Not surprisingly, classical Jewish sources do not contemplate such a question because such corporations did not exist. In recent decades, though, Jewish law has been stretched to address a whole host of issues that our ancestors did not know, especially regarding medical ethics.[27] To my knowledge, nobody has addressed this question, but the collapse of Enron, Worldcom, and other large companies due to fraud begs for such an analysis.

In the end, the board decided that it would take the Philip Morris money only on condition that the company not film those helped by the program to which it was contributing and only if it would not advertise the contribution altogether. Philip Morris agreed to these conditions. Truthfully, if the contribution had been larger, I wonder if the last condition would have been made or agreed to—and that raises the sticky and disturbing issue of whether our moral scruples can be bought for the right price.

Preferential Treatment

Among the many other moral issues that nonprofit organizations face, one common one is the request of a major donor or someone active in volunteering for the institution to put himself, herself, or a family member ahead of others seeking services. Should such people be accommodated in recognition of their support of the organization? Can an institution hope to gain additional donations by allowing this policy, and, if so, how should the policy be crafted and administered? By contrast, should it be a matter of fairness to accept people for service only on a strict, first-come, first-served basis?

The Jewish Homes for the Aged in Los Angeles have this very problem. Offering a warm environment and top-quality assisted living and skilled nursing care, the Jewish Homes have a long waiting list as well. That is only likely to increase as the American Jewish population ages. Do board members, volunteers, and donors deserve to have their relatives placed at the front of the queue? If so, does this policy effectively transform donations and volunteer work into pre-payments for a privilege not granted to others? On the other hand, a nonprofit organization cannot survive without the money and service given by such people, and morally the organization does owe a debt of gratitude to its volunteers. What is the fairest way, then, of honoring people's contributions of time and treasure while yet preserving access to scarce resources to those who either have not or cannot contribute in such ways?

Just to make it clear that these things do not happen in Los Angeles alone, the *New York Times* on November 16, 2002 printed an article entitled, "Private Preschool Admissions: Grease and the City."[28] Places in private preschools in New York are at a premium, and so it is apparently a widespread practice of people to contact friends on the board of directors to exert whatever influence they can to get their children admitted. Moreover, rich people also arrange for substantial donations to such schools, either personally or through the companies for which they work. The article began with the story of Jack Grubman, the former star telecommunications analyst at Smith Barney, who arranged for the Chairman of Citigroup, Smith Barney's parent company, to give $1 million to the 92nd Street YMHA to underwrite lectures and other events so that his twins could be accepted into the Y's preschool. The article quotes one board member as saying: "Look, it's a well-known fact that when you send your child to an independent school in the city, if you have the money, you're expected to pay a lot more than the $20,000 tuition. In many cases parents are paying $50,000 to $100,000 a year."[29] Mr. Grubman himself voiced amazement at this:

> We are going through the ridiculous but necessary process of preschool applications in Manhattan. . . . For someone who grew up in a household with a father making $8,000 a year and for someone who attended public schools, I do find this process a bit strange, but there are no bounds for what you do for your children. . . . Given that it's statistically easier to get into the Harvard freshman class than it is to get into preschool at the 92nd Street Y [by the way, this is a correct statement], it comes down to "who you know."[30]

How shall we think of such "greasing" of the wheels and such influence peddling? In a legal setting, the Torah establishes crystal-clear guidelines:

> You shall not be partial in judgment: Hear out low and high alike. Fear no man, for judgment is God's.[31]

> You shall not render an unfair decision; do not favor the poor or show deference to the rich; judge your kinsman fairly.[32]

> When a stranger resides with you in your land, you shall not wrong him. The stranger who resides with you shall be to you as one of your citizens; you shall love him as yourself, for you were strangers in the land of Egypt: I the Lord am your God.[33]

The rabbis of the Talmud and the Middle Ages added many more procedural rules to ensure impartial treatment. For example, one litigant may not be required to stand while the other is sitting; both parties to the case must wear clothing of similar quality; judges must understand the languages spoken by the people before them; and witnesses may not be related either to each other or to the litigants.[34] Through rules such as these the Torah and the Rabbis made procedural justice a reality, and, if applied directly to our cases, such rules would require that no special privileges apply to rich donors or to volunteers.

But are the rules for courts appropriate for admissions decisions made by nonprofit organizations? In some ways they are. Like courts, those making these decisions on behalf of a nonprofit institution must be concerned with questions of fairness, for that moral (and Jewish) duty applies to all people and groups. Moreover, nonprofit organizations are well warned to "hear out high and low alike," for otherwise they stand in danger of failing to help some of the very people they were created to serve.

In other ways, though, nonprofit organizations differ from courts. First, while courts are established and funded by communities, nonprofit institutions depend for their very existence on the voluntary service and donations of people who believe in their cause. Furthermore, for justice to happen judges must not be influenced by debts owed to anybody; indeed, even the process by which American judges must either seek election or political appointment threatens the objectivity of courts, and hence the rule for some courts is to appoint judges for life. Nonprofit institutions, though, use not only paid help but unpaid board members and volunteers, and they ask people to donate money. As a result, by their very nature they cannot be fair and objective.

In fact, on two different grounds one could reasonably argue that nonprofit organizations *should not* be completely objective and fair. First, the money and effort that some people contribute to their cause creates a debt of gratitude. Volunteer work and donations may not be counted as *quid pro quo* payment for special treatment, for that would undermine the very character of the gift that they presumably had given. In other words, it would be morally less worthy and possibly even wrong for someone to donate money to an institution *for the sake of* getting special treatment. That is the kind of situation educational institutions sometimes encounter when a rich donor suggests that he or she will finance the school's new building but only on condition that his or her child is admitted. Many nonprofit institutions are not able to resist such financial pressure, but surely everyone involved understands that such gifts are not really gifts; they are a price that the donor is paying to buy a place in the class—and, perhaps, the moral scruples of those who run the school. On the other hand, when someone has been donating to an institution or working for it on a volunteer basis for a long time and only then needs a special favor, there does seem to be a debt of gratitude that the institution has toward that person. The extent of that debt and what the institution should be prepared to do in response will appropriately vary with the size of the donated money or service and the length of time over which the relationship has occurred. But Jewish sources recognize such debts of gratitude: one is supposed to recognize favors (*hakarat ha-tov*), not only in words but also in deeds.[35]

There is another consideration that would argue for special treatment in these cases. Jewish law—and general morality—recognizes that duties flow out of relationships. Thus, according to the Talmud my obligations to my family are greater than my duties to my community, and those, in turn, are greater than my obligations to other human beings.[36] Ultimately, my duty to preserve myself comes before my duties to all others, for as Rabbi Akiba pointed out, the Torah demands that you help others "so that your brother can live *with you*," but that is only possible if you yourself are alive.[37] In our cases, though, through donating money and/or time, the person has established a relationship with the institution and is part of its extended family. Viewed this way, special treatment for such people would be justified as what one should do for those near and dear beyond that which one should do for anyone else.

To avoid even the taint of unfairness, however, nonprofit organizations would be well advised to establish policies defining these forms of special treatment and who is eligible for them. The Jewish Homes for the Aged has, in fact, done that. Members of the board of directors and its committees and long-time or major donors do get preferential treatment according to a formula discussed and approved as institutional policy by the board of directors. That way, everyone is put on notice that these will be the rules of the game and that the institution will adhere to them fairly. This does entail the danger that people will give to the institution *in order to* get the special favors later on, thus sullying at least somewhat the purity of their gifts; but the longer the relationship with the institution, the less that that is a problem.

An economic analysis of this situation would support this policy. As Professor Katz pointed out, the nursing home provides a costly service that we want to distribute to people on an equitable basis, including those who cannot afford to pay its true costs. We, the board of directors of the nursing home, propose to provide it to them at below cost (or even for free) on the basis of a sliding scale based on ability to pay. We can only do that by charging more to those who are willing and able to pay more; this is *cross-subsidization*. (We also engage in fund raising to supplement that source of income.)

With perfect information, we could charge each would-be consumer exactly the right amount, but that information is hard to acquire because people have an economic incentive to understate how much they are willing and able to pay. The fact that there is a waiting list means that we are currently charging less than the market price. We could eliminate the queue by charging everybody more, but that would frustrate our distributive goals.

The cheapest, easiest, and most effective way to get those willing and able to pay more to reveal their willingness and ability to do so is precisely to adopt a policy of letting relatives of large donors jump ahead in the queue. We have to be careful, though, not to specify too precisely how preferential their treatment will be because the clearer the *quid pro quo* nature of this policy is, the less like a gift it is for tax purposes.

We could apply a similar preferential policy to volunteers, but an economic perspective would have us be more selective in the kinds of volunteers to whom we extend such privileges. We would give them to board members, gerontologists, nurses, psychologists, physical therapists, and entertainers who volunteer their time, but probably not to candy stripers. That is because, after all, such spots have a clear economic worth, and in awarding them we must be constantly aware, especially as the population ages and demand increases, that other people who would bring in more money might fill them instead.

In this case, then, our moral principles and economically sound policy work in sync. Moreover, it is important to recognize both sides of the issue, for if we look only at the moral side, we may be doing the morally right thing while dooming the institution to bankruptcy, but if we look only at the economic side, we might feel morally troubled by the preferential treatment that the economics of the situation has led us to adopt. As it happens, after thorough analysis, we find that in this case the moral and economic factors coincide to suggest the limited kind of preferential policy that the Jewish Homes in fact established.

These moral and economic factors suggest that there are at least three categories of preferential treatment, with varying levels of moral legitimacy. The Grubman case and those like it are the hardest to justify because they are based solely on money: Grubman had had no relationship with the school before arranging for the contribution. On the other end of the spectrum is the Jewish Homes case, where money alone is not the criterion, but rather an ongoing relationship is a significant factor. Furthermore, fairness is preserved through a policy that specifies who will be treated more kindly than others, together with the reasons why that sort of discrimination is warranted. This way, anyone can do what is necessary to get into the favored group. In between the Grubman case and the Jewish Homes case is the policy of many universities to give preferential treatment to children of alumni ("legacies"), especially to those who have continually contributed to the school. There a long-term relationship exists, but only alumni and their children can qualify.

Two Special Issues for Synagogues

Lay and professional leaders faced with establishing and carrying out the policies of a synagogue often find themselves adrift in a sea without moral moorings. In large measure, this is because a synagogue is, by its very nature, a unique institution. It is not a business whose daily operations and whose interactions with customers are determined by the goal of making a profit. It is not even exactly like a nonprofit educational or social service agency, whose relations with students or clients are limited to one function at a time. In some ways, a synagogue is like an extended family, with all the complicated rights and responsibilities of familial relationships. Families, though, emerge out of births or out of serious and intended long-term commitments like marriage, while synagogue membership is completely voluntary and can be relinquished at any moment. Moreover, even families must run with some degree of efficiency in order to fulfill their missions, and the same is all the more true of public institutions like synagogues. Officers and professional managers of synagogues thus find themselves in situations without clear precedents primarily because they are heading a unique type of institution that has analogies to other institutions but no straightforward parallels.

To respond to the many moral issues that synagogues face, leaders should first try to get as clear a picture as possible of their goals. They undoubtedly want their synagogues to carry out functions effectively and efficiently. That means that they must have a clear sense of exactly what their mission is in the religious, educational, social, social action, ethnic (Zionist, interfaith, etc.), and cultural areas of life that synagogues usually address. They need to determine which of those areas are the most important in creating their ideal synagogue. They must also consider how those goals should affect not only *what* they do, but *how*. This would include how they run the support mechanisms that make their activities possible, including personnel, building and grounds, finance, publications, publicity, and so on. Most generally, they must think about how they want their synagogues to *feel*—like a place of holiness, an extended family, a community, an educational center, a social action center, a Jewish cultural center, or something else.

These general considerations will undoubtedly affect the way synagogue leaders address specific moral issues. To the extent that the synagogue is an extended family, for example, it will tolerate more from its members than a business would. That would mean that it might extend its services to some of its members in financial straits at reduced rates or even for free, just as families do for each other but as businesses rarely do. At the same time, it would also expect that members take responsibility for each other far beyond the duties that businesses have to their customers or even those that psychological professionals have to their clients. This might include visiting the sick, participating in synagogue efforts on behalf of the homeless and others in need, taking on some of the responsibility for the worship and educational functions of the synagogue, and perhaps assuming a leadership role in the synagogue. At the same time, to the extent that the synagogue is a public institution, it must insist on dues, on effective personnel, and on efficient administration. And as a Jewish religious institution, it must seek to work toward exemplifying the highest moral standards in whatever it does. Carrying out these many roles is admittedly very difficult, but having a clear understanding of the multifaceted and unique entity that a synagogue is can help both to alleviate frustration and to discern what the synagogue should do to resolve its moral problems.

One problem that synagogues face continually will make this clear—namely, the dues structure. Because synagogues are not businesses, they seek to make it possible for anyone to join, regardless of a congregant's financial ability to pay dues or to contribute. Even for those who are reasonably well off, dues cannot be set too high, lest they decide not to join altogether. In order to balance the budget, then, synagogues must raise only a portion of their money from dues, relying on donations from their most committed and financially able members to provide the rest of what is needed.

One aspect of the problem, then, is determining how to evaluate the claims of some people that they cannot afford the dues. The process by which the synagogue determines whether a claim for dues relief is justified is very important and also very sticky: the committee must be sure that the synagogue is not being cheated out of what it should fairly get and, at the same time, the committee needs to protect the privacy and dignity of those who apply for dues relief.

The Jewish tradition, in fact, speaks at considerable length about the importance of protecting people's privacy and dignity. While I have discussed this issue at some length elsewhere,[38] it will be helpful to summarize some of the relevant factors here. The Jewish concern with privacy begins with a provision in the Torah itself that bans intrusion for the purpose of collecting a debt:

> When you make a loan of any sort to your countryman, you must not enter his house to seize his pledge. You must remain outside, while the man to whom you made the loan brings the pledge out to you.[39]

Later Jewish law narrowed the debtor's right against intrusion. Because Jewish law does not permit creditors to charge interest on a loan to fellow Jews, the rabbis worried that if collecting the loan became an onerous process, people would no longer be willing to lend money to those who needed it, and that would, in the Talmud's phrase, be "locking the door in the face of [future] borrowers." The rabbis also wanted to prevent debtors from using their homes to hide items that could be used to repay the loan.[40]

Even with these later restrictions, the Torah's law prohibiting intrusions was taken very seriously. Creditors, after all, are justified in trying to recover the property owing to them in pledge, and even so the Torah limits their access to the debtor's home. Those like synagogue administrators or lay leaders who lack such grounds for entry, then, are all the more required to respect the privacy of those who dwell within. In fact, the general rule of Jewish law is that people may not enter someone else's home without permission, and if they do, the owner may eject them even by force, if necessary.[41] Furthermore, the rabbis advise people not to enter even their own home without warning lest they surprise and embarrass someone inside.[42] In one passage, they use God as the model: God called out to Adam, "Where are you?" to warn him that God was coming— and we should learn such good manners from the Holy One.[43]

In line with these principles, when the mail system expanded in the Middle Ages, Rabbenu Gershom (Germany, c. 960–1028) issued a decree prohibiting mail carriers and others from reading other people's mail lest they learn trade secrets or spread gossip, thus violating the prohibition of tale-bearing (Leviticus 19:16). According to the decree, violators would be subject to excommunication even if they did not publicize the contents of the improperly read letter. He thus recognized privacy as an important value in its own right apart from its importance in protecting people from harm.[44]

In the collection of taxes, probably the closest analogy to synagogue dues, Jewish communities also sought to insure confidentiality. Some demanded that the collectors be sequestered while working. The Frankfurt Jewish tax collectors refused to reveal entries in their books even to their superiors, the city treasurers; and the Hamburg community imposed severe fines for breaches of confidence.[45]

These privacy issues are compounded by economic ones. The case of the synagogue is harder to resolve on economic grounds than the last one discussed above, for the nursing home had a limited number of spaces and getting one would motivate people to reveal their ability to pay. By contrast, during most of the year the synagogue has plenty of space for more worshipers and would actually welcome them. How, then, can a synagogue motivate people to join and pay their fair share when the economics of the situation encourages them to take a free ride? One way is to restrict some of the synagogue's goods and services to members, as most synagogues do in requiring High Holy Day tickets, for then spaces are indeed at a premium. Similarly, a synagogue's youth program could be restricted to children of members, and some synagogues do exactly that. Synagogues, though, are reluctant to restrict other services because they see them as a form of outreach to encourage new people to join, and many even feel guilty about restricting seating on the High Holy Days to members. Ultimately, then, there is no good economic way to force people to pay their fair share; instead, the synagogue must appeal to moral motivations to get people to do that. Such motives would stress the unfairness of enjoying services without paying for them, the shame and guilt that one should feel if one does that, and the social pressure to assume one's rightful responsibility as a member of the group. Here the same factor discussed above of the depth of relationships applies, although in the opposite direction: the more that one becomes part of the group, the more one gains not only privileges, but responsibilities.

How, though, can a synagogue preserve the privacy of those who are willing to join but request reductions in dues while still fairly and effectively funding its operations? Many synagogues avoid the problem altogether for at least part of their membership by establishing lower dues for categories of people who generally have little money. This is also intended to encourage such people to join the synagogue. A common practice, for example, is to set dues for people younger than thirty years of age at a considerably lower rate than the standard dues, and many synagogues extend free membership to newly married couples during the first year of their marriage.

What about the majority of the membership, though? One synagogue, Temple Emanuel in San Francisco, sent its members a table of what the board set as "fair share" dues correlated to income, and it left it to members acting on the honor system to pay dues according to that structure. That synagogue did this both to avoid any invasion of privacy and also to entice people to join, for many who cannot afford to join a synagogue prefer to stay away from synagogues rather than subject themselves to a process of revealing their financial status to a committee. The synagogue actually collected more money using that method than it had by setting a fixed sum for dues that had provisions for relief for those who could not afford the cost. Other synagogues, however, have tried just such a plan and have regrettably not collected what the synagogue needed.

The other side of the problem is convincing the wealthiest members to contribute more than the dues structure demands so that the synagogue can have the money it needs. The English language calls that *charity*, from the Latin word for love; or *philanthropy*, from the Greek, meaning "love of man." These words establish the expectations of English speakers who use them—namely, that contributing charity is a generous act, going beyond what can be legitimately expected of anyone. The Hebrew word for such contributions, though, is *tzedakah*, from the root meaning "justice." That term well articulates the viewpoint in

Judaism that everyone has the duty to contribute to the welfare of others. Even if a poor person gives a coin to another poor person, and the latter just gives it back, every Jew is duty-bound to contribute to the poor and to other communal needs.[46] Those with money have all the more of a duty to support communal needs. Thus according to the Talmud and later Jewish law, the court can compel one who refuses to give charity—or who donates less than his means allow—to give according to the court's assessment, on pain of flogging, and if he still refuses, the court can forcibly appropriate his property for charity in the court's assessed sum.[47]

Modern fundraisers would undoubtedly love to have this authority! In countries like the United States, with a separation of church and state, however, fundraisers for Jewish causes like the synagogue must instead convince the wealthy to contribute of their own accord. Such organizations typically use honors of various sorts, but they also appeal to the potential donors' sense of responsibility, for Jews learn very early in their lives that their tradition sees philanthropy as a duty, not a supererogatory act.

While the best method to finance a synagogue's operations may vary from community to community and while every method may involve risks and problems, several things are clear: synagogues have a right to tax their members for synagogue services; they have a duty to all those who pay fairly not to let other people cheat the synagogue; they must, to insure honesty and fairness, specify objective, financial criteria for dues relief while also being open to modifying those criteria in cases of unusual need and to considering how applicants contribute to the synagogue in other ways; they have a duty to make the process of dues relief as dignified and private as possible; they have a Jewish duty to attract Jews to become members, including those who have little money; and they have a right to expect wealthy members to contribute significantly, even if a synagogue can no longer use legal means to extract such contributions. The method that a synagogue adopts should account as well as possible for all these factors.

Maintaining Morality and Holiness in a Nonprofit's Mission

By definition, nonprofit institutions are established to provide a needed service without the incentive of earning money in the process. There is thus a sense of nobility involved in what they do, a sense that motivates people to support them through their finances, time, and effort. Because nonprofit institutions are human creations, however, and because they must remain financially solvent, they inevitably run into moral problems.

In some of the cases I have discussed, conscious and careful attention to the issues involved and to setting public policy occurred, while in others people did what they thought they had to do to maintain donor loyalty, even if the methods raised moral qualms in the staff, volunteers, and other donors. Acknowledging the issues straightforwardly and then creating a fair process to deal with them can not only minimize any damage to the institution, but can actually strengthen its sense of mission and morality. With such careful ethical thinking, combined with equally careful economic and managerial analysis, the institution will be known not only as an idealistic undertaking, but one that succeeds in translating ideals into concrete reality.

Toward that end, the Jewish tradition, among others, can help. By definition, the moral problems that nonprofit institutions face are problems—that is, they present new or ongoing issues that require a balancing of goods, an avoidance of evils, and the wisdom and keen sense of judgment to do both while still maintaining the financial solvency and effectiveness of the institution. Thus it is not surprising that even the proponents of any one religion may not agree on what is to be done in response to a morally sticky situation. But in providing a clear picture of who we are and ought to be, together with long experience in applying that vision to the concrete realities of human life, Judaism, like other religions, provides the moral moorings and the experience that can suggest how nonprofit agencies can best deal with their specific moral issues and thereby strengthen their sense of mission and holiness.

For Jews and for others as well, this is not only a matter of morality, as important as that is; it is also a matter of holiness. In Leviticus 19:2, God says: "You shall be holy, for I, the Lord your God, am holy." That serves as the chapter heading for a long list of laws that include ritual ones, like observing the Sabbath and the prohibition of eating meat with its blood, and moral ones like respecting parents and ensuring honest weights and measures. Thus for Judaism, acting morally is required of us if we are to have good relations not only with other people, but also with God. Resolving the kinds of moral issues discussed in this essay, then, makes us not only more moral and humane, but also more holy as we seek to use God's law to imitate God and thereby become more like God.

Notes

The following abbreviations apply to all notes:

    M. = Mishnah (edited c. 200 C.E.)
    B. = Babylonian Talmud (edited c. 500 C.E.)
  M.T. = Maimonides's *Mishneh Torah* (1177)
  S.A. = Joseph Karo's *Shulhan Arukh* (1565)

1.   I would like to thank all the contributors to this project for their suggestions for revising the first draft of this essay. In particular, I would like to thank Drs. David Craig and Amy Kass, who were assigned the role of being the prepared respondents to that draft and who carried out that task thoroughly and perceptively, and yet kindly. While I am clearly responsible for what I say in this essay, I owe my co-authors much in helping me treat these topics more clearly and helpfully.

2.   Elliot N. Dorff, *To Do the Right and the Good: A Jewish Approach to Modern Social Ethics* (Philadelphia: Jewish Publication Society, 2002), Chapter 1.

3.   Elliot N. Dorff, *Love Your Neighbor and Yourself: A Jewish Approach to Modern Personal Ethics* (Philadelphia: Jewish Publication Society, 2003).

4.   On the New Testament's view of the Pharisees, see, for example, Matthew 3:7; Matthew 23; Luke 18:9–14, in which they are variously called "hypocrites" and "offspring of vipers." The Rabbis themselves recognized the insincere among their numbers, whom they called "sore spots" or "plagues on the Pharisaic party" (M. *Sotah* 3:4; B. *Sotah* 22b). With the exception of the relatively favorable depiction of Rabban Gamliel in the Acts of the Apostles, though, the New Testament paints the Pharisees with quite a broad, negative brush, particularly for being legalistic in their approach to Jewish law—and then, to make matters worse, for acting hypocritically in violation of that law (at least as the New Testament writers see things). For the dispute between Jesus and the Pharisees over the details of Sabbath laws, see Matthew 12:9–14; Mark 3:1–6; Luke 6:6–11, 13:10–17, 14:1–6; John 5:1–18. For Jesus's dispute with the Pharisees over divorce, see Matthew 19:1–12; Mark 10:1–12. For the replacement of law with spirit, see, in particular, Paul's Letter to the Romans 7:1–8:8, 9:30–33, and his Letter to the Galatians 5:16–26.

5.   This is evident, for example, in the recent work of this generation's most distinguished and quoted Reform theologian, Rabbi Eugene Borowitz, who emphasizes that for a decision to be identifiably Jewish, the Jew making it must be a *Jewish* self, steeped in the Jewish tradition and rooted in the covenant between the Jewish People and God. See his *Renewing the Covenant* (Philadelphia: Jewish Publication Society, 1991), pp. 284–99, reprinted in Elliot N. Dorff and Louis E. Newman, *Contemporary Jewish Ethics and Morality: A Reader* (New York: Oxford University Press, 1995), pp. 106–17. It is even more authoritatively evident in the last two official platform statements of the Reform rabbinate. Thus the 1976 Centenary Perspective says (in plank #4) that "Within each area of Jewish observance Reform Jews are called upon to confront the claims of Jewish tradition, however differently perceived, and to exercise their individual autonomy, choosing and creating on the basis of commitment and knowledge." The 1999 Pittsburgh Platform similarly says that "We are committed to the ongoing study of the whole array of *mitzvot* [commandments] and to the fulfillment of those that address us as individuals and as a community. Some of these *mitzvot*, sacred obligations, have long been observed by Reform Jews; others, both ancient and modern, demand renewed attention as the result of the unique context of our times." See http://ccarnet.org/platforms.

6.   For some examples of a variety of methodologies that do that, all of which recognize the importance of these factors but use them and the Jewish tradition in varying ways, see the Borowitz reading cited in note 5 above and the chapters by S. Daniel Breslauer, Richard J. Israel, David Ellenson, Louis Newman, Elliot Dorff, Aaron Mackler, and Laurie Zoloth-Dorfman in Dorff and Newman, *Contemporary Jewish Ethics*, pp. 94–105, 118–93, 219–46.

7.   Jacob Neusner, *Tzedakah: Can Jewish Philanthropy Buy Jewish Survival?* (Chappaqua, N.Y.: Rossel Books, 1982), pp. 67–79. William Sullivan, one of the contributors to this project, noted that in some ways this echoes Ahad Ha-Am's

famous *bon mot,* "More than the Jews have preserved the Sabbath, the Sabbath has preserved the Jews." Similarly, Sullivan suggests, "More than the Jews have preserved the commandment of *tzedakah, tzedekah* has preserved the Jews." A nice—and probably a true—adaptation of Ahad Ha-Am's insight for his time to ours—and by a Christian friend and observer!

8. For a description of those motivations and directions, see my book *To Do the Right and the Good: A Jewish Approach to Modern Social Ethics* (Philadelphia: Jewish Publication Society, 2002), Chapter 6.

9. Conversation with Robert A. Katz, Associate Professor of Law and Philanthropic Studies, Indiana University School of Law—Indianapolis, Center on Philanthropy at Indiana University, September 22, 2003.

10. Admission in civil matters is "like 100 witnesses": B. *Gittin* 40b, 64a; B. *Kiddushin* 65b; B. *Bava Metzia* 3b. No self-incrimination in criminal matters: B. *Yevamot* 25b; B. *Ketubbot* 18b; B. *Sanhedrin* 9b, 25a. See Aaron Kirschenbaum, *Self-Incrimination in Jewish Law* (New York: Burning Bush Press of the Jewish Theological Seminary of America, 1970).

11. Deuteronomy 23:17–19.

12. M. *Gittin* 5:5; B. *Gittin* 55a; B. *Bava Kamma* 95a.

13. M.T. *Laws of Theft (G'naivah)* 5:3.

14. Ibid., 6:1.

15. Deuteronomy 17:8–13; T. *Rosh Hashanah* 1:18; B. *Rosh Hashanah* 25a–25b. For a discussion of the role and authority of contemporary judges to interpret Jewish tradition, see Elliot Dorff and Arthur Rosett, *A Living Tree: The Roots and Growth of Jewish Law* (Albany: State University of New York Press, 1988), pp. 185–245, esp. pp. 187–98 and 223–27.

16. B. *Bava Kamma* 46b; B. *Bava Batra* 23b–24a, 92b–93a.

17. For a more thorough description of *teshuvah,* including the reasons why people are wary of forgiving but want forgiveness themselves and the reasons that prompt people to forgive along with the Jewish sources on all of this, see my article, "The Elements of Forgiveness: A Jewish Approach," in Everett L. Worthington, Jr., ed., *Dimensions of Forgiveness: Psychological Research and Theological Perspectives* (Philadelphia: Templeton Foundation Press, 1998), pp. 29–55 (reprinted in paperback in 2001 as *Forgiveness: Theory, Research, and Practice*) and Chapter 6 in Dorff, *Love Your Neighbor and Yourself.*

18. M. *Bava Metzia* 4:10; B. *Bava Metzia* 58a.

19. B. *Pesahim* 50b; B. *Sotah* 22b, 47a; B. *Sanhedrin* 105b; B. *Horayot* 10b; B. *Arakhin* 16b.

20. The principle is used to establish law in many places: B. *Ketubbot* 11a, 36b, 39b; B. *Sotah* 16a; B. *Gittin* 55b; B. *Bava Kamma* 39a; B. *Menahot* 6b; B. *Niddah* 4b. It is also used to object to a proposed legal ruling: B. *Yevamot* 92b; B. *Bava Kamma* 38a; B. *Avodah Zarah* 2b.

21. Deuteronomy 24:16.

22. B. *Berakhot* 34b.

23. M.T. *Laws of Repentance* 7:4.

24. The latest case is a $10.1 billion verdict—the largest ever except for the $144.8 billion verdict against cigarette makers in the Engle case in Florida— in a Madison County, Illinois court against Philip Morris for defrauding the public about the extra dangers of "light" cigarettes. There are four other pending class-action suits regarding "light" cigarettes, two against Philip Morris and

one each against R. J. Reynolds Tobacco Company and Brown and William-son Tobacco Corporation, the latter two also in Madison County, Illinois. Both the Engle case and the new Illinois case are being appealed. See Myron Levin, "Philip Morris Loses Lawsuit," *Los Angeles Times*, March 22, 2003, pp. C-1 and C-3.

25. Giving misleading or dangerous information violates this prohibition: *Sifra* on Leviticus 19:14. So does suggesting a bad business deal: B. *Hullin* 7b.

26. Offering alcohol to a Nazarite, one who has taken a vow not to drink alcohol (and, by extension, to an alcoholic), constitutes putting a stumbling block before the blind: B. *Pesahim* 22b. Similarly, one may not sell wood to those who would use it for idolatry: B. *Nedarim* 62b. Both the one who lends money on interest and the one who agrees to borrow money on interest violate this law of putting a stumbling block before the blind, as does one who lends money to someone without witnesses: B. *Bava Metzia* 75b. Striking one's grown child violates this prohibition as well: B. *Mo'ed Katan* 17a; B. *Kiddushin* 30a.

27. For a number of methodologies to gain moral guidance from the Jewish tradition, see Dorff and Newman, *Contemporary Jewish Ethics,* chapters 6–15.

28. Stephanie Strom, "Private Preschool Admissions: Grease and the City," *New York Times*, November 16, 2002, pp. B1 and B4. The quotations are on p. B4.

29. Ibid.

30. Ibid.

31. Deuteronomy 1:17; see Exodus 23:2, 6.

32. Leviticus 19:15.

33. Leviticus 19:35–36.

34. Both parties must sit or stand: B. *Shevu'ot* 30a; M.T. *Laws of Courts (Sanhedrin)* 21:3. Both must wear clothing of similar quality: B. *Shevu'ot* 31a; M.T. *Laws of Courts (Sanhedrin)* 21:2. Witnesses may not be related to each other or to the litigants: M. *Sanhedrin* 3:1, 4. That the judges must understand the languages of the litigants: B. *Menahot* 65a; see M.T. *Sanhedrin* 2:1, where Maimonides mentions a number of thing judges must know, but not this explicitly.

35. This is clearly true with regard to God, for the Mishnah says that "A person must thank God for the bad as well as the good. . . . One must thank God for whatever He measures out to you very, very much" (M. *Berakhot* 9:5). Similarly, one needs to show gratitude to human beings who have benefited us. Thus the Rabbis interpret the biblical command, "Do not take vengeance nor bear a grudge, but rather love your neighbor as yourself" (Leviticus 19:18) as follows:

> The Rabbis taught: What is vengeance and what is bearing a grudge? If man A said, "Lend me something of yours," and man B said "No," and the next day B said [to A], "Lend me your ax," and A said, "I will not lend it to you, just as you did not lend [what I asked] to me," that is revenge. If A said, "Here it is. I am not like you, who did not lend me [what I asked]," that is bearing a grudge. (B. *Yoma* 23a)

The Rabbis thus understand failure to be forthcoming to another individual in such situations as a violation of the Torah's laws prohibiting vengeance, even when one does not owe the other person anything; how much more would that be the case when one does. Along these lines, Rabbi Joseph Ibn Migash (1077–1141), in his Responsum #202, discusses the Talmudic saying,

"Into the well from which you have once drunk water, do not throw clods" (B. *Bava Kamma* 92b). If, says Ibn Migash, this applies to inanimate things, how much more should one's gratitude be shown to human beings. Thus there are two reasons why a friend of one of the litigants may not act as a judge in that case: First, he may be biased in his friend's favor, but second, if honesty compels him to decide against his friend, he will be guilty of ingratitude. See Louis Jacobs, *Theology in the Responsa* (London and Boston: Routledge and Kegan Paul, 1975), p. 41.

36. *Sifre* on Deuteronomy 15:7; M.T. *Laws of Gifts to the Poor* 7:13; S.A. *Yoreh De'ah* 251:3.

37. B. *Bava Metzia* 62a. The verse cited is Leviticus 25:36.

38. For much more on this, see Chapter 2 of Dorff, *Love Your Neighbor and Yourself.*

39. Deuteronomy 24:10–11.

40. That Jews may not charge interest on loans to fellow Jews: Exodus 22:25; Leviticus 25:35–38; Deuteronomy 23:19–21; M. *Bava Metzia,* Ch. 5. The concern to keep loans available appears, for example, in the laws of testimony necessary to establish that a loan was made: B. *Sanhedrin* 2b-3a. That debtors' homes could be invaded where the creditor suspected that collectable items were being hidden: Tur, *Hoshen Mishpat* 97:15. See also B. *Bava Metzia* 115a, where the right against intrusion is held to apply only to debts arising from loans, not to debts stemming from contracts or other obligations. According to M.T. *Laws of the Creditor and Debtor* 3:7, only the home of the debtor was protected, not that of his surety.

41. He is, however, liable for any injuries he causes, "for he has the right to eject him, but not the right to injure him": M.T. *Laws of the Injurer and Damager* (*Hovel u'Mazik*) 1:15. If the landlord did not intentionally injure the trespasser, however, he is not held liable (B. *Bava Kamma* 48b; S.A. *Hoshen Mishpat* 421:7), even though a person is generally responsible for unintentional wrongs (M. *Bava Kamma* 2:6; M.T. *Laws of the Injurer and Damager* (*Hovel u'Mazik*) 1:11.

42. B. *Pesahim* 112a; B. *Niddah* 16b. The rationale of not surprising and embarrassing someone inside is articulated by Rashi commenting on both of those passages. See also *Avot d'Rabbi Natan* 7:3.

43. *Derekh Eretz Rabbah* 5:2.

44. Louis Finkelstein, *Jewish Self-Government in the Middle Ages* (New York: Jewish Theological Seminary of America, 1924), pp. 31, 171ff, 178, 189. "*Herem d'Rabbenu Gershom,*" *Encyclopedia Talmudit* 7:153, footnotes 877–904 (Hebrew), cites Ashkenazic and Sephardic codes and responses that adopted and extended Rabbenu Gershom's mail decree.

45. See Salo W. Baron, *The Jewish Community* (Philadelphia: Jewish Publication Society, 1942), vol. 2, p. 281.

46. B. *Gittin* 7a.

47. B. *Bava Batra* 8b; see B. *Ketubbot* 49b; M.T. *Laws of Gifts to the Poor* 7:10. For more on Judaism's approach to poverty, see Dorff, *To Do the Right and the Good,* Chapter 6.

6 Philanthropy's Inconstant Friend, Religion

Philip Turner

So then, as we have opportunity, let us do good to all people, but especially to those of the household of faith.

—Galatians 6:10

According to the *Oxford English Dictionary,* the word *philanthropy* made its first appearance in English usage in the seventeenth century. John Dryden noted that there was no proper word in English to express its meaning, and so a word had to be borrowed from the "Grecians." The borrowing was, however, quite successful. By the next century, the century of "enlightenment," this borrowing from the "Grecians" had become a common notion. That period of history now lies almost in the distant past. Kant's little pamphlet "What is Enlightenment" appeared over two centuries ago—in 1784, to be exact. Seminal ideas of this great intellectual movement originated in such a distant past that we fail to realize that ideas once considered radical have become commonplace. Among these is *philanthropy,* understood as a love for humankind as such, expressed in generous (humanitarian) acts directed (potentially) to any, perhaps even all, who might benefit.

Like the Stoics before them, the advocates of enlightenment and their latter-day heirs seek a concept of human value that is rooted not in any particularizing personal or social characteristic but in something common to human beings as such. Freedom and reason are the *propria* thought to confer this special moral status, and it is from this moral leveling that our current opinions about philanthropic activity in large measure stem. Philanthropy finds its intellectual and moral niche within this set of assumptions. Consequently, philanthropy, so common public opinion in America holds, is properly directed, without respect to the differential characteristics of people, either to the improvement of some area of social life or to what in today's *news speak* are termed "humanitarian issues." People in New York, London, Kosovo, Afghanistan, or South Africa, regardless of race, religion, or political conviction, qualify as appropriate objects of philanthropic activity. The only relevant moral differences between them, in so far as true philanthropists (and humanitarians) are concerned, involve the character of the opportunities and needs addressed.

Philanthropy and humanitarianism are, if you will, close cousins who have escaped family ties to espouse a more inclusive responsibility. This generalized responsibility for the human condition is particularly strong in America, the only polity I know of that has been self-consciously founded upon the notion of a social contract between agents whose moral status is defined exclusively by their possession of freedom and reason. From these origins, I believe, springs a widespread and deeply held conviction that there is something morally suspect about giving special consideration to coreligionists or members of a particular ethnic group in the distribution of what we now call "charitable giving." Particularizing characteristics of this sort create, if you will, an uneven moral playing field, and for this reason are to be viewed with suspicion. There are, of course, notable instances wherein these suspicions are set aside in favor of obligations engendered by what might be called "special moral and/or religious relations." Nevertheless, within American society, these forms of charity, though tolerated, are viewed with some suspicion. Acts of charity directed to one's own are not prohibited, but they are, in the minds of many, morally questionable.

It comes as quite a surprise to most Americans when they discover that many, if not most, of the peoples of the earth do not share these suspicions. Indeed, for most people, decisions about what we call charitable giving are determined almost exclusively by moral obligations that stem from particular moral or religious relations. Among the most important of these particular relations are those that bind coreligionists, and serve, along with particularizing beliefs, to distinguish them from the devotees of other religions. It is this observation that brings me to the title of this essay. Generally speaking, religion, because it draws attention to a particular relationship, has proven and continues to prove an inconstant friend to both philanthropy and humanitarianism. The inconstancy of religion's relation with philanthropy stems (1) from the religious beliefs that give a privileged status to some that is not accorded to others, and (2) from a tension between a perceived duty to fellow believers and a more generalized duty to provide benefits to the general population and relief for suffering human beings regardless of their religious identity.

The purpose of this essay is to explore this inconstant religious support for philanthropy and humanitarianism, and, in the first instance, I shall do so by means of what I hope is a well-chosen example, namely, the Christian missionary effort in East Africa—particularly in Uganda. I have chosen to focus on East Africa and Uganda both because, having spent ten years there, I know this area of the world well, and because, for reasons that will become clear, it is very difficult to argue that the activities, "philanthropic" or otherwise, of the Anglican and Roman Catholic missions were carried out simply in the name of an imperial power.[1]

In tracking this missionary effort and examining its results, the tensions mentioned briefly above will appear in bold relief. It will become obvious that in respect both to motive and practice, Christian "philanthropic" activity in this area of the world has been driven by religious concerns that have given priority both to making coreligionists and to caring for them in a way that allows for what might be called the "right practice" of the faith. It is not that "humanitarian concern" has been lacking. It is simply that this concern has rarely, if ever, appeared in a pure form. The "philanthropy" of the missions and their latter day converts has always been directed by specifically religious purposes—purposes implying that considerable weight is attached to the particularizing difference of religious belief and practice.

Historical Notes: Christianity and Islam

Just how did the missionaries who entered East Africa in the second half of the nineteenth century view what we at first sight might call philanthropic activity? In Roland Oliver's almost magisterial account, *The Missionary Factor in East Africa*, we have a more than adequate picture of the currents and cross currents of missionary thought and practice in the late nineteenth and early twentieth centuries. The earliest Protestant missionaries in what is now Kenya were German pietists, trained in Basel. They held a strong prejudice against "good works," largely because they feared that a focus on what we might call "philanthropic activity" would detract from a pure presentation of the Gospel message. These early Protestant missionaries saw the "Negro" as "fallen humanity" rather than as "suffering humanity." Their primary aim, along with that of their sponsoring society, the Church Missionary Society (C.M.S.), was to assure salvation rather than the amelioration of the wretched conditions that confronted them on every side.[2] Indeed, they viewed these conditions as indications of the fallen state of their prospective converts. The conditions in which their prospective converts lived provided strong support for evangelistic activity, but not necessarily for "good works." Johann Rebmann, the most stalwart of the early pietist missionaries, wrote, "The deep fall of man from his Creator shows itself in these countries especially in the circumstance that nature exercises its full dominion over him, while he has been appointed to subject it to himself."[3]

The earliest Roman Catholic missionaries had distinctly different views. They worked in large measure with freed slaves whom they gathered into villages. Naturally enough, these villages provided a setting for introducing the techniques and culture of what the missionaries viewed as a more advanced civilization. It would be a mistake, however, to view their work among freed slaves as an unalloyed expression of philanthropic zeal. Their purpose, like that of the early Protestant missionaries, was primarily evangelistic. However, their evangelistic endeavors were linked with efforts to spread the benefits of civilization. As Oliver notes, "To the Catholic mind it was the Church that civilized the 'cultural heritage' of Greece and Rome, and it is the Church that remains the source of all 'true civilization.'"[4] What was true for Greece and Rome was true also for Africa, as previously it had been true for Latin America. Thus, in contradistinction to the more evangelical Protestants, conversion and the benefits of civilization were linked realities in the minds of the Roman Catholic missionaries. It was their view that conversion could not be simply an internal event. It required as well incorporation into the church. If this was to occur, an ordered social life of a new sort was required—one that served both to convert and convey a new form of life. Hence, the creation of villages and plantations in the context of which incorporation into the sacramental and disciplinary system of the Roman Church could occur. With this incorporation, it was thought, came the benefits of both salvation and a better form of life on earth.

The issue of freed slaves led even the C.M.S. into founding villages. As early as 1855 they established a village for freed slaves in India, and in time they came to believe, along with most other Protestant missions, that it was necessary to found Christian communities in Africa if they were to create a "bulwark against Satan," and "a social system and moral atmosphere in which the Christian character could grow."[5] Still, evangelical subscribers to the C.M.S. viewed these mixed efforts with suspicion. They continued to pay and pray for conversions. R. N. Crust, a member of the C.M.S. Committee, put the matter this way:

> I am entirely in favor of the Lay Evangelist, the Medical Evangelist, whenever Gospel-preaching is the substantive work; but when it is proposed to have a pious Industrial Superintendent, or an Evangelical tile-manufacturer, or a Low Church breeder of cattle or raiser of turnips, I draw my line.[6]

It was David Livingstone who changed public opinion about the place of philanthropic activity in the mindset and efforts of the missions. To Livingstone more than anyone else we owe a shift in public opinion that led the people of England to view the peoples of Africa in the first instance as "suffering humanity" rather than "fallen humanity." Livingstone started out, like the other missionaries, zealous for conversions; and indeed he remained so. But as time went on, he came to believe that the alleviation of suffering and the spread of civilization were necessary precursors to this final purpose. There is no doubt that firsthand experience of the horrors of the slave trade served more than anything else to bring about this change in his views. In the 1860s, it is reckoned that between fifty thousand and seventy thousand slaves reached the coast of East Africa per year. These people were in large measure the captives of various tribes who, after capture, had been bartered to the slavers from the coast. We have no idea of how many more were taken but in fact never reached the slave block in Zanzibar. We do know from Livingstone's descriptions, however, how horrible were the ravages of the trade. In his *Last Journals* he writes:

> We passed a woman tied by the neck to a tree and dead. . . . We saw others tied up in a similar manner, and one lying in the path shot or stabbed for she was in a pool of blood. The explanation we got invariably was that the Arab who owned these victims was enraged at losing his money by the slaves becoming unable to march. Today we came upon a man dead from starvation. . . . One of our men wandered and found a number of slaves with slave-sticks on, abandoned by their master from want of food. . . . We passed village after village and gardens, all deserted.[7]

Most know his extraordinary words, spoken just before his death, that appear on Livingstone's tomb in Westminster Abbey: "Heaven's rich blessing upon everyone who would help to heal this open sore of the world." Livingstone's view was that the introduction of trade and commerce would pave the way for conversion and so would close the open sore that surrounded him on every side. He wrote in a letter from Mabotsa in 1844:

> If we call the actual amount of conversions the direct result of Missions, and the wide diffusion of better principles the indirect, I have no hesitation in asserting that the latter are of infinitely more importance than the former. I do not under-value the importance of the conversion of the most abject creature that breathes: it is of overwhelming worth to him personally, but viewing our work of wide sowing of the good seed relatively to the harvest which will be reaped when all our heads are low, there can, I think, be no comparison. . . . Time is more important than con-centration.[8]

David Low, in his study *Buganda in Modern History,* has tracked the effect of Livingstone's appeal on the British public.[9] When it appeared that for financial reasons the British East Africa Company was to withdraw from East Africa, and that for political reasons the ruling Liberal Party was not going to step in and declare Uganda a British Protectorate, Bishop Alfred Tucker, the Anglican Bishop of Uganda, made a personal appeal for sufficient funds to allow the company to remain for an additional year. He was successful, and during that year both religious and public figures mounted an extraordinary campaign to mobilize public opinion in favor of British annexation. Low's analysis of the memorials sent to the government shows how deeply Livingstone's ideas had taken root in the British public. With remarkable unanimity, they express fear of a return of the slave trade, the removal of the civilizing influence of the missions, and (a new concern) destruction of the fledgling church that had taken root in Uganda. In these memorials, as in Livingstone's writings, the suppression of the slave trade, the spread of civilization, conversion to Christianity, and preservation of the church are linked and reinforce each other.

In this history, one sees movement from Evangelical suspicion of what we would call philanthropic activity, through its annexation to evangelistic efforts, to its being granted pride of place in an effort to remedy human suffering and promote both civilization and conversion. To this movement, two more intervals need to be added. The first is that the C.M.S. missionaries in Uganda were successful in no small measure because the Baganda saw them as harbingers of a superior civilization. Their superior knowledge and technology were tied in the minds of the Baganda to their religion, and for this reason, in the early period, Christianity won out over Islam. "Philanthropic" activity in Buganda was a successful tool of evangelism. The success of this strategy is well known, and has been well chronicled.[10] The extraordinary number of conversions, however, confronted the C.M.S. with a pastoral issue of extreme urgency. If the myriad of new converts were to mature in the faith and remain faithful, the social conditions in which they lived had to be changed. It was not only the case that the old gods had to be put out of the picture, but it was also that conditions favorable to stable, monogamous marriages and the nurture of children in the faith of their parents had to be created.

This observation brings one to another aspect, the second movement. In order to insure effective pastoral care of the fledgling church, the C.M.S., at the end of the nineteenth century, began to bring in teachers, agriculturalists, and medical personnel. Mission work assumed a more "philanthropic" face and a less evangelistic one. Nevertheless, this "philanthropy," if indeed that is what it was, was directed by specifically religious purposes. Roland Oliver has made the point in this way:

> But as the Churches grew, and as increasing numbers of baptized Christians had to be disciplined on charges of witchcraft and polygamy, it came to be realized that the medical mission was necessary as a social institution of the Christian community. If the witch-doctor was to be eliminated, with all that he symbolized of the sub-Christian fears and hatreds, the missionary doctor must abandon his evangelistic itinerations, stay in his hospital and train African nurses and medical assistants to replace the diviner in village life. And equally, if the children of monogamous marriages were to survive in sufficient numbers to compensate for the renunciation of polygamy, then maternity work, child welfare and infant dietetics must all come within the missionary's sphere.[11]

I have in no way traced all the complexities of the early history of missions in East Africa, but a thorough history has not been my purpose. The purpose of this brief exercise has been to show the many and complex ways particular relations based on common belief stood "in, with and under" what we would call philanthropic activity. Even in Livingstone's case, evangelism was what Aristotle might have called the "final cause" of what we would call philanthropy. What Americans would now view with some suspicion, the Victorians viewed as a religious duty. The eternal state of the soul, the remedy of human suffering, the spread of "civilization," and the preservation of fledgling churches were of a piece. Religious belief stood behind all these concerns and, in respect to them all, religious belief created particular obligations of a religious nature that had to be given attention. From the beginning, the "philanthropic" activity of the missions had what we might call ulterior motives. Further, as time went on, the "philanthropic" activity of the missions, through work in education, medicine, and agriculture, was directed increasingly to their own converts in an effort to create conditions that would keep converts faithful in their practice. The good works of the missions sprang in the first instance not from a general humanitarian concern, but from particular relations engendered by a perceived obligation to care for the religious health of people who had become fellow believers. Religion spawned good works but not for what we would call "humanitarian" reasons. Its efforts might well overlap those of philanthropy, but were carried out for rather different ends.

The inconstant and ambiguous nature of the links between religious belief and practice and "humanitarian concern" (in the modern sense) appear clearly when one views the brief history recounted above in relation to the history of Islam in the same area. Arab traders brought Islam to East Africa at a time prior to the arrival of the first Christian missionaries. In Buganda, there was considerable interest in this new religion. Nevertheless, Islam eventually lost out to Christianity in large measure because Christianity was perceived to be the religion of a more powerful civilization. The early Arab traders brought no schools, hospitals, or technical skills. The Christian missionaries did and, as a result, the technology and learning connected with Christianity simply outshone what the Arabs had to offer.

In recent years, however, the tide has turned. It is now Islam, which has adopted the very methods of the early missionaries, that is making a concerted effort in East Africa to use schools, hospitals, and technical support as means to procure the conversion of both Christians and pagans to what they hold to be the true and only faith.[12] International support for Islamic organizations began to flow into East Africa during the 1960s from Arab organizations such as the Islamic Call Organization, from Arab governments, and from wealthy individuals, particularly in Saudi Arabia. This involvement was connected both with political aims and with religious piety following a pattern in which whereby "wealthy rulers consider it their religious obligation to help poorer brethren and to contribute to the spread of Islam in Eastern Africa."[13]

In Uganda, the turnaround must be linked to the regime of General Idi Amin. Prior to the coup that brought him to power in 1971, Muslims in Uganda had looked, as they had for two centuries, to the East African Coast and the Islamic cultures that influenced that area. Amin shifted the attention of the Muslim community in Uganda to the North—first to the Bari and Nubi peoples of the Nile Valley, and then beyond to political alliances with Libya, Egypt, and Saudi Arabia. This shift brought with it an increase in the number of Christians (and others) who converted to Islam.[14]

It would be misleading to suggest by this observation that the number of conversions from Christianity to Islam has been high. Indeed, it should be noted that tribal membership counted as much as religious affiliation for preferment during the Amin regime. In fact, the position of Muslims in relation to Christians throughout East Africa remained and remains disadvantageous.[15] Nevertheless, anxiety among Christians in East Africa about an Islamic push from the North is high. Knowledge of what is transpiring in Nigeria and other areas of West Africa and, even more, the long struggle between Christians and Muslims in the Sudan, have jointly served to heighten tensions between the religious groups.

The situation in the Southern Sudan is of particular importance. In 1983, General al-Numayri introduced what came to be known as the September Laws. These constituted a version of *Shariah*, and served to change the ideological landscape of the Sudan. From this date (if not before), there has been a steady attempt by an Islamist government in Khartoum to impose *Shariah* on the peoples of the South and to force their conversion. R. S. O'Fahey comments on this attempt:

> The Islamist perception of a theocracy based on the *Shariah* is based *de facto* on the *Shariah* reality that the only fully mature person in the eyes of that law is a mature, *compos mentis* Muslim male. The rights of all others—Christian, Jew, woman or minor—are less. A secular alternative, based upon some ultimately Western-inspired conceptions of human rights, is by definition unacceptable to the Islamists. . . . Other issues include the position of women, . . . the discriminatory effect of Islamic banking on non-Muslims, . . . and the questions of intellectual freedom.[16]

The fact is, once *Shariah* is imposed, Christians become second-class citizens in their own country, and pagans are left with no legal status at all.[17] In Southern Sudan, this legal inequality has been accompanied by rapacious practice on the part of the army and the Islamist government of an unusually cruel sort.[18]

There are many reasons to retell the recent history of East Africa and the Southern Sudan—many of which are "humanitarian" in the modern sense of that term. The area cries out for "philanthropic" activity of a non-sectarian variety. However, Christians who live in Uganda, Kenya, and Tanzania look at things rather differently than the average American. They do not see the generosity of the Arab "North" as philanthropy. Rather, they see state-sponsored attempts to evangelize. They see large sums of money pouring into their countries from Arab states, Arab organizations, and wealthy Arab individuals. This aid takes a similar form to that given earlier by the Christian missions, and it is given for the same purposes: to make converts and sustain them in their new faith.

It is important to note that this aid is being given at precisely that moment in history when Christian missions are withdrawing financial support from the churches that sprang from evangelistic efforts. It is given also at a time when Westerners prefer to give to human need through organizations like Oxfam or Save the Children. The question on the minds of many Christians in East Africa is this: do not our fellow believers in the West have a religious obligation to help us in our struggle with Islam? In our struggles against an aggressive religion, the ravages of poverty, AIDS and a host of other diseases, should not Christian aid come directly to the churches, not only to address human suffering but also to help us in our efforts to stem the Islamic advance, evangelize, and provide aid and pastoral care to those who have been converted? In struggles like the one we face with Islam and with the burdens of underdevelopment, is there not a religious obligation to come to the aid of fellow believers?

It is my impression that a question of this sort is a "no-brainer" to many Jews, Muslims, and Evangelical Christians. Their position would be to say, "In circumstances like these, of course we have an obligation to come to the aid of our coreligionists." Further, they can easily show that aid given to start schools, dispensaries, and other social services in fact produces conversions at a greater rate than if such support is not available.[19] Nevertheless, the answer is less obvious to those Christians (and perhaps Jews) who have been shaped more by the enlightenment ideas of freedom, reason, and human equality than by the particularities of religious belief. The question, of course, concerns where the truth of the matter lies. In the remainder of this essay, I ask if there are particular religious/moral obligations to fellow believers that limit the scope of philanthropy by directing eleemosynary activity, if not univocally, at least in the first instance, to fellow believers. I ask, in short, whether religion (and I have in mind particularly the Christian religion) is in fact a faithful, dependable friend to philanthropy; or whether, in certain circumstances, it constrains its devotees to show more care for one class of sufferers than another. In respect to human need, does religious belief constrain one to look upon the human condition with unprejudiced eyes; or does it, in certain circumstances, constrain one to focus for specifically religious reasons on those who believe as one believes?

Religious Commitments, Religious Obligations, and Philanthropy

If I am right in my assessment of the moral climate that now grips America, the questions posed above may be seen by many at first glance as offensive in themselves. As indicated above, however, they will appear as perfectly normal, indeed virtuous, to most people in other parts of the world. Are these people simply unenlightened or do they have a point? Does philanthropy, understood as a love of humanity as such, in some way trump these particularistic demands, or is it the other way around?

As a way into these questions, I propose to take another case, this one closer to home; and ask if there are circumstances in which Christians have special obligations to fellow believers that may cohere with humanitarian concerns but that Christians espouse for specifically religious reasons and with specifically religious purposes in mind. In the summer of 1996, according to the estimates of the National Council of Churches (N.C.C.), some ninety houses of worship were "attacked, desecrated, vandalized and burned" as the result of "racially motivated hatred."[20] In response to these atrocious acts, the N.C.C., in conjunction with other individuals, non-profit organizations, public corporations, and the U.S. government, raised some $25 million to aid these congregations. Despite its focus on the desecration of churches, the appeal itself was made as a generalized humanitarian effort with the particular purpose of combating racism. In the words of Joan Brown Campbell, General Secretary of the National Council of the Churches of Christ in the U.S.A.:

> The response to these tragic events has been overwhelming and encouraging. Almost spontaneous, certainly unplanned or organized, it has come from every sector of the Christian community, from communities of every faith, and from individuals of moral discernment and active good will who may not be participants in any faith community. Hundreds of thousands of people have actively responded through contributing funds, volunteering, reaching out to build healthier communities, and voicing a clear condemnation of racism.[21]

Here, it would appear, is a case of philanthropic activity in its proper sense. Though many of the contributors had religious motivations, the aid they offered stemmed more directly from a humanitarian concern to right a gross social wrong than from a particular religious/moral obligation to fellow Christians. Further, aid was given by a broad spectrum of people and institutions whose activities were religiously neutral. Finally, the primary reason given for the appeal by its organizers was that the fundamental rights and dignity of fellow citizens had been violated. The common reason for this eleemosynary effort was, broadly speaking, humanitarian.

The question I am posing is whether or not, as a Christian organization, the N.C.C. should have made such a religiously neutral appeal. Should they have made, instead or in addition, an appeal directed specifically to Christians and rooted in particular obligations Christians may have to their fellow believers? Two passages in the New Testament bear in a very direct way on this question. They are 2 Corinthians 8–9 and Romans 15:26–29. These passages concern Paul's collecting money among the Gentile churches of Asia Minor to aid the poor Jewish Christians in Jerusalem who were suffering through a famine.[22] A careful reading of these texts makes it impossible for Paul's efforts to be understood as a simple example of what we would call philanthropy. On the contrary, they display particular obligations based upon very particular religious beliefs, and they give particular religious weight to the needs of a certain class of fellow believers.

How so? A modern reader of the texts from Romans and Corinthians may well assume that Paul was pursuing a solely moral purpose in taking up this collection—that he was making an appeal for those who were better off to share with those who were in distress. If this were so, his appeal would have resonance with humanitarians even though they might question why Christians were to be the only recipients of the aid. The text, however, provides little support for this supposition. The reason given for the collection was not to offer a remedy to a suffering population. Rather, the collection had its inception in the context of a dispute over the probity of circumcised Jews extending the right hand of fellowship to Gentiles who were not circumcised. Given this context, it is likely that the reason for Paul's collection was not in the first instance sympathy for the poor in Jerusalem (though he certainly was sympathetic to their plight), but a perceived obligation to make clear both to Jewish Christians and to the newly converted Gentiles what it means to be engrafted into God's people. The primary point of the collection was to make clear to both Jew and Gentile their unity within the Church. Or, to put the matter another way, the basic point of the collection was what Paul perceived to be the primary purpose of God, namely, the unity of all people and all things "in Christ Jesus" (Romans 9:11; cf. Ephesians 1:9–10; 2: 11–22).

Paul himself gives the collection this specifically religious interpretation. In referring to the money collected by the Gentile churches, he speaks not of money but of "grace," "communion," "ministry," "church service" and "blessing." In referring to the collection itself, he speaks of "this grace," and he goes on to mention in connection with the collection "the grace of God which has been given in the churches of Macedonia (2 Corinthians 8:1). Paul is making the point that the generous gift of the Gentile churches gave concrete expression to the grace they received in Christ; and that the Jews, to whom they are sending aid, had received the same grace. Both Jew and Gentile share the same benefits. Thus, the sacrifice of the Macedonians is to be viewed as a sacrificial gift that imitates Christ's gift to both Jew and Gentile. Sacrificial giving, particularly to those from whom one previously had been estranged, serves as a symbol of and witness to the basic truth about the purposes of God and the nature of the Church. Commenting on these verses, L. S. Thornton once said, "St. Paul, by his choice of words, was sometimes suggesting deliberately the connection of commonplace things (e.g., a collection for the poor) with the highest mysteries of the Gospel" (i.e., the unity of all believers in Christ regardless of their earthly distinctions).[23]

If viewed through the lens of Paul's collection, how ought Christians to consider the collection taken by the N.C.C.? Should they see it as a humanitarian act of racial justice, or as a religious duty owed specifically to coreligionists and devolving from the purposes of God for the Church? Paul's collection, I believe, suggests that as the Gentile churches in Macedonia (because of the fragility and importance of Jewish–Gentile relations within the Church) were under special obligations to give concrete expression to their unity with Jewish Christians, so also is it reasonable to assume for similar reasons that Christians in America have a specifically religious obligation to show that racial divisions have no place in the life of the churches. Just as divisions between Jew and Gentile gave the lie to God's purposes for the Church, so also do racial divisions between white and black Christians.

There are, in fact, a number of reasons to suggest that the collection for the burned churches would have been more adequately conceived by Christians (and the N.C.C.) not as a philanthropic act to counter (in some general sense) racism, but as a religious duty owed specifically to coreligionists that stems from a shared set of beliefs and practices that had been grievously compromised. Among these are the particular history between white and black Christians in America, the analogy that exists between this history and the earlier history of relations between Jewish and Gentile Christians, and the central importance of reconciliation and unity within Christian belief and life. Indeed, I would go so far as to say that in circumstances like these that there appears what can fairly be called a primary religious obligation for Christians; namely, to undertake actions directed specifically to coreligionists that serve to rectify others that compromise the beliefs and practices serving to provide a common religious identity to both giver and receiver. These actions may cohere with those performed by others for purely humanitarian reasons, but their primary motivation and purpose is, in certain important respects, quite different. Further, because their purpose is to manifest a fundamental religious belief, in certain circumstances (like those that obtained in Jerusalem and now obtain in East Africa), they may be legitimately focused on fellow believers rather than upon the general population.

In the light of these observations, are the questions now being posed by the Christians of East Africa to their coreligionists in North America and Europe appropriate? From the African point of view, there is a binding obligation that exists between their churches and those of North America and Europe. It is from Christians in these latter places that they, the Africans, first heard the Christian message preached. There is also a long history of aid from Western churches directed specifically to strengthening the abilities of the churches in East Africa not only to make converts but also to support them in their new faith. There is the additional factor that Christians from North America and Europe were involved, if not in the East African slave trade then most certainly in the West African dealings. The Christians of East Africa, therefore, ask if this history does not suggest obligations on the part of their Western coreligionists, which continue into the present—obligations that give expression to something fundamental to the faith of both. The obligations arise because of a long history of fraternal relations because of Europe and America's involvement in the slave trade and, perhaps most of all, because it is of central religious importance for Christians to give support to others who may be suffering for their common faith. In combination, these religiously significant factors make it imperative for Christians in the West to give aid to their coreligionists in Africa who are being subjected to such adverse pressures by followers of another faith.

To put the matter in another way, it is the view of many Christians from East Africa that the faith shared by African Christians and those from Europe and North America is now at risk in two senses. First, fellow believers with whom the West has a long history are under threat from an aggressive and hostile religion, and second, the institutions which serve to spread and sustain Christian belief and practice now lack the resources to sustain the faithful and make the sort of witness that needs to be made if effective evangelism is to take place. The withdrawal of aid from the Western churches is thus viewed as desertion in a time of trial, and a denial of the sort of unity and mutual responsibility that are essential aspects of Christian belief and practice.

I have provided two examples on the basis of which it can reasonably be argued that, in these circumstances, special religious obligations appear that direct the support of Christians specifically to fellow believers rather than generally to all who may in some way be suffering in a similar way. In both cases, it would seem that if these obligations are not assumed, something essential to Christian belief and practice is denied. The moment one makes such an observation, however, at least two rather perplexing questions present themselves.

The first is whether a similarly strong obligation arises for Christians with means whenever and wherever fellow believers find themselves hard pressed by hostile forces—racist, religious, or political. Certainly, the view of Christians that, in belonging to Christ, they belong to a single body in which the suffering of one member affects all members, suggests an obligation to suffering or deprived coreligionists that does not fall under the general rubric of humanitarian concern. In the cases mentioned above, however, the obligation takes on particular strength because of a long history. This history serves both to create a special obligation and to give particular significance to its fulfillment. It seems reasonable to say, therefore, that *prima facie* religious obligations focusing on coreligionists come into play whenever and wherever actions essential to belief seem called for, but that these *prima facie* obligations become more stringent when they arise in the context of a shared history. To put the matter another way, it would be virtuous for Christians in other parts of the world who have no particular relation to Christians in Syria, to come to their aid where possible. It would, however, be a sort of betrayal of Christian belief if Christians in Great Britain simply turned their backs on the Christians of East Africa if faced with a serious threat from Islam. What was perceived to be the case by the British public in the late nineteenth century is no less the case today.

The second question concerns how extensive duties to coreligionists are. I have already mentioned the way in which *Shariah* causes economic, social, and political disadvantages to those who are not Muslims. By suggesting that there may be religious duties to coreligionists that take precedence over duties to others of suffering humanity, does one suggest thereby the propriety of something like a "Christian Yellow Pages"—a favoring of coreligionists over others? If one says, as I believe Christians must, that participation in the life of the Christian people carries with it particular obligations to fellow believers, does that mean that one's religious and moral obligations are located, perhaps inordinately, within the circle of one's coreligionists?

This question exposes what might well be the dark side of religious loyalty and the positive side of humanitarianism. Do particular obligations to coreligionists effectively cancel out what we now call "humanitarian concern?" There are few places in the world where this question is not relevant—so much so that I have been plagued throughout by doubts about the moral wisdom of pursuing the question of particular duties to fellow believers. To this point, I have tried to show that Christian religious belief is not an unqualified friend to philanthropy. I now wish to show that it is not, therefore, necessarily its enemy. Or to put the matter another way, I want to show that Christians ought to look upon humanitarianism with a kindly eye even if their reasons for undertaking similar action are not always the same as those of humanitarians.

Let me begin by returning to David Livingstone. It was he who brought "suffering humanity" rather than "fallen humanity" to the mind of the British public. His example and its broad appeal suggest that there are resources within Christian belief that make it possible for devotees to look upon the human condition and respond to its vulnerable state with a sympathy that extends beyond the circle of fellow believers and with actions that are not directly tied to evangelistic effort. Indeed, Livingstone's example, along with the views of human dignity and equality that are constitutive of both philanthropy and humanitarianism pose an important question to any religion; namely, what are the resources within to direct sympathy and aid in significant ways beyond the circle of coreligionists?[24]

I lack the knowledge even to attempt an answer to such a question from a Jewish or Islamic perspective, and I certainly cannot answer for Hindus or Buddhists. I can, however, speak as a Christian; and from this perspective, there are several beliefs that make it difficult for Christians to insist that any and all acts of charity on their part be tied to evangelistic endeavor or to the provision of aid to fellow believers. The first belief maintains that human beings are all created in the image of God. As such, they have a special place within the creation, being commissioned by God on the basis of the image they bear to care for its good order and fruitfulness. The second belief states that Christ died for all. The third is that God wills all to know and love him. The fourth is that God's purposes include more than the state of the Church at a given time. Indeed, at any given time and in any given circumstance those more extensive purposes may take precedence over the state of the Church. Any one of these or any of them in combination drives the moral and religious concerns of Christians beyond the circle of fellow believers. Further, in each case, every human emerges as a being of special value to God; each is the recipient of special divine favor and love.

These beliefs suggest that there are Christian reasons for a concern for human suffering as such—concerns that are rooted in the special value human beings have in the eyes of God. This special value, however, is not rooted in any *proprium* that humans may possess (be it freedom, reason, or both), but in a divine favor that is a matter of divine choice. It is, furthermore, a favor that is not lost when freedom and reason are impaired. Accordingly, the favor extends to the weakest and most vulnerable members of the species. It is finally a favor that calls forth "charity" toward those in need on the part of all those who likewise enjoy this favor.

If the structure of Christian belief and practice requires charitable activity that is connected to evangelism and directed, in certain circumstances, particularly to coreligionists rather than to a general population, it also requires a concern for suffering humanity as such that need not be linked directly with either making or supporting fellow believers. East Africa once more provides a first-class example of this particular contrast between particular and generalized concern. The AIDS crisis serves to focus the issue. In some countries (Zimbabwe, for example) some 50 percent of the population is thought to be HIV-positive. The percentages are only slightly lower throughout East and Central Africa. The mind shrinks back in dizziness when one contemplates the degree of suffering and social chaos these figures suggest. If there ever were a case for pure philanthropy, the AIDS epidemic in Africa would seem to be it. Here if anywhere, eleemosynary activity ought to be directed to human beings without reference to religious purposes or duties to fellow believers. But is the case for Christians as simple as that? Should they funnel their aid through a humanitarian organization like Oxfam or should they direct some, perhaps even all, of their giving directly to churches with the specific purpose not only of addressing the AIDS crisis but also of strengthening their evangelistic and pastoral ministry?

Given God's compassion and love for all people, and given the fact that the AIDS virus is no respecter of religious persons, even if they be Christian, it would seem contrary to Christian belief to limit Christian efforts to stem the AIDS epidemic and treat its victims only to fellow believers. A Christian hospital that turned away AIDS sufferers on the basis of religion (or non-religion) would seem to deny a fundamental tenet of Christian belief. On the other hand, given the fact that Christians hold that belief in Christ is (in some form) necessary for salvation, it would not be unreasonable for Christians to link the aid they give in the midst of this epidemic to efforts at evangelization. Further, it would not be contrary to faith to make special provision for believers who are suffering from AIDS. Thus, the AIDS epidemic provides an excellent example of the push toward humanitarian concern on the one hand and the pull toward special obligations to fellow believers on the other. Both are implicit in what might be called the structure of Christian believing.

Particular Relations and Humanitarianism: The Arena of Virtue and Moral Imagination

How does one balance, and perhaps even relax, the tension between the push of humanitarian concern and the pull of particular religious (and/or other) obligations? Because the words *balance* and *relax* rather than *eliminate* are used, it may be taken as a given that I do not believe that (for Christians) the tension can be surmounted, eliminated, or bypassed. It is programmed into the DNA of Christian belief and practice. On the one hand, the arenas of family, friends, fellow countrymen, and coreligionists provide the primary context in which one's religious and moral life is lived. To leap over the obligations that define these relations in the name of a love for humanity as such, if adopted as a general rule of practice, would both leave social life in chaos and produce no small number of moral monstrosities. Hence, the weight given to obligations to fellow believers is a matter that must be determined in relation to the obligations accompanying other particular relations. These relations provide the primary context in which the religious and moral life is lived, and it is certain that attention to them provides the best way not only to care for those to whom one is (in a social sense) most closely bound but also to insure the health of society in general. Indeed, a strong case can be made for saying that the goal of humanitarianism (the promotion of human welfare as such) is best served by close attention to the particular people to whom one is in one way or another obligated.

In this respect, I have suggested that (in addition to family, friends, neighbors, and fellow countrymen) there are particular obligations to fellow believers of a particularly binding sort that come into play when a matter central to common faith is threatened with compromise and when there are significant historical and social links. I have suggested also that these obligations legitimate charitable giving directed to making or aiding fellow believers rather than to a humanitarian cause that is in some sense "recipient blind." I have suggested, as well, that Christians in East Africa have good reasons to appeal to these religious obligations in their relations with Western Christians. On the other hand, there is within Christian belief and practice strong precedent for saying something is amiss if no giving is "recipient blind." To quote Ephesians out of context, God cares both for those who are far off and for those who are near (Ephesians 2:17). To shut out the stranger, particularly if that stranger is an enemy or potential enemy, runs counter to a very fundamental Christian belief, namely, reconciliation. It would, therefore, be wrong for Christians in East Africa to chastise their American or European counterparts simply because they support Oxfam rather than their own ministries and organization.

At best, then, the tension between the push and pull mentioned above can be balanced or relaxed. It cannot be eliminated. Neither can it be neatly sorted out. It strikes me as overreaching to seek a casuistry that would help one decide, in a given set of circumstances, whether to give preference to sending one's child to private school, increasing giving to one's local church, giving to public radio, making a bequest to one's university, supporting the Church in the Southern Sudan, or contributing to Oxfam. These are all matters that might impinge upon an educated and sensitive conscience informed by Christian belief and disciplined by Christian practice. Decisions about the weight given to these and other matters of charitable concern will be determined not by a refined casuistry but by the interplay of circumstance, knowledge, virtue, and moral imagination.

Thus, having given (in certain circumstances) particular importance to religious obligations, one ought not to go on to say that these obligations automatically take precedence over others. What one can say is that a conscience informed by Christian belief and a life disciplined by Christian practice will perforce direct what we call charitable giving to the salvation of fallen humanity, the care of fellow believers, the relief of suffering humanity, and the enrichment of human social life in general. One can say also that this breadth of care in the end proves finally friendly, though not identical, to philanthropic concern. To return to the place we started, it seems to me that Livingstone provides an icon of a right balance between the push of philanthropic concern and the pull of special religious obligation. His example makes clear why, in Christian piety, contemplation of the lives of the saints is a richer resource for living what Christians call a faithful life than the necessary and helpful distinctions of casuists. Through these lives, attention is focused on life's major issues, thought is clarified, virtue is increased, and imagination is both set loose and disciplined.

It would seem, then, that Christian belief and practice are at one and the same time the friends of philanthropy, its critics, and its would-be instructors. They are philanthropy's friends in that they call attention to God's care for all people, and in that they provide strong motivation and precedent for the promotion of human welfare and the alleviation of human suffering. Indeed, a strong argument can be made for saying that they provide a stronger basis for philanthropic concern than the valorization of human *propria* like freedom and reason. They are also philanthropy's critics in that they call attention to the fact that commitment to humankind in general leads to moral abstractions that carry but little motivating force. They are, finally, philanthropy's would-be instructors in that they lift up the significance of particular relations, and suggest that attention to these limited engagements is perhaps the best way to promote the welfare of all.

Having made statements such as these, I must immediately confess to have spoken with an idealized picture of Christian belief and practice in mind. One of the things that the history of Christianity and Islam in East Africa serves to display is that the thought and motivation of Western Christians has undergone significant alteration since the nineteenth century. It does not seem an overgeneralization to say that philanthropic interest has overtaken religious commitment as a motivating force among Western Christians, at least among those who belong either to the Roman Catholic Church or to the magisterial Churches of the Reformation. Among these Christians, a generic appeal to overcome some social ill or promote some social good appears to have more power than an appeal based upon the need to convert nonbelievers or care for believers and the churches to which they belong. It would seem that the quality of life on earth and the alleviation of human suffering, more than eternal destiny and religious identity, serve as the motivating forces that stand behind the eleemosynary activities of more liberal Christians and humanitarians alike. Religion, for many Christians, has become an increasingly private affair that carries with it few corporate duties. The welfare of the earthly city is a matter of common concern. Religion is a more individual matter, and so the support of fellow believers is at best problematic and at worst wrong. To return to Livingstone and to take note of results he never intended—in the American context, among more liberal Protestants and Roman Catholics, suffering (or deprived) humanity appears now to have obscured fallen humanity from view.

It is precisely this situation that is so utterly clear to Christians in East Africa, and as a result they turn for aid increasingly to the more evangelical forms of Christianity for whom fallen humanity remains the primary category. It is this situation also that leads the churches of East Africa to ask the Churches from which they sprang if, in their espousal of a more humanitarian form of concern, they have forgotten something essential: namely, that there are particular obligations that obtain between coreligionists—obligations that are not hostile to humanitarian concern but obligations nonetheless, that can be ignored only at the cost of compromising beliefs and practices central to their common identity as Christians. If the answer to this question is yes, then it might be appropriate to ask this question by way of conclusion. If it is the case, as I have argued, that religion is a friend, though an inconstant one, to philanthropy, is philanthropy in any way a friend to religion? The question suggests the need for another essay, but one can give a tentative response. The answer perhaps depends on the nature of the religion in question and the way in which philanthropic activity is construed. If, on the one hand, philanthropy is construed in such a way as to deny the legitimacy of religious claims that give special importance to fellow believers, then the answer is likely to be no. If, on the other hand, philanthropists are open to the special significance of religious loyalties and the religion in question is of a sort that gives importance to caring for strangers, even enemies, then one may assume that common cause is possible and desirable, even if the reasons for making common cause are not the same. If, however, religion is of the sort that makes rather extreme distinctions between fellow believers on the one hand and strangers and enemies on the other, then the answer most certainly is no.

Notes

1. I speak only of the Anglican and Roman Catholic efforts at evangelism. There were, however, efforts to link the cause of empire and that of the Gospel in the case of German missionary efforts in what is now Tanzania. See Roland Oliver, *The Missionary Factor in East Africa*, 2nd ed. (London: Longmans, Green and Co., 1965), pp. 94–97.

2. The sponsorship of German pietists by an Anglican missionary society is explained by the fact that for a time the Church Missionary Society found it difficult to recruit people from England for the new field they wished to open in East Africa. The German pietists were willing to undertake work that English people at that time thought, because of the rigors of the climate, overly dangerous. See ibid., p.5.

3. Ibid., p. 9.

4. Ibid., p. 20.

5. Ibid., p. 24.

6. R. N. Crust, *An essay on the prevailing methods of evangelizing the non-Christian world* (London, 1894), p. 16.

7. Cited by Oliver in *The Missionary Factor in East Africa*, p. 32.

8. D. Chamberlin, *Some Letters from Livingstone, 1840–1872* (London: Oxford University Press, 1940), p. 70.

9. David Low, *Buganda in Modern History* (Berkeley: University of California Press, 1971), pp. 55–83 passim.

10. See especially John V. Taylor, *The Growth of the Church in Buganda* (London: SCM Press, 1980).

11. Oliver, *The Missionary Factor in East Africa*, p. 211.

12. Donal B. Cruise O'Brien, "Coping with the Christians, the Muslim Predicament in Kenya," in *Religion & Politics in East Africa*, ed. Holger Bernt Hansen and Michael Twaddle (Athens: Ohio University Press, 1995), p. 210.

13. François Constantin, "Muslims & Politics: The Attempts to Create Muslim National Organizations in Tanzania, Uganda & Kenya," ibid., p. 26.

14. Omari H. Kokole, "Idi Amin 'the Nubi' & Islam in Uganda Politics 1971–1979," ibid., pp. 47–48.

15. O'Brien, "Coping with the Christians," ibid., pp. 200–19 passim.

16. R. S. O'Fahey, "The Past in the Present: The Issue of the Shariah in Sudan," ibid., p. 42.

17. Ibid., p. 40.

18. For a terrifying description of the methods used to impose Islam on the peoples of the South, see Mark Tooley, "Struggling against Radical Islam," *Good News* 35, no. 3 (January/February 2002). See also Michael Tooley, "Sudanese Christians Struggle against Radical Islam," *AFA Journal,* April 2002, pp. 20–22.

19. See Oliver Duke, "The Development and Growth of Mayo Congregations," in *Land of Promise: Church Growth in a Sudan at War,* ed. Andrew Wheeler (Nairobi: Paulines Publications Africa, 1997), pp. 39–60.

20. The Rev. Dr. Joan Brown Campbell, "The Burned Churches Project," Testimony before the U.S. House of Representatives' Committee on the Judiciary, March 19, 1997, p. 7.

21. Ibid., p. ix.

22. For a more detailed rendition of the argument that follows, see Philip Turner, "The Burning of Churches and the Communion of Churches," ibid., pp. 48–57.

23. L. S. Thornton, *Common Life in the Body of Christ* (Westminster: Dacre Press, 1941), p. 27.

24. I am aware that the account I have given of David Livingstone, and indeed of other missionaries and their efforts, does not mesh well with much contemporary thinking about the colonial period. I wish neither to defend colonialism nor its advocates. I do, however, believe that, despite the fact that David Livingstone and many of his fellow missionaries shared often unwarranted and inadequate attitudes toward Africa and Africans, it is inaccurate to depict their efforts, after the manner of Charles Foucault, simply as exercises in power, control, and domination. The facts in the cases I have cited do not fit the theory. It is difficult to believe that the missionaries who went to Central Africa in the latter part of the nineteenth century did so to increase the sway of the British Raj. Because of the prevalence of disease, their expected life span was eighteen months and they knew it.

Part Four: The Importance and Insufficiency of Charity

7 The Sense and Sensibility of Philanthropy as a Moral Citizenship of Care

Paul G. Schervish

The leading question of this chapter is how to understand the moral dimensions of philanthropy as a spiritual sense and sensibility. My purpose is to elaborate a modestly integrated analysis of several aspects of philanthropy that make it a morally oriented behavior in the lives of individual donors. My general approach is akin to what Anthony Giddens calls the double hermeneutic of social analysis: to interpret how others interpret their lives.[1] Here, this means providing an analytic interpretation of how donors interpret their giving as a morally oriented or spiritual matter. By the term *spiritual* I mean the ensemble of deeply seated moral sentiments, inclinations, and duties that people recognize and live out in relation to their ultimate purpose. An ultimate purpose, explains Aristotle, is that self-determined end or final cause that people identify as the goal of life. It is known implicitly or explicitly, says Aristotle, as that end which cannot be identified as an intermediate goal or instrument for attaining another end.[2]

Max Weber calls such morally oriented behavior connected to ultimate purpose *wertrational,* or value-rational action, as opposed to *zweckrational,* or instrumentally rational action. While instrumentally rational action involves choice about the "relative importance of different possible ends," value-rational action is "motivated by the fulfillment of . . . unconditional demands," such as those "required by duty, honor, the pursuit of beauty, a religious call, personal loyalty or the importance of some 'cause.'"[3] There are numerous formulations of what people consider to be their ultimate purpose or value-rational goal. For Aristotle it is an educated happiness, for Heidegger it is participation in Being, and for Aquinas it is the unity of love of God, love of neighbor, and love of self. The general term I will use for a life implicitly or explicitly directed toward an ultimate end is moral biography or "gospel," that is, a life with the ultimate goal of exercising capacity in the service of doing what is needed.

This essay is empirical, theoretical, and partially normative. It is empirical in that I formulate a general understanding of the meaning and motives of caring behavior by drawing on what I have learned over the years from intensive interviews and surveys with wealth-holders and middle-income individuals.[4] It is theoretical in that I pull together several strands of my thinking about the morally oriented behavior of donors under a loosely defined theory that I call the moral citizenship of care.[5] The essay is normative in that I consciously invite others to consider whether, and in what way, my notions of moral biography, care, and the moral citizenship of care contribute to a more theoretically integrated, emotionally rich, and practically consequential understanding of philanthropy and philanthropists.

Throughout the chapter, I use the term *moral* in a way similar to how Philip Selznick uses it in his book, *Moral Commonwealth*. His seminal work offers a nondualistic understanding of the natural convergence between self and community—a convergence John Langan also emphasizes in his discussion of the communal nature of the individual and the inviolable individual as a communal being (see his chapter in this volume). Concurring with Emile Durkheim and John Dewey, Selznick maintains that the "moral" dimension of social relations is rooted in the actual value-motivated association of individual agents through which they forge social bonds and construct a self through the very same daily practices:

> [H]uman values are rooted in the troubles and strivings of organic life, especially in the transition from immediate impulse to enduring satisfaction. They arise out of the continuities of social existence, including the need to nurture what is immature and unstable. . . . Friendship, responsibility, leadership, love, and justice are not elements of an external ethic. . . . They are generated by mundane needs, practical opportunities, and felt satisfactions.[6]

It is within this framework of "mundane needs, practical opportunities, and felt satisfactions" that I will discuss several aspects of the moral foundations of philanthropy, particularly in regard to the donor. These moral foundations revolve around the nature of human inclination toward happiness, the meaning of "care" as meeting the true needs of others and oneself simultaneously, the motivational matrix of identification that generates care, and the distinguishing characteristic of philanthropy as a form of direct care.

In what follows, I address five aspects of the moral sense and sensibility surrounding philanthropy as a spiritual exercise. In the first section, I discuss moral life in general as a moral biography or "gospel" that combines material capacity and moral compass with the goal of fulfilling the ultimate end, for example, happiness, for oneself and others. Second, I describe the moral content of a moral biography as engaging in practices of care aimed at meeting the true needs of others. In the third section, I discuss the motivating inclination of care as residing in the ethics of identification and gratitude. The social relations of care are a single fabric extending from heart and home to the world, and are practices not of a selfless agent, but of one who embraces the unity of love of God, love of neighbor, and love of self. In the fourth section, I offer a positive definition of philanthropy as a social relation of care in which individuals respond directly to people in need rather than to the medium by which needs are expressed, as is the case in commercial and political relations. Fifth, I extend my argument from the personal to the communal level by indicating how the moral biography of individuals serves as the foundation for the social and cultural dispensation of a moral citizenship of care. In the conclusion, I describe discernment as the condition of possibility for all of the preceding considerations. Discernment is a process of conscientious decision making by which individuals clarify their capacity and moral purpose and how the two are to be connected in the conduct of life and philanthropy. I also discuss the broader general implication that the sense and sensibility of philanthropy which I have set forth is a particularly formative element of what is required if we are to animate cultural and spiritual life in an age of burgeoning affluence.

Moral Biography as a Gospel of Capacity and Character

The starting point for understanding philanthropy as a moral enterprise is to understand how life is a moral biography or what I call a gospel. In the *Nicomachean Ethics,* Aristotle says that the goal of life is happiness and that happiness is achieved by closing the gap between where one is and where one wants to be. This gap is closed by a life of virtue, that is, by making wise choices. A moral biography, then, is the perpetual migration from genesis to telesis, from history to aspiration by the exercise of wise choices. Wise choices, insists Aristotle, require both the freedom to act voluntarily and the virtue of wisdom. There can be no virtue without freedom and no true freedom without virtue. Without capacity there is no possibility of choice, just as without virtue there is no possibility of directing capacity. Making wise choices is thus the practice of moral agency, the combination of capacity and character.

Given this, a life is a moral biography or a gospel to the extent that it combines empowerment and moral compass, capacity and character, choice and wisdom, and freedom and purpose. Empowerment is the capacity to effect outcomes for oneself and others. It is the array of personal and material resources one can command as an agent. Moral compass is the strength of character or virtue that gives moral direction to the use of capacity.

An example of a life portrayed as a gospel is that of Moses as told in the Book of Exodus. As the story unfolds, we can see that it is the convergence of capacity and moral heading that matters. Moses is born a powerless son of Israelite slaves, yet soon becomes the adopted heir of the Pharaoh. Despite his princely empowerment and anticipated ascendancy to the throne, Moses learns that the capacity he has come to wield lacks moral heading, and so he takes flight to the mountains. Empowerment without moral compass, he recognizes, spawns arbitrary dominion. There, with no greater capacity than that of a stout shepherd and faithful spouse, he receives a mandate of moral direction from God manifested in the burning bush. Moses protests that he has been given moral compass but is bereft of empowerment. God tells Moses he will grant him an arsenal of miraculous powers to face down the Pharaoh, and that his brother Aaron will help him speak. In the end, Moses, imbued with a confluence of material capacity and moral purpose, breaks the resolve of the Pharaoh, parts the waters of the Red Sea, and, with moral compass becoming geographical bearing, leads his people through the desert from the clay towers of slavery to the land flowing with milk and honey. Nearing the final chapter of his gospel, Moses falters in trust and obedience. As punishment for the lapse in character, God arrests Moses's geographical progression at the outskirts of the promised land.

My purpose in citing the example of Moses is to indicate that in my thinking the ethics of doing good are rooted in a way of life revolving around how individuals tie together their capacity and character. Capacity is the array of resources, both personal and material, over which people exercise command, and is the foundation for choice. The greater the capacity, the greater the quantity and range of choice. In *Gospels of Wealth,* I described three interrelated components of capacity as (1) psychological empowerment—the disposition of great expectations, the legitimacy of those expectations, and the confidence to achieve them; (2) spatial empowerment—the capacity to establish a protective wall from intrusion and to extend one's influence geographically beyond one's immediate personal presence; and (3) temporal empowerment—the ability to reshape the past, forge the present, and bind the future.[7] Clearly, freedom of choice does not guarantee that individuals will make wise decisions and generate an offspring of happiness. It does, however, guarantee that such individuals will have a broad horizon of choice, that their choices will have the capacity to fashion the choices of others, and that they will harbor the potential to advance or impede the ultimate ends of themselves and others.

In addition to possessing the empowerment of a productive agency, a moral biography must include normative bearings. In *Gospels of Wealth,* I also described three interrelated aspects of moral compass: (1) the daily exercise of virtue or strength of character by individuals as they work through the opportunities and obstacles of the hand that life has dealt them; (2) the development of character that occurs from tests of moral fiber as individuals move through formative life-course transitions from one social status and personal identity to another; and (3) the impulse to make the big and small events of biography a redemptive process of life, death, and rebirth in the quest for healing, learning, forgiveness, and union. The quotidian exercise of virtue, dutiful commitment during transitions, and the quest for transformation are the aspects of character that, when married to psychological, spatial, and temporal empowerment, comprise the *general framework* of the sense and sensibility of a moral biography. The next question is, what constitutes the quintessential spiritual and moral *content* of such a moral biography? My answer: participating in the social relations of care.

The Content of a Gospel: The Social Relationships of Care

If the intersection of capacity and character constitutes the general nature of a personal gospel, carrying out social relations of care constitutes the moral sentiments and behaviors of that gospel in practice. In charitable giving, the capacity for choice takes the form of financial wherewithal, and moral compass takes the form of an orientation to care. The notion of financial or material wherewithal is straightforward enough, and does not require further discussion here. The notion of care, however, is not so clear-cut and needs further elucidation.

The first consideration concerns the nature of the moral sensibility of care. What rudimentary bearing, I ask, is substantial enough to be the basis for duty and yet familiar enough to be a natural inclination? It is the disposition of *care*. The term derives from the Latin *cura* and is an etymological cousin of *caritas* or interpersonal love.

Philosopher Jules Toner systematically formulates a notion of care grounded in a phenomenological analysis of *radical love*. Toner defines love as the affection by which a lover "affirms the beloved for the beloved's self (as a radical end) . . . [and] by which the lover affectively identifies with the loved one's personal being, by which in some sense the lover is the beloved affectively."[8] If love is the affection of identifying with another as a radical end, care is the practical or implemental aspect of love. Care is love directed at meeting the true needs of others. According to Toner, care

is an affirmative affection toward someone precisely as in need. It is not the need nor what is needed that is the object of radical care; radical care is of the one who has the need, under the aspect of needing. For example, I have an affection of care toward one who needs food or friendly words or a listener or instruction. As a consequence of care, I desire food for him, or friendly words and so on. If I have a care or concern for the food or words or instruction, etc., it is only . . . relative and derivative care [not radical care].[9]

Clearly, Toner's definition of care as meeting the true needs of others does not provide an answer to what would constitute care in any particular situation. He does, however, point us toward the proper question. First, he emphasizes that care is directed at another person as a radical end; we do not truly care for an object. Certainly people speak of caring for education or for the Boston Symphony. But for Toner, such concerns signify derivative care, and are not to be confused with, or substituted for, radical care directed toward the only worthy object—other human beings, the so-called "ultimate recipients" or "ultimate beneficiaries" of care.

Second, Toner insists that care, as the practical implementation of love, is an affective involvement in meeting others' *true needs*. Again, we can never know in the abstract what another's true needs are; nor does simply setting out to attend to someone's true needs mean that we actually do that. Yet by emphasizing the notion of *true* needs, Toner places front and center the obligation not just to respond to others in their needs, but also to respond effectively. According to Toner, taking the effort to figure out how to respond in a way that accomplishes a beneficial end (even if not always viewed as such by others or even by the recipient) is a crucial indication of how much we care in the first place. With care defined as the practice of meeting the true needs of others, the next question is to explain what animates care. The answer is that care is animated by the sense and sensibility of identifying the fate of another as linked to our own.

Thomas And Tocqueville: The Ethics of Identification and Gratitude

Along with situating philanthropy as a dimension of moral biography, and as a social relation of care, the third step in unpacking the meaning of philanthropy as a spiritual practice is to locate the natural inclinations that kindle care. I have reviewed elsewhere the primary motivations for care in the form of philanthropy.[10] The two I want to emphasize here are identification with the fate of others and gratitude for unmerited advantages. For my discussion of identification, I draw on the Judeo-Christian and American focus on the identity between love of neighbor and love of self. I recognize that there are other religious, spiritual, and philosophical traditions that I could appropriate to make my point. But the Judeo-Christian tradition and the associational dynamics of American civil society described by Tocqueville are the ones with which I am most familiar, and from which the discourse about philanthropy and care emerge in the United States.

My primary argument is that care entails not simply meeting the needs of another, but the creation of a collaborative relationship of care that fulfills the common true need of both parties for effectiveness and significance, or happiness. Toner explicitly makes this connection: "[T]he lover affectively identifies with the loved one's personal being, by which in some sense the lover is the beloved affectively." Notice two things about which I will say more in a moment. First, a true act of care is an act of identification with another. It is recognizing a radical affinity connecting the destinies of self and neighbor. Second, a true act of care is actually an act of self-love. We have now arrived at the point at which it is possible to specify a morality of natural inclination that is substantial and familiar enough to ground the duties and ideals of philanthropy. I call this morality the *ethics of identification*.

In modern discourse, self-identity revolves around the awareness of oneself as a distinctive personality. However, such a notion was not always prevalent. If our contemporary emphasis is on the notion of *self*-identity, the more classical emphasis of Thomas Aquinas, for instance, is on self-*identity*. To be clear, Aquinas did not share our modern conception of identity as a component of personality; he did not even use the word *identity*. But he did speak eloquently about mutual union as the basic condition of *caritas*—what Toner refers to as radical love implemented through care. As Aquinas puts it, "by the fact that love transforms the lover into the beloved, it makes the lover enter inside the beloved, and conversely, so that there is nothing of the beloved that is not united to the lover, just as the form attains the innermost recesses of that which it informs, and conversely."[11]

It is not stretching things too far to suggest that what Aquinas describes in scholastic terms as the fundamental mutuality of love is akin to what Tocqueville enunciates in civic terms as "self-interest properly understood." As Tocqueville explains, Americans "enjoy explaining almost every act of their lives on the principle of self-interest properly understood. It gives them great pleasure to point out how an enlightened self-love continually leads them to help one another and disposes them freely to give part of their time and wealth for the good of the state."[12] Harriet Martineau, a contemporary of Tocqueville who wrote six volumes on her travels in America, is equally persuaded that a sense of identification is at the heart of any situation in which "charity has gone deep as well as spread wide." According to Martineau, the spirit of charity becomes one with "the spirit of justice" only in those societies with a full-fledged "spirit of fraternity." Such a spirit of fraternity, she maintains, arises "from the movers feeling it their own concern that any are depressed and endangered as they would themselves refuse to be."[13]

It is inadequate to proffer an ethics of altruistic selflessness precisely in that area of human dedication in which the self is most involved. When it comes to *caritas*, what matters is the quality of the self not the absence of self; the quality of what we do in the name of identification not the absence of identification; the sensitivity of our interests not the absence of interests. This is congruent with David Craig's (see his essay in this volume) insistence that we should focus not only on what donors give to beneficiaries but also on the benefits that donors *take* from their giving. Aquinas recognizes and even extols this seeming paradoxical unity of duty and pleasure in the implemental aspects of *caritas:* As Gerard Gilleman says, "For St. Thomas there is no place in a morally good act of will for an absolute disjunction between love referred to self and love referred to another. The proper effect of love is to associate self with the other."[14] Rather than search for the realms of altruism or *selflessness* that are supposed to counter the utilitarian ethic of calculated self-interest, we have found it more fruitful to track the realms of self-identification with others. We agree, then, with M. W. Martin,[15] who also argues that it is philosophically more consistent and more practically productive to activate rather than remove a commonality of interests between donor and recipient. As such, it is the presence of an identified self, not the absence of self, that animates care and is therefore a sense and sensibility to be honored rather than eschewed.

In addition to the dynamics of identification, a second formative inclination is that of gratitude. Over the course of two decades, my colleagues and I have interviewed over 250 individuals from across the economic spectrum about their motivations for care. A virtually universal disposition that we encountered is the propensity that many summarize by the simple yet heartfelt phrase "to give back." It turns out, however, that upon probing we unearth an impetus that is even more vital than this salutary phrase suggests. Invariably, beneath the desire to give back is a sense of gratitude, and behind that gratitude is an appreciation of blessing, grace, gift, luck, or fortune. Gratitude is an active, mobilizing sentiment; a discerning encounter with blessing animates a response of care for others.

Theologian Robert Ochs remarked in a lecture years ago that there are three ways to take a gift. It may be taken for granted, taken with guilt, or taken with gratitude. We have found in our interviews that the most positively formative disposition of philanthropic consciousness and conscience involves taking the gifts of fortune with gratitude. Those who take their gifts with gratitude approach the world with a more emotionally abundant, secure, and gracious disposition. They recognize their material and personal capacities as dependent on the providence of God, people, or circumstances. And they discern from experience more than from tenet that because so much has been given to them, so much can be given by them.

In a perceptive way that brings us back full circle to identification, those who experience such blessing and gratitude also formulate the moral logic by which a spiritual experience of blessing engenders a pragmatic practice of care. The most consequential corollary of apprehending one's life as imbued with gift is the generative recognition that just as my fortune is not due entirely to my own merit, others' misfortune may not be completely attributable to their own failure. Such an insight forges an identification between donor and recipient as the offspring of a common heritage of unmerited positive and negative fortune, and as the source of a common destiny. Those who have been dealt a friendly hand care for those who have been dealt an inauspicious one. Blessing breeds gratitude and gratitude breeds identification, and, again, identification breeds generosity.

Fortunately, identification, gratitude, and care are not foreign endeavors. By inclination we identify our fate with the fate of others, even if these others are at first family and our closest associates. By inclination, we experience unmerited advantage and seek to provide it to others. Experience imbues us at least with embryonic sentiments of radical love and radical care. As the Book of Deuteronomy says, the law of love

> is not too hard for you, neither is it far off. It is not in heaven, that you should say, "Who will go up for us to heaven, and bring it to us, that we may hear it and do it?" Neither is it beyond the sea, that you should say, "Who will go over the sea for us, and bring it to us, that we may hear it and do it?" But the word is very near you; it is in your mouth and in your heart, so that you can do it.[16]

Identification and gratitude, then, are familiar in two senses. They are dispositions that are not only common to experience but are common because they are born in and borne by the family, and are often expressed in familial metaphors. Our research indicates that we are first inclined to help those we perceive to have a fate that parallels our own fate or the fate of our spouse, parents, siblings, or children. It also consistently reveals that all who care for others out of gratitude regard their activity as an active engagement, rather than an absence, of self.[17] How the general understanding of moral biography, identification, and gratitude helps specify what is distinctive about the particular arena of philanthropy is the topic of the next section.

The Distinctive Characteristic of Philanthropy as a Form of Care

Moral biography, care, and identification are three pillars of philanthropy. A moral biography is capacity married to moral compass; care is the content of a moral biography; and identification is the animating inclination of care. Within this framework, philanthropy is a distinctive mode of identification, a type of care, and an element of moral biography. Philanthropy is important because it is a relationship of care and is constitutive of moral biography. It is distinctive because, as I will explain, it is a direct relationship of care; it is not privileged because, as I will also explain, it may not be the most important relationship of care for any particular individual at any particular place and time. Philanthropy is one specific relationship directed toward meeting the true needs of others.[18] As such, philanthropy stands alongside many other relations of care—such as those of parent and child, spouses, friends, employer and worker—and is not privileged when understood in its conventional sense. However, when and where philanthropy is the best way to combine capacity and moral compass in a particular situation, it is a cardinal moral practice.

Most efforts to conceptualize philanthropy emphasize the presence of a special dedication to the public good or philanthropy's connection to the nonprofit sector. However, neither of these aspects gets to the essence of what distinguishes philanthropy from politics and commerce in a positive rather than a derivative way, as is indicated by its residual appellations of *third, nongovernmental,* and *nonprofit* sector.

In my view, the defining characteristic of a philanthropic relation of care is what activates its attention. In *commercial* relations, needs elicit a response largely to the extent that they become expressed in dollars—that is, they are translated into what economists call "effective demand." Similarly, in *political* relations, needs elicit a response largely to the extent that they can become expressed as campaign contributions or as votes—which in fact is another form of effective demand. What makes commercial and political demand "effective" in eliciting a response is that these forms of demand are presented through a medium upon which suppliers depend for their material existence. Neither businesses nor politicians can long afford to ignore such concrete indications of their clients' will. On occasion, commercial and political agents may attend directly to people's needs, in which case they incorporate a philanthropic dimension. However, for the most part and over the long run, commerce and politics respond not to the inherent value of the people in need but indirectly to the medium through which people express their needs, and on which commercial and political actors rely for their survival.

In philanthropic relations, the focus is not on the medium of votes or dollars that communicate needs but directly on the people who have the needs. The immediate object of attention is the people in need. In contrast to commercial and political relations that are mobilized by the medium of effective demand, philanthropy is mobilized directly by what I call an affective demand that activates the recognition of and identification with others in their needs. A construction company builds homes not just because someone has a need for a home, but because that need is expressed with dollars. Habitat for Humanity builds a home because someone needs a place to live.

Recall that in *Les Misérables*, Jean Valjean consoles the dying Fantine by agreeing to bring Fantine's daughter, Cosette, under his care. This reflects a philanthropic relation with both Fantine and Cosette not simply because Valjean is attempting to do good, nor because his help is tax deductible or housed as formal philanthropy within the boundaries of the nonprofit sector. It is philanthropic because it matches the resources of a giver to the needs of a recipient through a social relation that is directly mobilized and governed by a strength of character and moral compass born of identification with another as a radical end in need. It is interesting to note that Jean Valjean carries out his care for Cosette essentially as a family relationship of father to daughter (replacing his lost relationship with his sister's daughter) and his care for Fantine as a relationship of surrogate spouse (replacing his relationship with his sister). He also carries Marius on his shoulders through the sewers of Paris as his son, soon to be wedded to Cosette. Significantly, Valjean is an industrialist and mayor who could have cared for Cosette through commerce by employing her in a fairer labor contract than the innkeepers, Monsieur and Madame Thernardier, or through the polity by placing her in a state guardianship established by town policies.

Once again, philanthropy is motivated by identification and can be seen to be familial. It is familial in that Valjean relates to those he helps as flesh of his flesh. It is also familial in that philanthropic relationships emulate family relationships; both attend to others in need because of the value of those in need rather than because of the value of the medium through which needs are communicated. Finally, philanthropy is familial in that it is a relationship of mutual care. Jean Valjean fulfills his happiness as he bestows it on others. Just as donors express care by supplying material and spiritual capacity to meet the needs of recipients for effectiveness and significance, so do donors receive care by having their needs for effectiveness and significance met as well. In this sense, philanthropy becomes a *collaborative* relationship of mutual care between donors and recipients. When such relationships of care, rooted in the identifications and practices of family, become extended in kinship, space, and time, they help create a public way of life I call the moral citizenship of care.

The Moral Citizenship of Care

Up to this point, I have discussed several elements of the spiritual inclinations and affections of individuals that constitute philanthropy as moral practice. These include the understandings that a moral biography is the pursuit of an ultimate goal through the confluence of what I have referred to variously as capacity and character, empowerment and moral compass, choice and virtue; that the content of moral compass is care or the meeting of the true needs of others; that care is motivated not by philosophical altruism or absence of self but by an identified self, with self-love being a constituent ingredient; and that the defining attribute of philanthropy is responding because others are in need rather than because others are able to express their needs through a medium of effective demand.

I now draw together my considerations by indicating how what I have described about philanthropy as a personal practice provides the foundation for a caring society, that is, the organic link between what is personal and what is communal or cultural. Just as for individuals the sense and sensibility of philanthropy revolves around a caring relationship directed toward simultaneously meeting the true needs of others and oneself, for society the sense and sensibility of philanthropy revolves around how personal relations of care become translated into what I call the moral citizenship of care.

By introducing the notion of a moral citizenship, I seek to name a vibrant, yet often ignored, aspect of what constitutes the moral health of a society in general, and of the United States in particular. This entails drawing out two implications of what I said in the foregoing sections for understanding the foundations of a caring society. Conceptually, I recommend complementing our notions of political and economic citizenship with the notion of moral citizenship, which focuses on the motivations and practices of mutually beneficial identification and the social relations of care spawned by such identification. Empirically, I suggest the need to recognize that in addition to formal philanthropy, the moral quality of a culture emerges from and, in turn, animates a fuller range of informal relations of care that pervade daily life. Although there are several implications of my sanguine portrait of moral interdependence for the debate on the social capital and civil society, I will not here repeat what I have said elsewhere.[19]

I propose the notion of moral citizenship of care as a conceptual framework for understanding and making broader interpretive sense of the full range of practical social relations of care—of which formal philanthropic giving and volunteering are but two important components. As far as I know, the term *moral citizenship of care* has not been used anywhere else, but what I mean by it is straightforward. I have already discussed at length the meaning of *care* as the attention to others in their true needs, and I have indicated that I am using the notion of *moral* in Selznick's sense as the constellation of mobilizing affections and values that arise not from an external ethic but from the everyday engagements surrounding "mundane needs, practical opportunities, and felt satisfactions."[20]

The combined term *moral citizenship* requires more explanation and can be clarified by contrasting it to political and economic citizenship. First, moral citizenship shares with political citizenship the proposition of equivalence among individuals. But with moral citizenship, this equivalence is not primarily before or under the law. Rather, the equivalence is before and under the sentiment of self-recognition in others and self-identification with the needs of others. If the instrumental trajectory of political citizenship revolves around exercising the legal rights and duties of democratic processes, the instrumental trajectory of moral citizenship revolves around fulfilling the inclinations and obligations of the contents of care—extending from the familial to the global.

Clearly, the rights and duties of political citizenship can be congruent with the objective of advancing the social relations of assistance and can contribute to their improvement and operation—indeed, the rights and duties of citizenship derive from, imply, and even add an array of pro-social desires, sentiments, and dispositions, especially having to do with the aspect of universalism.[21] However, because political rights and duties are by constitutional mandate limited in their reach, they are neither profound nor broad enough to be the primary ethic for identifying, inspiring, and nurturing the fundamental character of a free society. As salutary as political citizenship is, it is mainly an adjunct to, rather than the source of, a moral community. Moral citizenship is the ground or social foundation of political citizenship and is the end for which political citizenship is a means. Moral citizenship resides in and fortifies the interstices and ultimate goals of life where political citizenship never does, or should, reach. Moral citizenship provides the content for the processes and content of political citizenship.

Moral citizenship is equally more profound than economic citizenship, something Adam Smith readily acknowledged. In *The Theory of Moral Sentiments,* Smith insists that economic markets (and political institutions) cannot be expected to produce beneficence in society. For Smith, the economic citizenship of the free market provides a framework and a floor for rudimentary well-being within society, but not for greater well-being:

> Society may subsist among different men, as among different merchants, from a sense of its utility, without any mutual love or affection; and though no man in it should owe any obligation, or be bound in gratitude to any other, it may still be upheld by a mercenary exchange of good offices according to an agreed valuation. . . . Society may subsist, though not in the most comfortable state, without beneficence.[22]

The additional voluntary moral sentiments of beneficence are required to establish a deeper moral commonwealth in which the needs and injuries of others are responded to from love, gratitude, friendship, and esteem:

> All the members of human society stand in need of each other's assistance, and are likewise exposed to mutual injuries. Where necessary assistance is reciprocally afforded from love, from gratitude, from friendship, and esteem, the society flourishes and is happy. All the different members of it are bound together by the agreeable bands of love and affection, and are, as it were, drawn to one common centre of mutual good offices.[23]

In contrast to moral citizenship, both political and economic citizenship are intermediate goals of life. They focus foremost on access to and participation in a process of determination rather than directly on the content of that determination. There are, of course, substantive contents that people seek to obtain via political and economic citizenship. However, in order to obtain these contents, those seeking them must express their desires largely through electoral processes and market mechanisms rather than directly as needs. In other words, the practice of political and economic citizenship revolves around the process of effective demand that I described previously. Political and economic citizenship can be counted on in the long run to produce outcomes for those in need only to the extent that those in need can materially discipline political or economic decision makers by providing or withholding votes and dollars. Still, and this is crucial, where a vibrant moral citizenship exists, political and economic decision makers sometimes in fact do transcend the dynamics of effective demand and respond directly to those needs that are signaled by the categorical worth of the people who have those needs. Hence, we do find policy makers taking principled stands that may cost them political capital, and business owners and corporations providing pro bono or discounted goods and services that cost them financial capital.

As a practical ethic and as a way of life, the moral citizenship of care is that sphere of thinking, emotion, and behavior that begins in the tribulations and aspirations surrounding what is close at hand and extends to an ever-broadening horizon of others in need. Moral citizenship does not divide the private from the public, the local from the distant; instead, it speaks of the levels and distribution of moral capital rather than of social and financial capital. The moral citizenship of care focuses on the extension and expression of care, rather than on the extension and expression of civic life, membership, and participation, as the cornerstone of cultural health. The moral citizenship of care leads us to focus on the informal and formal relations of care in which people are currently engaged and which they need to take up, rather than foremost on the derivative social and political relations that can thrive only by attending to effective demand. The moral citizenship of care sets the agenda for political and economic citizenship by designating the injuries of existing law and commerce and specifying directions to rectify the current dispensation. The moral citizenship of care is the public and communal outcome of the moral biography of care as the latter extends to broader concentric circles of human kinship, time, and space.

Conclusion: The Formation of Moral Biography

In this chapter, I have set out a series of interconnected considerations about the moral dimensions of philanthropy. The motif of the chapter is that dispositions and practices of care that individuals perform are part of what constitutes a life as a moral biography or *gospel*. This gospel is the intersection of empowerment and moral direction. The development of moral biography is the foundation for the quality of the commonwealth as the locus of a moral citizenship of care.

Throughout the chapter, I have emphasized the inclinations, dispositions, and sentiments that constitute moral biography and moral citizenship. I also maintain that life is dialectical such that every sense and sensibility leading toward care can be weakened or undercut by equal and opposite forces. As Amy Kass reminds us, "the Greeks understood that great misfortune may lurk in the shadow of great good fortune. They knew that a great windfall can cause a great downfall, and that gifts are equally conducive to benefit and harm, to joy and sorrow."[24] I have written frequently about the potential for capacity to lead to both blessing and curse under the rubric of the "dialectic of care and control."[25] By this I mean that every opportunity to follow moral compass also offers an opening to lose moral bearing. Ever present is the potential for capacity to become separated from care, and to choke off what needs to be done. For this reason, I want to conclude this chapter with a few words about how people learn, deepen, and recast their moral biography as time and circumstances change, and as they face countervailing forces that threaten to misdirect their moral biography. I have focused on the moral sense and sensibility of motivating care as familiar, attractive, and fulfilling rather than alien, unpleasant, and debilitating. The question is, How do people become attuned to what is truly familiar and fulfilling? How do they educate their sense and sensibility so as to care rather than merely control? The answer: through a conscientious process of clarification or discernment.

There are many traditions of discernment by which individuals discover and implement their practical vocation in the light of faith, and I am undertaking a study of them. For now, I will say a few words about the method of discernment with which I am most familiar, that offered by Ignatius Loyola, the founder of the Jesuit religious order, and subsequently fleshed out by others.

In Ignatian spirituality, discernment is the process by which individuals learn their duty, not by eliminating predilections but by discovering them at a deeper level. For those generally and regularly oriented toward good—"going from good to better," as Ignatius puts it—what is to be done is discovered by a convergence of intelligence and affection in the light of movement toward one's ultimate end. Theologian Michael Buckley, writing on the elements of discernment, says that the ultimate end in religious terms is "transforming union." But it is not enough to have this end; we also need a concrete means "of contacting or of being guided by God." The religious person, says Buckley, "is vitally persuaded not only that God has offered himself as such a possibility and fulfillment, but that he will guide human life towards this realization; God offers not only finality, but consistent direction."[26]

The term *discernment* derives from the Latin *cernere*, "to sift," and *dis*, "apart." Discernment is a process of archeological discovery in which the *discreta* or discrete aspects of life are sifted through and ordered into meaningful patterns and purposeful decisions. In practice, discernment is a process of self-reflection often aided by the questioning and direction of an advisor or spiritual director who encourages individuals to clarify and set the course for carrying out decisions in an environment of liberty and inspiration. Liberty is the material and psychological freedom from unfounded presuppositions, assumptions, fears, and anxieties. Inspiration is the personally ascertained array of desires that provide the direction for commitment. Discernment is not carried out to eliminate aspiration, inspiration, and inclination, but to make them clearer. It is, in the end, the identification of a *munus suavissimum,* that most pleasant duty that enlists the aptitudes, intelligence, and aspirations of a person to embrace what is pleasing as a path to happiness. In an address at Boston College, theologian Howard Gray said discernment aims not at finding the most difficult thing to do, but the most inspiring thing to do.

In regard to charitable giving, discernment helps individuals to uncover for themselves, rather than simply be told, the prospects and purposes of their financial life in the context of the prospects and purposes of their spiritual life. Through discernment, individuals clarify their level of charitable capacity, clarify the people and causes they care about, and unearth how to translate their capacity and care into specific philanthropic endeavors that are personally formative for both themselves and those they seek to help.

The content of such discernment varies from individual to individual. Still, we have found that virtually all those we have interviewed develop their own sense and sensibility about philanthropy by addressing and answering some version of the following four questions:

- Is there anything you want to do with your material capacity?
- That meets the true needs of others?
- That you can do better through philanthropy than through government or commerce?
- That enables you to identify with the fate of others, fashion a financial morality for yourself and your children, and achieve greater happiness by expanding the effectiveness and significance of your life and the life of those for whom you care?

In the end, while financial gifts flow to fulfill the true needs of recipients for happiness and to close the gap between the beneficiaries' history and aspiration, moral and spiritual gifts flow to the donors as a result of charitable giving that fulfills their true needs for happiness—developing the interstices of a caring society characterized by a moral citizenship of care. Although the moral citizenship of financial care has always been part of an ascetic way of life, it is an especially valuable element of spiritual life in an age of affluence. As personal and social wealth expand the horizon of choice for individuals, it becomes increasingly important that we develop a positive spirituality for affluent living and for making wise choices among the obstacles and opportunities of affluence.

A key personal and cultural question of the twenty-first century for an increasing segment of the world's population is, how do I fashion my own and my community's spiritual life in an age of affluence? How will the vast growth in the quantity of choice be translated into a deeper development in the quality of choice? Answering these questions requires clarifying the level of our financial capacity and deciding how best to allocate it with moral compass. This, I believe, will increasingly include conscientious decisions about financial care in the form of charitable giving. To animate such a spiritual life in an age of affluence, we are not without the resources of inclination toward care, the dynamics of identification, and the process of discernment by which individuals link choice and wisdom, capacity and character, and empowerment and moral compass.

From this perspective, the ethics of doing good is neither alien nor automatic. I concur with Aquinas that grace builds on nature, and compliance with grace entails the conscientious self-formation of discerned decision making in the light of one's ultimate end. In order for doing good to fill the interstices of daily life, it must be voluntary. This means we need to enlist the motives and the methods to fathom the daily vocation of our moral biography as the connection of capacity and moral compass, the dynamics of care as attention to meeting the true needs of others, the place of philanthropy as one avenue for directly doing so, and the moral citizenship of care as the cultural and social fruit of the foregoing.

Notes

I am grateful to the T. B. Murphy Foundation Charitable Trust and the Lilly Endowment, Inc. for supporting the research on which this chapter is based, and to Todd Fitzpatrick, Caroline Noonan, and Glenda Murray for their competent and gracious editorial assistance. I also wish to thank David H. Smith and the members of the seminar on Moral Issues in Doing Good for their collegial encouragement and insightful assessments of my chapter.

1. Anthony Giddens, *The Constitution of Society* (Los Angeles: University of California Press, 1984), p. xxxv.
2. Aristotle, *Nicomachean Ethics*, 2nd ed., ed. and trans. Terence Irwin (Indianapolis: Hackett Publishing Company, Inc., 1999), I. 2. 1. & I. 7.
3. Max Weber, *Economy and Society,* ed. Guenther Roth and Claus Wittich (New York: Bedminster Press, 1968), pp. 24–26.
4. Paul G. Schervish and Andrew Herman, *Empowerment and Beneficence: Strategies of Living and Giving among the Wealthy,* Final Report on the Study on Wealth and Philanthropy (Chestnut Hill, Mass.: Social Welfare Research Institute, Boston, College, 1988); Paul G. Schervish, Platon E. Coutsoukis, and Ethan Lewis, *Gospels of Wealth: How the Rich Portray Their Lives* (Westport, Conn.: Praeger, 1994); Paul G. Schervish, Mary A. O'Herlihy, and John J. Havens, "Agent-Animated Wealth and Philanthropy: The Dynamics of Accumulation and Allocation Among High-Tech Donors," Final Report of the *2001 High-Tech Donors Study* (Chestnut Hill, Mass.: Social Welfare Research Institute, Boston College, 2001).
5. Paul G. Schervish and John J. Havens, "The Boston Area Diary Study and the Moral Citizenship of Care," *Voluntas: International Journal of Voluntary and Nonprofit Organizations* 13, no. 1 (Spring 2002).
6. Philip Selznick, *The Moral Commonwealth: Social Theory and the Promise of Community* (Los Angeles: University of California Press, 1992), p. 19.
7. Schervish, Coutsoukis, and Lewis, *Gospels of Wealth.*

8. Jules Toner, *The Experience of Love* (Washington, D.C.: Corpus Books, 1968), p. 183.

9. Ibid., p. 75.

10. Paul G. Schervish and John J. Havens, "The New Physics of Philanthropy: The Supply-Side Vectors of Charitable Giving—Part 2: The Spiritual Side of the Supply Side," *The CASE International Journal of Higher Education Advancement* 2, no. 3 (March 2002): 221–41.

11. *Thomas Aquinas's Commentary on the Third Book of the Sentences* by Peter Lombard, division 27, question one, article one, response to fourth objection, cited in Gerard Gilleman, S.J., *The Primacy of Charity in Moral Theology* (Westminster, Md.: The Newman Press, 1959), p. 126.

12. Tocqueville, Alexis de, *Democracy in America,* trans. George Lawrence, ed. J. P. Mayer (New York: Harper Perennial, 1966; 1835), p. 526.

13. Harriet Martineau, *How to Observe Morals and Manners* (New Brunswick, N.J.: Transaction, 1989; 1838), p. 218.

14. Gilleman, *The Primacy of Charity,* p. 125.

15. M. W. Martin, *Virtuous Giving: Philanthropy, Voluntary Service, and Caring* (Bloomington: Indiana University Press, 1994).

16. Deuteronomy 30:11–14.

17. Paul G. Schervish and John J. Havens, "Social Participation and Charitable Giving: A Multivariate Analysis," *Voluntas: International Journal of Voluntary and Nonprofit Organizations* 8, no. 3 (Summer 1997); Schervish and Havens, "The Boston Area Diary Study."

18. Susan A. Ostrander and Paul G. Schervish, "Giving and Getting: Philanthropy as a Social Relation," in *Critical Issues in American Philanthropy: Strengthening Theory and Practice,* ed. Jon Van Til (San Francisco: Jossey-Bass, 1990).

19. Schervish and Havens, "The Boston Area Diary Study."

20. Selznick, *The Moral Commonwealth,* p. 19.

21. Ibid., pp. 193–201.

22. Adam Smith, *The Theory of Moral Sentiments* (Amherst, N.Y.: Prometheus Books, 2000; 1759), p. 124.

23. Ibid.

24. Amy Kass, ed., *The Perfect Gift: The Philanthropic Imagination in Poetry and Prose* (Bloomington: Indiana University Press, 2002), p. 1.

25. Paul G. Schervish, "Adoption and Altruism: Those with Whom I Want to Share a Dream," *Nonprofit and Voluntary Sector Quarterly* 21, no. 4 (Winter 1992); Paul G. Schervish, "The Sound of One Hand Clapping: The Case For and Against Anonymous Giving," *Voluntas: International Journal of Voluntary and Nonprofit Organizations* 5, no. 1 (1994); Paul G. Schervish, "The Modern Medici: Patterns, Motivations, and Giving Strategies of the Wealthy," paper presented on the panel "The New Philanthropists" at the inaugural forum "What Is 'New' about New Philanthropy," University of Southern California Nonprofit Studies Center, Los Angeles, January 20, 2000. See also Schervish, O'Herlihy, and Havens, "Agent-Animated Wealth and Philanthropy."

26. Michael J. Buckley, "The Structure of the Rules for Discernment of Spirits," *The Way,* Supplement 20 (August 1973): 21.

8   Philanthropy, Charity, Subsidiarity, and Solidarity
A Basis for Understanding Philanthropy in Catholic Social Teaching

John Langan, S.J.

From its very beginning, this chapter seems to be menaced by two major difficulties. In the first half of the title, I am offering a string of abstractions, the first two of which are familiar and will seem to many people to be virtually equivalent, while the second two are not totally unknown but have a certain vague and puzzling character to them. In the second half, I turn to a specific religious tradition as a way of understanding a complex and increasingly secular network of activities carried on in a highly pluralistic society. I will argue that subsidiarity and solidarity, when taken together, provide a better basis for understanding important social dimensions of philanthropy than does the notion of charity. They actually provide a framework that will be useful to persons of very different religious and nonreligious perspectives for thinking about the social functions and social responsibilities of philanthropy.

Philanthropy and Charity

My formative academic training was in moral philosophy in the analytic tradition, which took metaethics and the study of the nuances of moral language very seriously and approached these matters in a resolutely secular spirit. But my mentor, William Frankena of the University of Michigan, always encouraged his students to acknowledge the relevance of the history of ethical theory and the contribution of the major religious traditions to apparently secular forms of ethical thinking.[1]

As a result of this training and even more deeply because of my own views about the interplay of religious and ethical influences in shaping ethical reflection in our culture, I have often taken a class or two in the early part of a course to discuss with students a number of biblical passages bearing on the issues of the course. In an age of widespread religious illiteracy, this can lead to some surprising reactions. The one I remember most vividly occurred in a class for which I had assigned the thirteenth chapter of Paul's first letter to the Corinthians. This is one of the most famous passages in the New Testament; and it is very often used as a reading at weddings. It is a soaring affirmation of the enduring value of love or charity or, to use St. Paul's original Greek, *agape*. One of the students came up to me after class and said that she liked the reading but that it sounded very much like something she had once heard in church. I tried gently to suggest that this was not a coincidence, and that she had in all likelihood heard this very passage many times before; but she continued to find it incredible that something commonly read in church could actually be attractive and deeply moving.

The connections between charity as a theological virtue in the Christian tradition and the forms of philanthropy that have flourished in a diverse and increasingly secular society are bound to be complex, given the historical richness and complexity of Christian theological and ethical traditions and the many forms that philanthropy has taken over the ages. In this essay I will not attempt to trace the historical connections or to make an argument for the logical dependence of social norms on theological positions or to use religious considerations as a motive for philanthropic activity. Rather, what I propose to do is to explore a particular religious and ethical way of thinking about the social aspects of philanthropy, a way of thinking that is expressed in the body of church documents and encyclical letters of the popes commonly[5] grouped together under the heading of Catholic social teaching or Catholic social thought.[2]

This may well seem to be a less than promising approach, especially since this body of material says very little explicitly about philanthropy. It also directs our attention away from some of the themes that have been especially prominent in Christian approaches to philanthropy. Three themes that have had a powerful influence on readers of the New Testament and on the writings authored by "the Fathers of the church" in the early centuries of the history of the Christian church have been: (1) the concern for purity of motive in the giver, (2) the devaluation of the transitory goods of this world in comparison with the eternal goods of the life to come, and (3) the contrast between the perilous state of the affluent and the divine protection given to the poor.[3]

These are all themes that make the modern philanthropic world and the contemporary philosophical observer uncomfortable. The concern for purity of motive,[4] which leads toward evangelical radicalism or toward an altruistic universalism of a Kantian sort, has been largely subordinated in the practices of development and advancement offices of philanthropic institutions, in which large quantities of energy and ingenuity are expended on the task of enlisting the vanity or, at best, the magnanimity of potential donors. Motives are not to be looked at too closely; in general, they are presumed to be not much better or worse than those of the middling run of humanity, *l'homme moyen sensuel*. It is not assumed that the class of big donors and the class of real saints coincide perfectly. The devaluation of the goods of this world[5] is often seen as either incoherent or subversive. If a comfortable and secure way of life, good health, and civilized pleasures are not seen as goods worth pursuing and worth having, then education, health care, and measures for the relief of poverty lose much of their point. Asceticism[6] seems to be at odds not merely with egoism but with the goals of philanthropy. The perilous state of the affluent, while strongly affirmed in some striking New Testament parables as well as in some vehement prophetic denunciations,[7] seems to contradict the biblical connection between faithfulness to God's covenant and the enjoyment of the blessings of prosperity that is promised in Scripture. Here, too, we can note the current reluctance of even churches and church-related organizations to rely on themes invoking fear, the sense of sinfulness, the precariousness of life, and the prospect of eternal punishment in the course of their exhortations to generosity.

Some Limits of Charity

Charity itself has an attraction ranging well beyond the community of the faithful. The ideals of sacrificial love and of service dedicated to the needs of others are, even when they are implemented in an imperfect and parochial fashion, appealing to people of many diverse backgrounds. As the basis for a Christian understanding of philanthropy, charity seems to have an impeccable religious pedigree. But it suffers from three limitations: one logical, one historical, and one spiritual.

The logical limitation is that the concept of charity is highly general and complex. It is presented as something necessary for and practicable by all persons in all states of society. It is a virtue that is supposed to motivate and guide slaves in the Roman empire, North African bishops, Dutch Calvinist merchants, Carmelite nuns, Australian convicts, discarded wives of once-polygamous chieftains, Alyosha Karamazov, Mother Teresa, and the Notre Dame football team. This is not to say that it is vacuous. It does rule out many kinds of behavior; but in doing so it has to rely on other normative concepts to give real content to its contribution to the moral life. Thus, my loving a person requires my showing respect for his or her rights. My acting in a loving manner toward a particular person requires that I be able to practice more specific virtues such as patience, fairness, liberality, and justice. The point here is not that charity or love or *agape* is irrelevant to an account of the practice of philanthropy, but rather that it is a notion that is inadequate to fulfill the task by itself.

The notion of charity as love or *agape* has a greater role to play in the lives of those who are looking to integrate their relations with their fellow human beings into a theological understanding of human life than it has for those who are looking for more specific guidance in answering questions about the range of beneficiaries and the scale of donations. In the Christian tradition, charity is a theological virtue. This means that God is both its source and its object. The last point is very important for our purposes here. Christians are called upon to show charity not merely to their neighbors but to God as well. This will sound less surprising to us if we put it in a form closer to the language of the Hebrew

Bible: Christians (and Jews) are commanded to love God above all things.[8] God, then, is the supreme object of charity or love. This implies that charity cannot be interpreted primarily or fundamentally as response to need, since God, at least the God of Abraham, Isaac, and Jacob (who in this respect is also the God of Augustine and Aquinas, Calvin and Pascal, Kierkegaard and Rahner) is not in need, is not the kind of being having needs that we could satisfy. Rather, charity with regard to God and to other beings who are valuable in themselves or who are to be treated as ends in themselves is a response to what is understood to be good or valuable.

Charity, including the love of a uniquely perfect God, can, however, be a motive for charitable action and charitable giving aimed at meeting the urgent needs of human creatures. In fact, the provision of resources to meet these needs and of means adequate to beings that are ends in themselves becomes an even more pressing demand in a world where disasters and crises rapidly become widely known. But there remains the task of explaining just how such a motive develops in the agent and does its work in society, as well as what norms it should be guided by, if the motive is to specify our philanthropic activity and thinking.

The accidental or historical limitation to understanding philanthropy in terms of charity is that in English and other languages, *charity* has taken on a more specific set of meanings exemplified in those situations where persons are unable to provide various goods and services (e.g., health care, education, food, and clothing) for themselves or to pay others to provide these services. *Charity* care suggests an absence of choices and alternatives, an inferior quality of the good or service being provided, dependence on the benevolence of others, and an inability to make effective claims in justice (whether these claims are to be understood in terms of rights or of merit). A good provided on a charity basis is taken out of the marketplace and its web of economic considerations and relationships; and brief reflection serves to remind us that this has both positive and negative aspects. The good is provided to the poor and the indigent, and that is widely judged to be an appropriate response to a pressing problem. When the good is provided to the affluent or to those who have access to it in other ways, we think that the good is being misused or that some kind of deception or "scam" is going on.

There is often the implication that one accepts the good because one must, but that one is also accepting a certain stigma along with the good, at least the stigma that comes with a confession of failure.[9] A good that is necessary for one's survival or flourishing cannot be provided by one's own exertions; and this readily becomes a cause for self-reproach and shame. The indigent person is pushed to the margins of a society in which agents are commonly expected to be self-determining and self-providing. The recipient of charity is reduced to a passive role and is widely regarded as a failure.[10] Something of the bitterness of the bread eaten in exile is felt in the acceptance of charity goods.

This is, however, a reaction that does not hold in all cases. It is true that when we are thinking of a good necessary for survival in the ordinary circumstances of life, and when we consider the feelings of those who have to admit that they cannot provide these goods for themselves, then we expect reactions of shame and a sense of failure. But when we think of extraordinary needs in overwhelming circumstances (earthquakes, hurricanes) or the needs that the desperately ill or the severely disabled have, we come to see such reactions as inappropriate and we try to dissuade people from having them or being influenced in their decisions by them. Indigence is an involuntary condition in such cases; when it is a matter for reproach, it is usually because we believe that matters could have been otherwise and that the impoverished person is at least partially responsible for his or her situation.

But it may be that indigence is freely chosen, and in such cases our reactions are more divided. In the Catholic tradition, as well as in the Buddhist tradition, mendicancy and a willingness to become the recipient of charity has been seen as a sign of religious commitment, a discipline for the transformation of the proud into the humble, and a constitutive virtue of the religious life. St. Francis of Assisi is the exemplary figure here.

The voluntary poverty of anti-bourgeois radicals over the last two centuries provokes different assessments, precisely because it is rooted in a different set of interpretative connections and social allegiances. Many elements in these forms of voluntary and involuntary poverty do not fit well into the contemporary world of philanthropic activity, in which complex organizations mediate between considerable numbers of donors and even larger numbers of recipients, and in which a much wider range of concerns is being addressed than the feeding and clothing of the desperately indigent. The "beggars" of the philanthropic world are themselves well educated and well spoken; they are gainfully employed, and they may even be affluent. They may not be the Medici, but they are certainly not primitive Franciscans.

There is a third reason why the notion of charity is a less than satisfactory basis for developing our understanding of the philanthropic world, and it has to do with the development of Christian spirituality not merely in Catholicism but also in Protestantism and Orthodoxy. It is that in the Christian churches there has been a powerful tendency to interpret the requirements of charity in terms of interior attitudes and intimate interactions among individuals. The core questions in this setting are not what should we do to direct our resources and the resources of others to the common good and how should we be contributing to the transformation of society and culture, but what should *I* do in order to relieve the sufferings of Lazarus, the prototypical beggar at the gate of the affluent, and how should I be regulating and ordering my desires for various types of goods? There are many factors in the Christian tradition responsible for this emphasis on the individual and on the interior in our practice of the virtue of charity. It seems proportionate to the abilities and social opportunities available to subjects in pre-democratic societies; it seems to be exemplified in certain scriptural passages such as the parable of the Good Samaritan; and it offers a response to human need that does not focus on the troubling and often morally perplexing aspects of social choice and social action.

There is an understandable desire on the part of many sensitive and generous people to find ways to express their compassion for other individuals without raising such issues as "the problem of dirty hands" and without having to consider competing claims of distributive justice and the possibility of unintended consequences. There is a worthy and widespread desire to run a soup kitchen, free from theory and free from moral anxieties and criticisms, simply to do good things for needy people. In certain settings, especially where there is an emergency and where some needs are so comprehensive and so urgent that almost anything people want to do will bring real benefit to the victims, such a desire should prevail. More generally, it should be given a place of respect in our deliberations and in our understanding of the motives of activists and the exemplars of sacrifice. But there continue to be questions about how to understand philanthropic activity and how to conduct it which will not yield to a simplistic call to do good and to feed the hungry. These questions push us in the direction of *social* ethics; answering them requires clearness of mind as well as goodness of heart.

Subsidiarity

The development of the Catholic tradition of social thought has brought to wider attention two notions that, I believe, can be of considerable use to us as we work through these questions. They are the principle of subsidiarity and the virtue of solidarity. The principle of subsidiarity was first articulated by Pius XI in his 1931 encyclical, *Quadragesimo anno:*

> It is a fundamental principle of social philosophy, fixed and unchangeable, that one should not withdraw from individuals and commit to the community what they can accomplish by their enterprise and industry. So, too, it is an injustice and at the same time a grave evil and a disturbance of right order to transfer to the larger and higher collectivity functions which can be performed and provided for by lesser and subordinate bodies. Inasmuch as every social activity should, by its very nature, prove a help (*subsidium*) to members of the body social, it should never destroy or absorb them.[11]

This passage was later quoted approvingly by John XXIII in his social encyclical, *Mater et magistra* (1961) in a political and social context considerably different from Pius XI's original affirmation. Four observations need to be made about this text and its repetition by John XXIII. First, its original intention was to set a limit to the increasing reliance on state solutions to social and economic problems, a reliance that found its fullest expression in the political movements of the 1920s and 1930s that supported the establishment of totalitarian states and more generally relied on the expansion of government activities to deal with the consequences of economic catastrophe.

The first of these states was, of course, the Soviet Union controlled by the Communist party, to which the church was consistently and vehemently opposed. The relationship of the church to other totalitarian regimes in Italy, Germany, and smaller countries in Europe was more complex; but the church was always uncomfortable with the concentration of power in the totalitarian state, even if only because it feared for its own freedom and because it distrusted the more rabid forms of nationalism and militarism that provided a great deal of the emotional energy propelling these regimes. The principle of subsidiarity is clearly intended to affirm and to endorse the existence of a public social space that is not controlled by the state or by a political party.

Second, the affirmation of the principle of subsidiarity takes place within a systematic context in which the natural legitimacy of the state and its responsibility for ordering society toward the common good are strongly affirmed. In opposing totalitarianism, the popes do not wish to endorse individualism, which they explicitly stigmatize as "evil."[12] There is no intention to dismantle the state or to move toward libertarian or contractualist interpretations of political life. Catholic social teaching continues to affirm that the state is a natural entity, something that has its reality and its legitimacy prior to particular choices.

Third, the affirmation of the principle of subsidiarity is intended to form part of a view of society that takes as both a foundational principle and a supreme goal the value of differentiated harmony. Catholic social thought has constantly manifested a distrust of strong forms of both libertarianism and egalitarianism, which both in different ways threaten the value of differentiated harmony. Libertarianism puts harmony at risk and can, at least in limiting cases, seem to offer nothing better than anarchist isolation in its stead. Egalitarianism, when applied in isolation, threatens to reduce all persons to one level or one pattern and to eliminate diversity. Both of these outcomes are incompatible with the Catholic sense of community. But, if neither liberty nor equality can be taken as a unique value or principle in structuring a modern society, neither can subsidiarity.

Especially in Pius XI, the principle of subsidiarity forms one element in an organicist conception of society. In such a conception of society, the Marxist theory of class conflict, which sees violent revolutionary struggle as both an inevitable historical process and as a cause that gives rise to a moral obligation of support and participation, is out of place. The prevailing assumption is that the interests and demands of various groups in society are to be articulated and coordinated in such a way that conflict will be minimized and cooperation in working toward the common good will be realized.

Thus, immediately after enunciating the principle of subsidiarity, Pius XI went on to endorse a form of syndicalism in which the more adversarial forms of labor–management relationships—within which workers in most developed countries cast their demands for justice and human dignity and the improvement of their condition—were to be transcended by a cooperative form of organization according to "functional groups . . . binding men together not according to the position they occupy in the labor market, but according to the diverse functions which they exercise in society."[13] This became one of the bases for commending the syndicalism of Salazar's Portugal and Franco's Spain, in which the demands of the poor and the working classes and the political activities of liberal and socialist parties were largely suppressed in the name of social harmony.

The archetype of this way of organizing society was to be found in the syndicates of fascist Italy under Mussolini, a regime that aimed at both the suppression of internal dissent and the expansion of aggressive imperialism. This was a connection that proved over time to be highly embarrassing; it accounts for the discredit into which the notion of subsidiarity fell for a long while. It also illustrated the ability of particular political groups to use the language and the categories of Catholic social thinking to promote ends that fell significantly short of the universalist, humanitarian objectives that the popes wished to set before the societies of the developing and industrializing countries of Europe.

A more benign, acceptable, and intelligible way of fitting subsidiarity into morally promising patterns of social development is found in the encyclical of John XXIII, *Mater et magistra,* which notes "the multiplication of social relationships, that is, a daily more complex interdependence of citizens, introducing into their lives and activities many and varied forms of association, recognized for the most part in private and even in public law."[14] John XXIII makes it clear that he believes in the progress of society and that he thinks the special responsibility of public authorities is to promote the common good. His approach makes it clear that the invocation of subsidiarity is not meant to stand in the way of national and international development or to restore a condition of idealized harmony that obtained in the past.

One plausible way of interpreting the principle of subsidiarity is to see it not as articulating a universal demand in terms of which we are to judge societies and their institutions, but as expressing a complex set of preferences that should guide prudential decisions taken within a given political and cultural context. The set of preferences would run as follows: when dealing with social problems and needs, give preference to private solutions over public, to national solutions over international, to regional and local solutions over national. This set of preferences is to be applied within society's orientation to the common good and its commitment to human rights, which both serve as standards for assessing the range of solutions being offered.

This implies that the preferences in the set are not absolute, but are *ceteris paribus,* other things being equal; they must yield when serious harm to the common good or to the rights of persons would result. Both the preferred private, national, and local solutions and the less preferred public, international, and national solutions are to be scrutinized for the empirical results that they produce. We must, however, acknowledge that this leaves a considerable indeterminacy in the application of the principle of subsidiarity because our knowledge of future outcomes is sketchy and is likely to be molded and even distorted by our biases and hopes. Also, because the principle is being applied within a cultural context, the history and the different circumstances of various cultures and the constitutional arrangements that they have chosen to adopt will lead to important differences in the way the principle is applied in different societies.

The much disputed but clearly powerful attachment of many Americans to "states' rights," the anxiety of many Québécois about maintaining a distinctive religious and linguistic community in a continent of Anglophones, the need felt in the nineteenth and early twentieth centuries by most European states to promote centralization for the sake of national security, the "tyranny of distance" that has so profoundly shaped Australian history, the tensions inherent in the multilingual and multiethnic fabric of India, the persistence of tribal conflicts in much of Africa, and the opportunities created by the development of vast integrated systems of transportation and communication have all meant that the principle of subsidiarity needs to be applied with considerable sensitivity to local conditions and preferences.

In all these contexts, the principle of subsidiarity stands in opposition to totalitarianism and to the more drastic and brutal forms of centralized control. It creates a presumption in favor of smaller, more locally sensitive responses to problems; and it favors a polycentric distribution of power and resources. It leaves the boundaries between public and private initiatives, between local and national programs, between national and international institutions, open to be settled by a mixture of democratic deliberation, market forces, individual decisions, and historical accidents.

At this point, we can begin to see how the principle of subsidiarity bears on our understanding and practice of philanthropy. It forms part of an understanding of society that is wary about turning all significant social problems and needs over to the state, even though the state will always have more resources and more opportunities to resolve these problems in an apparently definitive fashion than will any private institution or group. In this way of understanding society, local particularism is not dismissed as a failure to achieve consistency and rationality; private initiative is not denounced as a self-interested effort to diminish public capacity; national projects and preferences are not seen as concessions to parochial and partisan ways of dealing with social reality. The commanding center is not the sole source of life, understanding, and value. Precisely because individual persons living within a social milieu are capable of acts of creative imagination and unregulated generosity, we can see that rigid and comprehensive centralization, whether it be in the bureaucratic and *étatiste* style or in the revolutionary and messianic mode, is bound to be destructive of social creativity and of a wide range of goods that are best achieved locally and spontaneously.

Thus, from the perspective of Catholic social thought, private philanthropy should be seen as a vitally important form of activity in a nontotalitarian society. It contributes to fulfilling two key functions of the state: the achievement of the common good and the protection of human rights. But it does so in a way that diffuses rather than concentrates power. It complements the efforts of the state because of its greater flexibility and range. It goes where the state cannot or will not go. It can reach out to those persons and groups whom public programs fail to help adequately or whom current fashions neglect. It can provide resources and encouragement for those projects in the arts and sciences that seem overly specialized or that have become too controversial for public funding. It can direct attention to those projects that seem small on the national scale but that are profoundly important to local communities. It can affirm the challenged, sustain the neglected, and challenge the parochial and self-satisfied.

A specific responsibility that falls on private philanthropy, in a constitutional democracy that treats the separation of church and state as a fundamental feature of its constitutional structure, is to support those activities that link the broad range of everyday human concerns to the ultimate issues of meaning and value that we regard as religious. These are activities that we have wisely decided to take out of the range of those things that are to be subject to political regulation or open to financial support from the government. In a society with our sort of secular constitutional arrangements, the task of supporting religion and its ministers and their activities is an especially important form of philanthropic activity open to ordinary citizens.

Philanthropy conceived as the promotion of the innovative and controversial has affinities with the promotion of a diversity of ways of life, of experiments in living of the type envisioned in Chapter 3 of John Stuart Mill's *On Liberty* and in the discussion of *demoktesis* in Robert Nozick's *Anarchy, State, and Utopia,* even though these would seem unlikely allies for a Catholic vision of society.[15] But in the present situation of contemporary culture where religion is not established and where it faces numerous challenges, Catholicism and its institutions probably have more to fear from an imposed secular uniformity than from the toleration of heretical religious opinions.

Solidarity

Where subsidiarity looks primarily to diversifying and balancing the ways in which society organizes its efforts toward the common good, solidarity looks especially to the inclusion of the marginalized and the neglected within the range of persons who benefit from the attainment of the common good. It faces the task of correcting the outcomes that the broadest and most comprehensive institutions of society (the state, the market, the corporation) bring about in their ordinary functioning when these outcomes leave people at risk of losing their lives and their human rights. Solidarity is one of the main themes in the encyclical, *Sollicitudo rei socialis,* which John Paul II issued in 1989; his adoption of the term was clearly influenced by the celebrated Polish trade union, which did so much to weaken the hold of the communist regime in Poland and which provided an example of a broad and inclusive political movement. He insists that solidarity "is not a feeling of vague compassion or shallow distress at the misfortunes of so many people," but that "it is a firm and persevering determination to commit oneself to the *common good:* that is to say to the good of all and of each individual, because we are *all* really responsible *for all.*"[16] Here we should note that the pope is clearly modeling his language about solidarity on the definition that Thomas Aquinas offers for the virtue of justice in the *Summa Theologiae,* where he says of justice understood as a virtue in the human subject that it is the "lasting and constant will of rendering to each one his right."[17]

Whereas Aquinas sees justice as a disposition in the will of the subject rectifying his or her dealings with other individuals, John Paul II proposes the common good as the direct object of the moral commitment found in solidarity; the commitment is obligatory and not optional. In setting forth his view of solidarity, John Paul II wants to combine the rigor of demands in justice with the extensive range of responses in charity. Solidarity is an ethical conception that is parallel to and responsive to the enormous increase of interdependence in the international order, especially in the international economy. It is clear from the ease with which he moves from talk about interdependence (which relies on a base of factual information and empirical analyses) to normative discourse and practical exhortations, that he regards the increasingly dense world of social and economic interaction not as a universe that develops without moral content but as one that carries a great deal of normative material. For him, the gap between *ought* and *is*, between fact and value in this area of human life, is very small. Thus he writes:

> It is above all a question of *interdependence*, sensed as a *system determining* relationships in the contemporary world, in its economic, cultural, political, and religious elements, and accepted as a *moral category*. When interdependence becomes recognized in this way, the correlative response as a moral and social attitude, as a "virtue," is *solidarity*.[18]

The Pope's treatment of solidarity fits with two other prominent notions in the later phase of his social teaching, namely, the notions of structural sin and of the (preferential) option for the poor. These are notions that have their home in liberation theology, a movement that John Paul II regarded with coolness and caution because of its reliance on Marxist methods of social analysis and criticism and because of its readiness to support revolution in the face of entrenched injustice in some of the most heavily Catholic areas in the world. But the heart of the matter lies in his affirmation that sin is not to be understood purely in individual terms; thus, he speaks of "influences and obstacles which go far beyond the actions and the brief lifespan of an individual,"[19] and of "a *moral evil*, the fruit of *many sins* which lead to 'structures of sin.'"[20]

John Paul, writing at the very end of the Cold War, finds two attitudes that are most likely to lead to negative consequences for humanity; these are "on the one hand, the *all-consuming desire for profit*, and on the other, *the thirst for power*, with the intention of imposing one's will upon others."[21] Correcting these attitudes requires a moral conversion in which solidarity plays a key role. I take it that what the pope has in mind is something like the following process: (1) one has rights and benefits that arise from existing economic and social structures (e.g., interest from debts of Third World countries); (2) one sees that the people who have the corresponding obligations are undergoing great suffering and are in need of help; (3) one affirms one's identity with these people and one's commitment to their good (an implication of the virtue of solidarity); (4)

one sees that the structures are productive of evil and are in some sense sinful (even though they may enjoy a presumption of legitimacy and justice); (5) one realizes that one is called on to support a change in social attitudes on this matter; and (6) one does something (votes, contributes, persuades others, approves forgiveness of debt, supports more favorable terms for repayment or for earning money by trade).

The motivating factor in this process is the virtue of solidarity, which is more demanding than the virtue of justice and which pushes Christians and others to consider ways of meeting the needs and demands of others that are broader and more flexible than the application of previously established principles of justice. In the pope's view, this process is not an option that a few good-hearted people might take up as an expression of their generosity; it is a moral requirement (and in this respect it is akin to the demands of justice). This conversion process, which is both parallel to and subversive of the common understanding of justice, is especially important in our dealings with the poor and the disadvantaged, who are the people most likely to feel the effects of structural sin.

We can readily see the relevance of John Paul II's line of thought for such issues as globalization, distributive justice, and the economic aspects of human rights, even if we disagree with the way he shapes the argument. The relevance to philanthropy seems less clear. But John Paul II is calling our attention to situations where serious harm is occurring even though *prima facie* the principles of justice are still being observed, to situations where personal and group biases stand in the way of our heeding the demands for justice that people from other cultures and alien social milieu are making on us, and to situations where urgent needs threaten to overwhelm locally available resources. Contemporary communications media regularly bring to our awareness an increasing number of these situations. We must realize that the challenges to our compassion and our generosity arise on such a scale and at such distances that the paradigms of charitable action and personalized philanthropy provided by the parable of the Good Samaritan (and reinforced by generations of mutual aid within local communities) has to be replaced or revised in important ways.

The notion of solidarity points us to a space in our moral universe where action and advocacy in aid of the suffering and the marginalized need to cross the boundaries of nation, ethnicity, religion, class, and gender; where the flexibility and freedom characteristic of philanthropy can be combined with the scale of organization and the commitment to universal principles that are at the heart of altruistic efforts *in the political realm* to achieve justice for others. The response to the needs of others, which figures so centrally in our concept of charity, can blend with the respect for the freedom and dignity of others that is fundamental to the Kantian and Rawlsian conceptions of justice.[22]

Both subsidiarity and solidarity are ideas that can provide important connections between the general commandment of universal love and the normative structure of philanthropic activity. Without such connections, universal love or charity runs the risk of becoming a generalized and indiscriminate benevolence that requires so much that it requires virtually nothing because it is used to ground obligations that are beyond our capacity to fulfill. Or it may become nothing more than a bland exhortation to be "nice" to the people we encounter. Philanthropic activity, when severed from broader moral and religious notions, runs the risk of becoming an ad hoc set of responses to needs, demands, and requests.

Both solidarity and subsidiarity are notions rooted in the complex social learning process by which Western and now world society have become knit together in awesomely vast but imperfect networks of communication and cooperation. They are not distinctively or exclusively religious notions, since they are accessible to all who have come to understand the Scylla and Charybdis of modern societies: the centralization of power and choice in totalitarianism or the abandonment of millions of people who lack all power in both the market and the polity. People in those situations have no secure access to the resources they need in order to survive and to express their human dignity. More positively, the notions of subsidiarity and solidarity alert us to the possibilities for good that are too often neglected in the ordinary workings of our primary economic and political institutions. These possibilities include the potential for innovation and discovery that are often crowded out by the big battalions and the potential for the rescue of the neglected and defenseless from the evils that oppress them. Both sets of possibilities are, I would argue, the special responsibility of philanthropy.

Notes

1. Historical illustrations of the ways in which religious traditions have shaped philanthropic institutions can be found in David Hammack's essay in this volume; Frankena's interest and mine have been more in the connections between religious traditions and belief systems on the one hand and ethical concepts and practices on the other. The section of Patricia Werhane's essay that deals with Bishop Joseph Butler, Adam Smith, and Immanuel Kant shows the way in which the affirmation of benevolence by an Anglican bishop engaged in a theological and philosophical critique of Hobbes prepares the way for a moral understanding of capitalist institutions in Adam Smith and for a universalist rational ethic in Kant, an ethic that is itself rich in theologically significant concepts.

2. A standard collection of these writings is *Catholic Social Thought: The Documentary Heritage*, ed. David J. O'Brien and Thomas A. Shannon (Maryknoll, N.Y.: Orbis Books, 1992). The index has no entry for "philanthropy." This collection, like most studies of the subject, begins with the encyclical *Rerum novarum* (1891) of Leo XIII. While everyone agrees that there is within Catholicism a long tradition of thinking about both theoretical and practical aspects of social and political life, a tradition in which the most influential figures are St. Augustine and St. Thomas Aquinas, there is also a general recognition that Leo's encyclical is a decisively important development in that tradition. *Rerum*

novarum is part of an effort to reposition the church in a society that was to an increasing extent moving out from under the authoritative shaping force of Christianity. The French Revolution, the Industrial Revolution, and the rise of Marxism had all raised challenges to the church's understanding of its social role and had manifested the alienation of large sections of European society from Catholicism and from the established churches in general. There were also intensifying conflicts within the increasingly secularized political and economic orders, conflicts that produced internal divisions within the Catholic community and that raised doubts about the sustainability of its commitment to the values and the sense of order that had marked feudal society and the *ancien regime*.

3. An overview of relevant passages in the early Christian literature is provided by William J. Walsh, S.J. and John Langan, S.J., "Patristic Social Consciousness," in *The Faith That Does Justice*, ed. John Haughey, S.J. (New York: Paulist, 1977), pp. 113-51.

4. See, for example, Matthew 5:47-6:4 (from the Sermon on the Mount); Luke 10:29-37.

5. Matthew 6:24-34; Luke 12:13-34.

6. "Asceticism" is used here in a sense given to it by Mill, who was arguing against Carlyle's endorsement of "resignation" or *Entsagen*. Mill wants to affirm the instrumental value of asceticism and to acknowledge the significant social benefits that can arise from individual acts of sacrifice. But utilitarianism in his account of it "only refuses to admit that the sacrifice is itself a good." Cf. *Utilitarianism*, in Collected Works, vol. X: *Essays on Ethics, Religion and Society*, ed. J. M. Robson (Toronto: University of Toronto Press, 1969).

7. Luke 16:19-31; Amos 4:1-13.

8. Compare Luke 10:25-28 and Deuteronomy 6:4-5.

9. The emphasis on self-respect in the political and social thought of Booker T. Washington, which is discussed in the essay by Amy Kass, is an effort to counteract some of the negative implications of the standard nineteenth-century paradigm of Christian charity as well as the negative impact of forms of racism which proclaimed that the black person had no soul or self worth respecting.

10. Concern over the reduction of recipients of charity to merely passive involvement in the social transactions of philanthropy is a major theme in David Craig's essay. His reliance on the capabilities approach of Martha Nussbaum and Amartya Sen, a form of Aristotelianism, is something that easily fits with the conception of the agent finding fulfillment in distinctively human activity, a concept that is fundamental in the practical philosophy of Aquinas and is taken into the tradition of Catholic social thought. In more recent Catholic social thought, the notion of participation, which has roots in Neo-Platonic metaphysics, has been given a notably more social and active interpretation. Such an activist interpretation is necessary if the principle of subsidiarity is to be effective in large, differentiated society. It is also present in the role of citizenship as this is understood both by Paul Schervish and William Sullivan.

11. Pius XI, *Quadragesimo anno*, 79. It is customary to refer to these documents by the first words of the Latin text, which is official, if not always original, and to cite them by paragraph numbers rather than page numbers of a particular edition. Translations in this paper are those found in O'Brien and Shannon, *Catholic Social Thought*.

12. *Quadragesimo anno,* 78.

13. Ibid., p. 83.

14. *Mater et magistra* (1961), 59.

15. By *demoktesis,* literally, the fashioning of a people, Nozick refers to those utopian and normatively enriched forms of community that philosophers from Plato forward and religious visionaries and legislators have seen as embodying the comprehensive fulfillment of humanity. By depriving these visions of their universal claims and by ensuring for their proponents a space of liberty in which they can realize their ideals on a voluntary basis, Nozick wishes to reconcile the limited state, which he believes is all that can be justified and permitted on the basis of a fundamentally individualistic theory of human rights, with the wider aspirations for moral community which have had such wide appeal. A Catholic parallel to this can be found in the development of religious orders and communities, which both make higher demands on their members and offer them broader opportunities than could be universally realized in the church taken as a whole. One should, however, bear in mind that Catholic social thought would not accept the individualistic conception of human rights that Nozick takes as fundamental to his project in political philosophy and would not accept his conclusions about the very limited powers of the "night watchman state."

16. John Paul II, *Sollicitudo rei socialis,* 38. The Latin title, which does not come easily to Anglophones, is commonly translated as "On Social Concern." His conception of solidarity is in many ways akin to the conception of philanthropy as "common work" in Paul Pribbenow's essay on Jane Addams and fits well with Pribbenow's insistence on the moral requirement of accountability.

17. St. Thomas Aquinas, *Summa Theologiae* II–II, 58, 1, Thomas Gilby, O.P., translator (Cambridge: Blackfriars, 1975).

18. John Paul II, *Sollicitudo rei socialis,* 38.

19. Ibid., p. 36.

20. Ibid., p. 37.

21. Ibid.

22. In its understanding and application of the notion of solidarity, Catholic social teaching is strongly universalist and is not interested in the particularist bonds that are important themes in the essays by Philip Turner and Elliot Dorff. My sense is that Catholic and Jewish practices are not all that divergent, especially in a field such as health care. The particularist concerns that Turner sees arising especially from the connections between First and Third World churches are certainly a major theme in Vatican diplomacy.

Part Five: Retrospect and Prospect

9   Donors, Intermediaries, and Beneficiaries: The Changing Moral Dynamics of American Nonprofit Organizations

David C. Hammack

In thinking about the ethics of charity and philanthropy, about "moral issues in doing good," we should take carefully into account the context in which participants act. In many traditions of moral reasoning, context is taken for granted and discussions focus on what duties, care, and concern one individual owes to another. The focus is properly on the donor and on the recipient. But the ethical obligations of donors cannot be limited to the relation between giver and ultimate beneficiary, because these actors almost always relate to one another through larger human communities and institutions.

In the United States, a nonprofit, nongovernmental organization usually serves as the intermediary between donor and beneficiary when gifts flow outside the circles of family and friends. Nonprofit organizations provide charitable services, from religious activity to counseling and job training; from education, health care, and research to art exhibitions and musical performances. Nonprofits identify those who need assistance; they evaluate eligibility and merit. They assure donors, the public, and the courts that donations are used for appropriate and specified purposes. State laws allow nonprofits to hold property, to keep it exempt from state and local taxation, and sometimes, under "charitable immunity," to protect assets, donors, and volunteers from lawsuits. Federal law allows donors to deduct from taxable income some or all of their gifts to nonprofits, but not gifts to individuals.[1]

From the American Revolution into the 1960s, each nonprofit organization formed its own largely self-contained moral world. Over time, the moral worlds of American nonprofits became more and more numerous, more and more diverse, and in most cases more inclusive. In 1800, almost none was Catholic or Jewish, almost all excluded African Americans and women. All that changed, sometimes slowly, over the next 150 years. Within each organization, donors to particular causes engage other donors, large and small, as well as volunteers and workers for those causes—and also engage larger traditions of moral reasoning associated with particular beliefs and ways of thinking—Puritan, Calvinist, Evangelical, Quaker, Pietist, Anglican, humanist, aesthetic, Catholic, Jewish, any of several Native American, African, and African American traditions; in recent years increasingly Muslim, Buddhist, Hindu.[2] The diverse moral worlds of America's nonprofit organizations shaped and encouraged giving and volunteering. As *separate, parallel* sponsors of schools, clinics, and other efforts to do good in many ways, nonprofits also allowed followers of very diverse religious and political traditions to live as neighbors in something approaching harmony.

The separate, largely self-contained moral worlds of particular nonprofit organizations had many virtues, virtues that are explored and illustrated in several essays in this volume.[3] Separate, self-contained nonprofit organizations also faced some important limitations. They encouraged local and national unity only indirectly, and sometimes not at all. They failed to end racism, and although the opportunities for benevolence and civic participation they afforded women were very important, such opportunities were constrained and limited. Historically, U.S. nonprofits served well those who had full standing as citizens and access to resources, but provided little for minorities or the very poor, and never cared adequately for the children of the poor. Protected by states rights, controlled by heavy state regulation, blinkered by persisting racism and sexism, and limited in their ability to mobilize resources, they failed to provide universal access to education, to health care, to family assistance, to appreciation and accomplishment in the arts. From the late nineteenth century on, critics objected that separate, limited, self-sufficient organizations could never provide a national quality of life appropriate to a great nation.[4]

By the middle of the twentieth century, most Americans had come to the conclusion that it was necessary and possible to open their society more fully to all. With the New Deal, the federal government assumed substantial responsibility for the economy in general and began to provide significant resources for the disabled and elderly poor. The Civil Rights movement culminated, during the 1960s, in legislation and court decisions that protected the rights of individuals regardless of race, gender, national origin, religion, or sexual orientation. Women no longer allowed their lives to be circumscribed by duties associated with the kitchen, the nursery, the sick room, the church, and charity. A rush of legislation—creating Medicare, Medicaid, student grants and loans, and federal job training programs, expanding the National Institutes of Health and the National Science Foundation—opened the way to large and increasing federal appropriations to pay for the services that nonprofits provide. The extraordinary and rising prosperity of the American population after World War II enabled many more people to pay for education and other nonprofit services, transforming the environment for nonprofit organizations. Federal funds came with strings, of course, and purchasers of services insisted on receiving services they preferred. Federal policies and market forces would, henceforth, force American nonprofits—and their donors—to acknowledge the great moral community of the nation as a whole, and to pay particular attention to those who controlled the funds, votes, and court decisions. Organizations and donors alike would be forced to rethink their relationship to the particular traditions of moral reasoning that had long defined the nonprofit approach to giving and volunteering.

The Self-Contained Moral Worlds of Nineteenth-Century American Charities

The frequently restated formulation of Moses Maimonides, the twelfth-century Jewish philosopher, gives us a place to begin in thinking about the relation between donor, beneficiary, and institution. According to Maimonides, there are "eight degrees of *tzedakah* [charity, justice]":[5]

(1) The donor gives in such a way as to enable someone unknown to him to become self-sufficient; the beneficiary does not learn the name of the donor and loses no self-respect.
(2) The donor gives in such a way that neither the donor nor the beneficiary knows the other.
(3) The donor gives in such a way that he knows the beneficiary, but the beneficiary does not know the donor.
(4) The donor gives in such a way that he does not know the beneficiary, although the beneficiary knows the donor.
(5) The donor gives adequately and cheerfully, before being asked.
(6) The donor gives adequately, but only after being asked.
(7) The donor gives something, but less than fitting in relation to his circumstances.
(8) The donor gives less than needed or fitting, in ill humor.

Writing in the Muslim world of North Africa during the twelfth century, Maimonides emphasized the relation between the donor and the beneficiary. The Jewish communities he knew sometimes enjoyed toleration, but were not integrated into the Muslim societies and states that surrounded them. These communities were by no means always small and stable. Maimonides himself was forced to leave a Spanish community that had long been hospitable to Jews; his own repeated experiences as a refugee and newcomer make it clear that the Jewish communities of his time by no means consisted only of small populations in which everyone knew everyone else.

Maimonides's wonderful list of degrees of virtuous giving emphasizes the relation between donor and beneficiary, but it also takes the larger context into account. Classic examples of giving at his highest degree include the revolving loan fund, through which those who demonstrate ability can borrow to launch or expand a business, and the scholarship fund, which allows beneficiaries to understand that they have "earned" and "merited" assistance with school tuition. Such funds work only if they are managed by responsible groups that may include the donor but that derive a distinct identity and legitimacy from sponsorship by continuing institutions and from participation by people whose credentials are viewed as appropriate. Clearly Maimonides understood the operation of such funds by temples, schools, and mutual benefit societies in his own society. He took for granted the institutions that intervene between donor and beneficiary.

From the very beginning of the Republic, American nonprofits have worked, in a spirit very much like that of Maimonides, to encourage donors to help others in ways compatible with individual dignity and Republican citizenship.[6] Federal and state laws have always encouraged giving through autonomous, self-sustaining organizations that promote individual self-sufficiency while preserving self-respect; they continue to do so. But American nonprofits, which changed very slowly for 150 years after 1789, were transformed in the 1960s. Students of philanthropy are just now coming to grips with this transformation.

We can look first at the realities of nonprofit life from the Constitution to the 1960s. Nonprofit organizations were essential to religion and education from the 1790s on, and by 1900 they had come to play many key roles in U.S. society. In the mid-1890s, Albert Shaw and other very well-informed contemporary observers pointed out that private, nongovernmental organizations provided most of the secondary education in New York City (Manhattan did not have its first free public high school until after 1900) and almost all of the higher education and library facilities. Nonprofits provided much of the hospital care; many of the social services (especially care of orphans and the aged); and nearly all of the museums and orchestras in Boston, New York, Philadelphia, Chicago, and St. Louis.[7] Contemporary observers often noted that only the great cities of the Northeast and the Midwest, with their wealthy donors and great private institutions, provided high-quality adult education, hospitals, or cultural facilities. Research universities, medical centers, and arts organizations continued to grow on the basis of these institutions well into the twentieth century.

Throughout this long period, American nonprofits obtained the bulk of their resources from private donors and volunteers. American nonprofits always did receive some income from government, and they enjoyed important government subsidies, direct and indirect: exemption from property taxes and sometimes from water and sewer fees; "charitable immunity" from civil lawsuits; the privileges of self-government, continuous existence, and property rights that most American states granted to charitable corporations by the mid-nineteenth century. Nearly all American nonprofits, including Bible and tract societies and many orphanages,[8] also received significant funding from fees, charges, and other forms of earned income.

But donations of time and money accounted for the largest share of the income of most nonprofit organizations, making them truly *eleemosynary*—that is to say, based on the giving of alms, dominated by donors seeking to act morally. This becomes clear when we reconstruct the history of nonprofit resources. Nonprofit employment—which we can roughly estimate from census counts of clergy, women religious, charity workers, teachers, nurses, librarians, and from separate measures of the ratio of public to private school enrollments, hospital beds, etc.—amounted to a negligible share of all employment in 1800, to about

1 percent in 1900, 2 percent in 1930, and 3 percent in 1960.[9] We do not have good comprehensive estimates of nonprofit income for this long period, but most nonprofit expenditures have always gone to employees, who have generally received incomes that are near the average of all incomes. Until the 1950s and 1960s, government funding for nonprofit organizations (apart from support for veterans) came almost exclusively from the states and, where states permitted it, from local governments. State and local funding varied greatly from place to place, was always limited, and was usually tied to the provision of specific services to specific individuals through orphanages and secondary schools.

During these years when the nonprofit share of employment rose slowly to 1 percent, 2 percent, and then 3 percent, our best estimates suggest that the share of private giving of total national income hovered in the range of 1–1.75 percent.[10] Until the 1960s, private donations must have provided half or more of the incomes of most nonprofits. In Cuyahoga County (Cleveland), Ohio, for example, my rough estimate is that in 1930 the county's nonprofit hospitals obtained about 38 percent of their income from current private gifts and from endowment income; its private colleges obtained about 42 percent in that way; its private social services, as much as 70 percent. The proportions remained large thirty years later: 40 percent for private colleges and universities, and 58 percent for social service agencies, though the share had fallen sharply for hospitals.[11]

Into the mid-twentieth century, much of the work of nonprofit organizations was done not by paid employees, but by volunteers—by Sunday School teachers, by Catholic nuns and brothers, by missionaries at "home" as well as in "foreign lands," by "friendly visitors," by doctors providing "charity care," by "ladies bountiful" who not rarely brought vision and expertise to the boards of homes for the outcast, of schools and colleges and hospitals, of museums.[12] Paid employees, then and now, often accepted salaries lower than the incomes they might have earned in the general economy: in effect, workers volunteered part of their time, giving a substantial part of that essential resource through the nonprofit organizations for which they worked.

Under these circumstances, nonprofit organizations relied very heavily on donors and volunteers. Whereas tax-supported established churches had dominated the field in the colonial period, self-sustaining churches and religious charities invented remarkable fundraising schemes in the face of the disestablishment movement that came with the American revolution. *The Autobiography of Benjamin Franklin,* which was very widely read throughout the nineteenth century, contains a basic manual of fundraising techniques, and nineteenth-century religious leaders did much to advance the cause. When Connecticut eliminated government funding for Congregationalist churches in 1818, Lyman Beecher declared this "the best thing" because "it cut the churches loose from dependence on state support. It threw them wholly on their own resources and on God."[13] The first half of the nineteenth century saw remarkable innovations in fund raising and the creation of an elaborate vocabulary for fundraising appeals. Twentieth-century historians have documented these innovations in books whose titles echo the language of nineteenth-century religion: "Protestant crusade,"[14] "city mission movement,"[15] an "errand of mercy," the "evangelical united front,"[16] "moral stewardship,"[17] "religious benevolence," "their brothers' keepers,"[18] "the work of benevolence,"[19] a "warm friend for the spirit,"[20] "the Bible business."[21] The first half of the twentieth century saw the addition of a wide range of nonsectarian efforts of the same kind: the Community Chest, the Community Foundation, the March of Dimes, the alumni fund.[22]

Reliance on many donors, on volunteers, and on students and other clients willing to pay for services gave American nonprofits very much the appearance of "associations" that so impressed Alexis de Tocqueville.[23] Throughout this long period, institutional realities forced American donors to take account of the realities of nonprofit organizations. Each donor had to keep in mind the fact that he or she was only one of many donors: if an organization pursued an idea not accepted by its entire group of donors, it could lose resources and, perhaps, be compelled to change focus, or even be forced to close. Each donor had to remember the importance of earned income: if ideas and practices concerning pricing, cross-subsidies, programs, or values threatened to alienate important groups of students and other service purchasers, the organization could lose revenue and be forced to change. Each donor had to recognize that essential volunteers and underpaid workers might well leave if they became offended. Even the wealthiest donors—George Foster Peabody, Andrew Carnegie, John D. Rockefeller, Julius Rosenwald, Margaret Olivia Sage—had to work within limits imposed not only by the law and by public opinion, but also by other donors, volunteers, staffs, as well as by the clients of their day.[24]

A few examples will indicate some of the ways in which nineteenth-century American charities engaged donors, volunteers, and other close supporters in self-contained discussions of moral reasoning with one another and within larger communities, about doing good.

Many charities took a religious approach to moral reasoning for granted. After the Rev. Muhlenberg opened the third annual meeting of the nonsectarian Orphan Society of Philadelphia with prayer on January 6, 1818, the (entirely female) board of managers reported the opening of its new asylum, praising it for its "excellent accommodation for those who reside in it," but also as "a convenient chapel or meeting-house for public worship." The asylum was providing its fifty children "elementary education," and, "convinced that nothing is more important to their temporal interests, than a conformity to the circumstances in which they may be placed," had worked "to inculcate and exact habits of industry." It had kept "both boys and girls steadily employed: the girls in sewing and knitting, the boys in knitting." The board of managers ended with thanks to "Almighty God . . . for without his smiles, they are fully aware that their own labours must have proven abortive." They also thanked "a generous and extended list of patrons." Sarah Henry (a Protestant) and Rebecca Gratz (a Jew), serving as the finance committee, reported the receipt of subscriptions, donations, and offerings amounting nearly to $4,000; income from the sale of items made by the orphans, $36.32; tax funds from the guardians of the poor, $352.22.[25]

To the dismay of many evangelical Protestants, some charity leaders (especially in Boston, but also in New York, Philadelphia, and elsewhere) took a rational, humanistic approach that avoided direct reference to religion. Samuel Gridley Howe opened the *11th Annual Report* of the Perkins Institution and Massachusetts Asylum for the Blind (1843) with a critique of Diderot based on sympathetic observation and reasoning that referred to "nature" rather than God. The French *encyclopedist* had speculated that because "the blind can be affected only by the sound of groans, I suspect them generally of hard-heartedness." Close observation demonstrated the contrary to Howe, who reported that "Orin Moore, an amiable and interesting boy of nine years of age, who was much beloved by his teachers and all his comrades," had died during the previous year. Moore's blind classmates demonstrated through their grief that "the blind do not have any less acuteness and strength of the social affections than others, but on the contrary, these affections seem to be even more developed . . . nature, baulked of exhibiting her power in one direction, puts it forth with increased energy in another. Or rather, to speak more correctly, . . . the law of exercise applies to the social as well as to the intellectual faculties." Howe added, "the instinctive dread of death which nature plants in us for self-preservation, acts quite as strongly, perhaps indeed even more strongly among the blind: so that they need not the sight of the somber trappings 'and the suits of woe' with which others are wont to associate death . . . in order to make them shrink from dissolution."[26]

Very generous individuals launched the Perkins Institution (Col. Thomas Perkins gave his mansion and others added the very substantial initial sum of $64,000); but in 1843 the Institution obtained nearly all of its $12,981 income from the states of Massachusetts ($9,265) as well as Maine, Vermont, New Hampshire, Connecticut, and South Carolina; $266 from pay pupils; $110 from investments; and $432 from private donors. Donors, like the corporation's board and like Howe himself, had to take into account above all the preferences and moral views of legislators in Massachusetts and other states. They had also to consider, to a far smaller degree, paying pupils and private donors. Clearly, Howe believed that broadly phrased humanistic reasoning would appeal to the legislators.[27]

Evangelical Protestants who objected to the nonsectarian nature of some of these charities moved, from the 1820s onward, to advance institutions that were more explicitly Protestant. By 1843, Presbyterian leader Robert Baird could assert that evangelicals had successfully organized for a wide variety of purposes. Through independent charities, he concluded

funds are raised for the erection of church edifices, for the support of pastors, and for providing destitute places with the preaching of the gospel—this last involving the whole subject of our home missionary efforts. [Also for] education, from . . .

primary schools up to the theological seminaries and faculties. . . . [And for efforts to make] the press . . . subservient to the cause of the gospel and the extension of the kingdom of God . . . [and to] grapple with existing evils in society, such as intemperance, Sabbath breaking, slavery, and war, by means of diverse associations formed for their repression or removal . . . [as well as for the support of] beneficent and humane institutions.[28]

These various purposes often combined in a single evangelical organization. As historian Carol Smith-Rosenberg has shown, for example, the New York City Tract Society and its offspring, the Association for Improving the Condition of the Poor, made increasing use of paid agents to address the religious and moral needs of the city's poor. "There are localities in our city which are very repulsive, and which could not be reached" by volunteer visitors, the Tract Society's annual report for 1852 stated. These districts were "crowded with men and women sunk deeply in immorality, yet possessing immortal spirits and hastening to final judgment. For their especial benefit three assistant missionaries have been employed" to preach the gospel and at the same time to bring material relief and opportunity for regular employment.[29] The Reverend Theodore Cuyler added that "there is a tendency and a temptation to provide the gospel for the rich in goodly sanctuaries, forgetting that Christ came to save the lowly. It is to counteract this tendency . . . that this Society goes out on its mission of philanthropy."[30]

Catholic institutions, spurred by massive immigration from Ireland, Germany, and then southern and eastern Europe, operated in a world of similar values but distinctive moral conversations. In the absence of government support, Catholic leaders, like their Protestant counterparts, depended upon donations and fee-paying students, patients, and families. Among themselves, Catholics did debate ways to advance the unchanging message of the universal church. Some laymen argued that because associations had replaced aristocrats in republican America, lay boards should control church property and even nominate priests—as aristocrats sometimes did in Europe. Official Catholic policy came to require that donors subordinate themselves, in a formal sense, to the moral guidance of priests and bishops. In a pastoral letter of 1819, Archbishop Ambrose Marechal of Baltimore rejected lay trusteeship as Catholic doctrine, stating that "when a Bishop appoints a Priest Pastor of a congregation . . . the faithful who are committed to his charge, become immediately and in reality his flock; and he is invested with spiritual powers in their regard, which all the world can neither give nor take away. It becomes his duty to govern, and sanctify by his instructions and example, the faithful."[31]

In this spirit, the first American St. Vincent de Paul Society began in 1845, not by reasoning about the alleviation of poverty or by thanking individual donors, but by appointing its president "to wait upon the right Reverend Bishop to apprize him of the organization and purposes of the Society." At its second meeting, the president read the bishop's letter "fully approving the organization and objects of it, being designed to relieve and alleviate the suffering and wants of those in a poor and destitute condition."[32] To build schools and other institutions in the United States, bishops sought funds from French, Bavarian, and Austrian foundations: they also "literally begged from house to house . . . not only among the Catholics . . . in the diocese, but also outside of it."[33] Formal Catholic accounts typically credited to the bishop funds raised in this way, but it is clear that donors gave more willingly for some purposes than for others.[34]

Catholic institutions also sought resources from non-Catholics. In 1842, the agent of Vienna's Leopoldinen-Stiftung (a Catholic foundation supported by Austria's imperial family) reported that "the bishops and the faithful are obliged to assume the entire burden of financing" Catholic colleges in the United States. But he added that "Protestant students are accepted by Catholic colleges because . . . the income derived from Protestant students makes it possible for the college to provide better facilities . . . more teachers and better equipment." To attract Protestants, Catholic schools emphasized their "excellence" and "order," and excused non-Catholics from Catholic religious exercises.[35] Catholics built their nonprofit organizations through means very similar to those of Protestants, and in the service of most of the same values, but within a distinctive environment that emphasized dutiful deference to pastoral authority.

Jewish organizations also date from early in the history of the American republic. New York City's Sephardic Temple Shearith Israel opened a separate school by 1810. By the middle of the nineteenth century, Jewish communities were organizing general fundraising campaigns, not only on the east coast, but as early as 1854 even in Los Angeles.

Protestant religious denominations also on occasion developed general approaches to charitable activity. The Presbyterians, for example, organized national "boards" to fund and supervise outreach and educational activities across the United States and abroad. As the country plunged toward civil war in 1860, southern Presbyterians objected to the anti-slavery discussions then going on within many Presbyterian charitable organizations. At their urging, the denomination's governing general assembly thoroughly discussed the proposal that, because boards and independent charities were not "expressly enjoined or implied by necessary inference" in the New Testament, the denomination should eliminate them and confine charitable activity exclusively to its individual congregations. The proposal failed, and Presbyterian boards continued to supervise many charities, missions, and schools.[36]

Lacking large endowments and wealthy donors, Protestant schools often catered directly to the market for students. Francis Wayland, who served as president of Brown University for nearly thirty years, emphasized a sort of market morality to a British visitor in about 1850. Wayland aimed to convert Brown "from . . . an eleemosynary, into a self-supporting institution." A decline in enrollment had reduced Brown's income, threatening to leave it "an annual burden upon the Baptists." The enrollment decline, Wayland reasoned, could not have been due to the high price of tuition, because Brown charged less than schools that had more students. It was not due to lack of "public confidence" in the "teachers and system of teaching," because when Wayland tendered his own resignation to force the trustees to consider this point, a careful trustee inquiry determined that "the professors, the discipline, and the mode of teaching were . . . unexceptionable." Wayland concluded "that the article we offered the public in all these colleges was not what the public wanted; and that, therefore, they did not come to take it even when it was offered for nothing." What was wanted, "in our free country" where "every man has an equal right to education," was a collegiate education that taught "the application of scientific discoveries to the arts of life" rather than an education in Greek and Latin for ancient, learned professions that had fallen from favor.[37] Wayland's reasoning, emphasizing stewardship of Baptist resources and respect for student preferences, persuaded Brown's trustees to institute major changes in the curriculum.

It would be wrong to leave the impression that nineteenth-century U.S. practices left nonprofit organizations entirely unconstrained by public regulation. One of the chief lessons of the history of nonprofit law is that court decisions and legislation have always constrained nonprofit action, whatever the views of those within the little world of a particular organization.[38] Nineteenth-century legislatures and judges significantly limited the ability of donors in Virginia, New York, and other states to leave funds to charities at their deaths, especially when the charities were not incorporated.[39] And incorporation, indeed voluntary action of any kind, always required conformity to local law. In 1853, for example, a judge in Virginia sentenced a Mrs. Margaret Douglas to a month in prison for running a school for free black children; she was violating a law against teaching African Americans to read.[40]

The American nonprofit system attained general recognition in the second and third quarters of the nineteenth century. In 1879, a leading British authority on hospitals provided the following thoughtful review, emphasizing the moral conversations that animated the boards of voluntary hospitals:

> In order to understand how the pay hospital and the pay ward arose in America, it must be remembered that in colonial days—that is to say, before the establishment of the Republic—no single American hospital had an endowment of any kind. Under the Republic it became necessary, as there were no endowments, that some system for procuring an adequate and permanent income for these charities should be established if the hospitals were to be maintained at all apart from State aid. It was true that the public at large generously subscribed towards the maintenance of the medical charities at that time, but the voluntary income was found to be altogether inadequate for the purpose. Again, an American has very little, if any, sympathy with pauperism, and the poor-law system is regarded by him with something akin to disgust. In other words, the Americans strongly object to pauperizing methods in good works for their fellow men. It came to pass therefore that the hospital managers throughout America determined to establish paying wards.[41]

Modern American Nonprofit Organizations: More Resources, Less Autonomy

Behind their varied moral conversations, nineteenth-century eleemosynary organizations repeatedly emphasized the theme of responsible self-

192 *David C. Hammack*

sufficiency, for individuals and institutions alike. Another theme often lay just below the surface: the inadequacy of the charitable response. Nonprofit leaders always recognized their inability to begin to provide for all, or to meet the ideal standard of equal access for all to education, adequate work, health care, and the arts.[42] Poverty, traditions of strong state government, and a desire to maintain an old social order significantly retarded the development of nonprofit organizations of most kinds in the South and West. In the twentieth century, the search for resources by nonprofits and others led through the Social Security Act (payments to the elderly and the disabled supported an expansion of nursing homes), the National Institutes of Health, the G.I. Bill, the Hill-Burton hospital construction act, the National Science Foundation, and the National Defense Education Act, to Medicare, Medicaid, federal grants and loans to college students, federal job-training initiatives, and to the food stamps and rent supplements that now help sustain many halfway houses.[43]

These federal programs provided essential funds: they also came with strings. The Great Society legislation of the 1960s significantly increased federal funding, which probably surpassed private donations for most nonprofits in the 1970s. Congress appropriated funds for specific programs and often changed those programs. New nonprofits arose to provide federally funded services, and both new and established organizations worked to make programs eligible for federal funds, to twist programs into shapes eligible for more than one funding stream, and to change programs as federal priorities shifted.[44] At the same time, the federal civil rights legislation that made it possible for northern and southern congressional representatives to unite in creating Medicare, Medicaid, federal student grants, and other programs simultaneously limited the ability of nonprofits, as of other employers, to discriminate on the basis of race, gender, age, national origin, or religion. Other federal legislation gradually required nonprofits, like other employers, to improve the safety of their workplaces. All these factors limited the role of nonprofit boards.

Equally important, though much less noted in discussions of nonprofit organizations, is the fact that the extraordinary prosperity of most Americans transformed the nonprofit sector after World War II. The average American income (after inflation) grew rapidly after 1945, more than doubling between 1960 and 1990.[45] Incomes became more, not less, equal well into the 1970s, as nearly everyone benefited to some extent. Far wealthier than their depression-scarred parents, late-twentieth-century Americans spent much more on services of all kinds, including the health care, education, recreational and arts activities—and the advocacy—that nonprofit organizations provide.

The Civil Rights movement led to the removal of most state restrictions on who could set up a nonprofit and serve on its board, and also to the removal of restrictions on nonprofit purposes.[46] Utilizing rights now protected by the federal government, African Americans, women, people who face mental and physical challenges, and many others now moved to establish nonprofits for their own purposes.[47] Freed from traditional limitations on their sponsors and their purposes, nonprofit organizations became more and more diverse. Organizations pursuing distinctive causes became much more common. And the government protected more rights of individuals who worked for, or who used the services of, nonprofit organizations.

Legislation of the 1960s and 1970s opened the way for continuous increases in federal support for nonprofit organizations, enabling them to grow. Contrary to a widely shared misperception, federal spending for the services that nonprofits provide (health, education, research, job training, other social services) increased steadily from less than half of 1 percent of the U.S. economy in 1962 to 1.8 percent in 1970, 3 percent in 1980, 3.5 percent in 1990, and 4.4 percent in 1997.[48]

Federal funds came, of course, with new federal rules in addition to injunctions against discrimination.[49] Much of the early federal funding went directly to nonprofit organizations in support of their general missions as they defined those missions: Hill-Burton and subsequent federal funding for "community" (usually nonprofit) hospitals; National Defense Education Act funding for graduate study in social sciences as well as technical fields relevant to the Cold War; Civil Rights-era anti-poverty, Head Start, and community development funding for anti-poverty community organizations. Through the 1960s, federal funds greatly expanded the impact of decisions made by those who controlled nonprofit organizations.

But such direct federal grants to individual organizations soon proved to be politically unsustainable, except in fields such as defense, medicine, and scientific research where political pressures can be managed if not eliminated through the use of peer review and similar devices. In the face of the controversies spawned by civil rights organizations, by organizations that favored or opposed birth control and abortion, by organizations deeply committed to particular religious perspectives, Congress sought alternatives. The "rights revolution" made it increasingly attractive to provide federal funds directly to individuals, who could then select a service provider for themselves—on the model of the G.I. Bill. Following this logic, much federal funding shifted, over time, from grants to vouchers (rent supplements, food stamps, Medicaid and Medicaid payments for health care, and grants and subsidies for loans to students).

One result of the use of voucher-type programs of federal support for health care, higher education, and other services has been to reinforce the historic market focus of America's nonprofit organizations, a focus already strengthened by prosperity.

Greater measured incomes have come with a historic shift of women into paid work. Traditionally, women volunteers provided much of the labor for nonprofit organizations. Women's increasingly successful demands to be included in the paid labor force account for part of the increase in measured per capita income. This factor has also shifted the balance of work in many nonprofit organizations from volunteers to paid staff.

In general, U.S. nonprofits today earn about half of their income and obtain about a third from governments. Donors now provide only a sixth or less of nonprofit income—much less than the half or more donors accounted for just forty years ago. Francis Wayland's dream that a college might move beyond the dependent status of an eleemosynary institution and become fully self-supporting has, in this way, become a reality, for Brown University and for thousands of other institutions as well.

The proportions vary in complex ways, of course: arts organizations receive almost no government money, while social service organizations receive the largest share (unless we take the view that nearly all health-care funding is determined by federal policy; in that case, most health care is government-supported because federal corporate tax policy strongly encouraged employer-based health insurance). Measured by expenditures or by employees (and ignoring the considerable variations from one region to another),[50] about half of all nonprofit activity now occurs in health care; about a fifth in education; about 10 percent in social service and religion; and about 5 percent in the arts.[51]

But there is no question that while donors continue to work through nonprofit organizations, the share of nonprofit resources that comes from donors has dropped so sharply (except in organizations devoted to religious worship, the arts, and direct advocacy) that the relation between donor and nonprofit has been transformed. My own estimates suggest that in Cuyahoga County, Ohio in 1990, donations and endowment income *together* accounted for just 3 percent of the funds of nonprofit hospitals, 16 percent of the funds of private colleges and universities, and only 17 percent of the funds of social service agencies.

As we have seen, donors faced significant constraints before the 1960s. The constraints increased greatly after the mid-1960s. Donors must still give through nonprofits, but nonprofits have become ever more complex, and donors face many additional restrictions and much more competition for influence. Government agencies demand close accounting for funds, often in accord with widely varying fiscal years that track poorly with the operations of the nonprofit that uses the money. Federal laws and regulations now protect the rights of individuals: the U.S. Supreme Court has ruled that federal student aid funds cannot be given to colleges that discriminate on the basis of race or gender, even if that is the preference of a nonprofit community. The Court also ruled, in the case of *Rust v. Sullivan,* that Congress could refuse to pay for general obstetrics-gynecology and healthy baby services offered by a hospital program that did not forbid its doctors and nurses to discuss abortion with patients—even with patients who were not receiving federal support.[52] More generally, the Court held that Congress violated neither First Amendment rights nor the legitimate judgments of professionals when it appropriated funds for use *only* in offices that limited the speech of their employees.

On these and other questions, the moral discussions held within most nonprofit organizations are now subject to significant public review. Because their organizations operate under the closer supervision of a federal government now strongly committed to the quite universal protection of human rights, and because they depend to a much greater extent on government funds and on earned income, nonprofit boards, in all fields except religious worship and the arts, now operate in settings that are far from the closed moral universes of their nineteenth-century predecessors. Board members and other donors provide a much smaller share of the resources: the walls that set them apart can no longer exclude their neighbors. The neighbors—in the form of rights-empowered clients and staff, paying customers, and government rules—are now within the walls, sitting at the table, making the conversation more complex and more difficult.

Discussions of philanthropy too often ignore the reality that almost all gifts go through nonprofits. Discussions of philanthropy also ignore, too often, the extraordinary changes that have transformed the nonprofit sector in the United States. While donors and volunteers traditionally sustained American nonprofits, nonprofits now obtain five-sixths of their income from other sources. The result is that nearly all discussions of philanthropy greatly exaggerate the importance of gifts and volunteers and exaggerate as well the autonomy and the influence of donors. By the same token, most discussions of philanthropy greatly underestimate the importance of earned income and of government payments of all kinds.

Donors have legitimate moral interests in the uses to which their donations are put, and moral obligations to ensure that their gifts do as much good as possible. Donors also have legal obligations to follow the formal rules by which the public defines appropriate giving and tax-related behavior. And donors certainly have a strong interest in the effectiveness of the organizations through which they seek to "do good."

But the nonprofit organizations that receive nearly all gifts are obliged, now more than ever before, legally as well as morally, to consider other interests in addition to those of their donors. Schools, hospitals, and other service providers have legal and moral obligations to their students, alumni, and patients to provide services at "understood" levels of quality and in "agreed fashions," and at "acceptable" prices—and to continue to provide such services indefinitely in the absence of major changes in their environments. Nonprofit organizations have an obligation even greater than that of private enterprises to take into consideration the preferences, however diverse or reasonable, of their "customers," as well as the preferences of their donors. Armed with greater wealth, affluent nonprofit "customers" are more capable than ever of enforcing their own preferences. Government enforcement of recently recognized rights further strengthens the customer. And government-provided vouchers further reinforce the market.

Recent changes in the nonprofit sector—reflected in the decline of volunteering, increased recognition of individual rights, women's demands for inclusion and pay—have also strengthened the positions of nonprofit employees vis-à-vis the preferences of donors.

In the past, donors had to negotiate with other donors and with volunteer workers. Now donors must take into account the reality that different government agencies may and do seek different purposes. Donors must also consider that often a nonprofit organization finds it difficult to satisfy the conflicting demands of all the agencies from which it draws funds—or from which it would draw funds if it could find a way.

These new realities challenge nonprofits to maintain fidelity to their missions. They make it far more difficult than in the past for donors to evaluate the moral impact of their gifts. At the same time, they make nonprofit organizations more important than ever, in nearly every part of the United States. The new realities have greatly increased nonprofit resources. They greatly enhance the autonomy and integrity of employees and customers. Overall, they have greatly increased nonprofit responsiveness to the preferences of those who use their services. They have increased nonprofit accountability to customers and governments. Precisely because customers and voters so commonly disagree among themselves, they have made nonprofit accountability increasingly complex and contentious.

We should keep these changing realities in mind as we consider "moral issues in doing good."

Notes

1. For excellent introductions to the legal and functional aspects of nonprofit organizations in the United States today, see John G. Simon, "The Tax Treatment of Nonprofit Organizations: A Review of Federal and State Policies," in Walter W. Powell, ed., *The Nonprofit Sector: A Research Handbook* (New Haven, Conn.: Yale University Press, 1987), pp. 67–98; Lester Salamon, *America's Nonprofit Sector: A Primer* (New York: The Foundation Center, 1999); and Michael O'Neill, *Nonprofit Nation: A New Look at the Third America* (San Francisco: Jossey-Bass, 2002).

2. Princeton Seminary theologian Charles Hodge, a veteran of religious discussion and debate, observed in 1845 that "it is undeniable, that the members of each Christian denomination, in America, live in some degree apart, look at their respective cantons, and are ignorant of what other religious bodies are doing." Review of Robert Baird, *Religion in America; or an Account of the Origin, Progress, Relation to the State, and Present Condition of the Evangelical Churches in the United States,* in *Princeton Review* XVII, no. 1 (January 1845): 18.

3. The essays in this volume that focus on specific traditions of moral discourse in particular groups of institutions, notably the essays of David Craig, Elliot N. Dorff, Amy Kass, John Langan, and Philip Turner, provide remarkable discussions of the humanistic, Jewish, Protestant, and Catholic traditions.

4. England faced the same issue. "Philanthropists may induce all school boards to copy London, and found scholarships to carry the best boys from the lower schools to the secondary," James Bonar wrote in 1881. "But these are a favored few; and the middle class schools into which they are drafted are good or bad, according to the luck of the locality. For the masses, there is practically an infinite distance to divide an Oxford college, or even a 'public school,' with its multitudinous fees and strait exclusiveness, from a city board-school, with its nominal charges and indiscriminate admission of all comers." "A

Peep at French Schools," *Appleton's Journal: A Magazine of General Literature* 11, no. 63 (September 1881): 208.

5. Rabbi Moses Maimonides, Mishneh Torah 10:7–15, slightly restated from the version given on the "Sephardic Sages" website, http://www.sephardicsages. org/8.html, January 6, 2003, citing Rabbi Stephen Passamaneck, *An Introduction to the History and Sources of Jewish Law* (Oxford: Oxford University Press, 1996), pp. 277–89.

6. My own discussion of the development of the American nonprofit sector appears in David C. Hammack, ed., *Making the Nonprofit Sector in the United States: A Reader* (Bloomington: Indiana University Press, 1998).

7. Albert Shaw, "The Higher Life of New York City," *The Outlook,* January 25, 1896, pp. 132–39; Everett P. Wheeler, "The Unofficial Government of Cities," *Atlantic Monthly* 86 (1900): 370–76. On education in later nineteenth-century New York City, see David C. Hammack, *Power and Society: Greater New York at the Turn of the Century* (New York: Russell Sage Foundation, 1982), Chapter 6.

8. Peter J. Wosh, *Spreading the Word: The Bible Business in Nineteenth-Century America* (Ithaca, N.Y.: Cornell University Press, 1994); Timothy A. Hacsi, *Second Home: Orphan Asylums and Poor Families in America* (Cambridge, Mass.: Harvard University Press, 1997).

9. For a discussion of the evidence on the growth of the nonprofit sector, see David C. Hammack, "Nonprofit Organizations in American History: Research Opportunities and Sources," *The American Behavioral Scientist* 45, no. 11 (July 2002): 1638–74; and "Growth, Transformation, and Quiet Revolution in the Nonprofit Sector over Two Centuries," *Nonprofit and Voluntary Sector Quarterly,* June 2001, pp. 157–73. See also other essays in a special symposium that I edited on "The Quiet Revolution in the Nonprofit Sector: Law, Policy, and Commerce," especially Colin B. Burke, "Nonprofit History's New Numbers (and the Need for More)," *Nonprofit and Voluntary Sector Quarterly* 30, no. 2 (2001): 174–203.

10. Burke, "Nonprofit History's New Numbers."

11. David C. Hammack, "Foundations in the American Polity," in Ellen Condliffe Lagemann, ed., *New Scholarship on the History of American Foundations* (Bloomington: Indiana University Press, 1999), pp. 43–68.

12. Remarkable studies of volunteering, especially by women, include, Carroll Smith-Rosenberg, *Religion and the Rise of the American City: The New York City Mission Movement, 1812–1870* (Ithaca, N.Y.: Cornell University Press, 1971); Barbara Lee Epstein, *The Politics of Domesticity: Women, Evangelism, and Temperance in Nineteenth Century America* (Middletown, Conn.: Wesleyan University Press, 1981); John Patrick McDowell, *The Social Gospel in the South: The Woman's Home Mission Movement in the Methodist Episcopal Church in the South, 1886–1939* (Baton Rouge: Louisiana State University Press, 1982); Suzanne Lebsock, *The Free Women of Petersburg: Status and Culture in a Southern Town, 1784–1860* (New York: W. W. Norton, 1984); Nancy A. Hewitt, *Women's Activism and Social Change: Rochester, New York, 1822–1872* (Ithaca, N.Y.: Cornell University Press, 1984); Karen J. Blair, *The History of American Women's Voluntary Organizations, 1810–1960* (Boston: G. K. Hall, 1989); Kathleen D. McCarthy, *Lady Bountiful Revisited: Women, Philanthropy,*

and Power (New Brunswick, N.J.: Rutgers University Press, 1990); Anne Firor Scott, *Natural Allies: Women's Associations in American History* (Urbana and Chicago: University of Illinois Press, 1992); Evelyn Brooks Higginbotham, *Righteous Discontent: The Women's Movement in the Black Baptist Church, 1880–1920* (Cambridge, Mass.: Harvard University Press, 1993); Patricia Hill, *The World Their Household: The American Woman's Foreign Mission Movement and Cultural Transformation, 1870–1920* (Ann Arbor: University of Michigan Press, 1985); Mary J. Oates, *The Catholic Philanthropic Tradition in America* (Bloomington: Indiana University Press, 1995); Susan Yohn, *A Contest of Faiths: Missionary Women and Pluralism in the American Southwest* (Ithaca, N.Y.: Cornell University Press, 1995); Julie Roy Jeffrey, *The Great Silent Army of Abolitionism: Ordinary Women in the Antislavery Movement* (Chapel Hill and London: University of North Carolina Press, 1998); Judith Ann Giesberg, *Civil War Sisterhood: The U.S. Sanitary Commission and Women's Politics in Transition* (Boston: Northeastern University Press, 2000).

13. Benjamin Franklin, *Autobiography,* and Lyman Beecher, *Autobiography,* both excerpted in Hammack, *Making the Nonprofit Sector in the United States,* pp. 70–84; 120.

14. Ray Allen Billington, *The Protestant Crusade, 1800–1860: A Study of the Origins of American Nativism* (New York: Macmillan, 1938).

15. Smith-Rosenberg, *Religion and the Rise of the American City.*

16. Charles I. Foster, *An Errand of Mercy: The Evangelical United Front, 1790–1837* (Chapel Hill: University of North Carolina Press, 1960).

17. Clifford S. Griffin, *Their Brothers' Keepers: Moral Stewardship in the United States, 1800–1850* (New Brunswick, N.J.: Rutgers University Press, 1960).

18. Lois W. Banner, "Religious Benevolence as Social Control: A Critique of an Interpretation," *Journal of American History* 60 (1973): 23–41.

19. Lori Ginzberg, *Women and the Work of Benevolence: Morality, Politics, and Class in the Nineteenth-Century United States* (New Haven, Conn.: Yale University Press, 1990).

20. F. T. Waite, *A Warm Friend for the Spirit: A History of the Family Service Association of Cleveland and its Forbears* (Cleveland: Family Service Association, 1960).

21. Wosh, *Spreading the Word.*

22. John R. Seeley et al., *Community Chest* (Glencoe, Ill.: The Free Press, 1957); David L. Sills, *The Volunteers: Means and Ends in a National Organization* (Glencoe, Ill.: The Free Press, 1957); Merle Curti and Roderick Nash, *Philanthropy in the Shaping of American Higher Education* (New Brunswick, N.J.: Rutgers University Press, 1965); Mayer N. Zald, *Organizational Change: The Political Economy of the YMCA* (Chicago: University of Chicago Press, 1970); Peter Dobkin Hall, *The Organization of American Culture, 1700–1900: Private Institutions, Elites, and the Origins of American Nationality* (New York: New York University Press, 1982); David C. Hammack, "Community Foundations: The Delicate Question of Purpose," in *An Agile Servant,* ed. Richard Magat (New York: The Foundation Center, 1989), pp. 23–50, revised version reprinted in Hammack, *Making the Nonprofit Sector;* Peter Dobkin Hall, "Cultures of Trusteeship in the United States," PONPO *Working Paper* #153 (May 1990); Eleanor L. Brilliant, *The United Way: Dilemmas of Organized Charity*

(New York: Columbia University Press, 1990); Kathleen S. Kelly, *Effective Fund-Raising Management* (Newark, N.J.: Lawrence Erlbaum Publishers, 1998).

23. Alexis de Tocqueville, "Of the Use Which Americans Make of Public Associations in Civil Society," in *Democracy in America* (1840), reprinted in Hammack, *Making the Nonprofit Sector in the United States*, pp. 149–53.

24. An excellent discussion of this point for nineteenth-century Boston is Robert F. Dalzell, Jr., *Enterprising Elite: The Boston Associates and the World They Made* (Cambridge, Mass.: Harvard University Press, 1987), Chapter 5, "Philanthropy and the Uses of Wealth." Also see Steven Wheatley, *The Politics of Philanthropy: Abraham Flexner and Medical Education* (Madison: University of Wisconsin Press, 1988); Ellen Condliffe Lagmann, *The Politics of Knowledge: The Carnegie Corporation, Philanthropy, and Public Policy* (Middletown, Conn.: Wesleyan University Press, 1989); David C. Hammack and Stanton Wheeler, *Social Science in the Making: Essays on the Russell Sage Foundation, 1907–1947* (New York: Russell Sage Foundation, 1994); Jeffrey Sosland, *A School in Every County: The Partnership of Jewish Philanthropist Julius Rosenwald and American Black Communities* (Washington, D.C.: Economics & Science Planning, 1995); Abigail A. Van Slyck, *Free to All: Carnegie Libraries and American Culture, 1890–1920* (Chicago: University of Chicago Press, 1995); Eric A. Anderson and Alfred A. Moss, Jr., *Dangerous Donations: Northern Philanthropy and Southern Black Education, 1902–1930* (Columbia and London: University of Missouri Press, 1999).

25. Philadelphia Orphan Society, *Third Annual Report* (Philadelphia: The Society, 1818).

26. Trustees of the Perkins Institution and Massachusetts Asylum for the Blind, *Eleventh Annual Report to the Corporation* (Boston: 1843), pp. 4–5. For a characteristic evangelical denunciation of Boston rationalism and transcendentalism, see Charles Hodge's insistence, in his review of Robert Baird's *Religion in America:* that Unitarianism's "coldness" led its "pulpits to resound with harangues on Slavery, Spirituous liquors, Capital punishment, Texas, Aesthetics, any thing but Christ," rather than with orthodox Calvinist Christianity. *Princeton Review,* January 1845, p. 39.

27. Ibid., p. 47. For an extended discussion of donors to the Perkins Institution and Boston's leading philanthropies, see Dalzell, *Enterprising Elite*, pp. 126ff.

28. Robert Baird, *Religion In America; or, An Account of the Origin, Progress, Relation to the State, and Present Condition of the Evangelical Churches in the United States: With Notices of the Unevangelical Denominations* (New York: Harper: Blackie and Son, 1844); excerpts from selection reprinted in Hammack, *Making the Nonprofit Sector in the United States.*

29. Quoted in Smith-Rosenberg, *Religion and the Rise of the American City,* p. 193.

30. Ibid., pp. 193–94.

31. *Pastoral Letter of the Archbishop of Baltimore to the Roman Catholicks of Norfolk, Virginia,* 1819, section reprinted in *Documents of American Catholic History,* John Tracy Ellis, editor (Milwaukee: Bruce Publishing Company, 1956), pp. 229–30. On the complex and extended history of the trusteeship controversy, see Patrick W. Carey, *People, Priests, and Prelates: Ecclesiastical Democracy and the Tensions of Trusteeism* (Notre Dame, Ind.: Notre Dame University Press, 1987).

32.	Minute of the society quoted in Daniel T. McColgan, *A Century of Charity: The First One Hundred Years of the Society of St. Vincent de Paul in the United States* (Milwaukee: Bruce Publishing Co., 1951), pp. 79–80; reprinted in Ellis, *Documents of American Catholic History,* p. 296.

33.	Michael Heiss, Report on Wisconsin Catholicism to the directors of the Ludwig-Missionsverein, Munich, August 30, 1861, *Salesianum XL,* Augustine C. Breig, translator and Peter Leo Johnson, editor (October 1945), pp. 169–80, reprinted in Ellis, *Documents of American Catholic History,* p. 368. Ellis also notes substantial donations from the French Society for the Propagation of the Faith (p. 252) and the Austrian Leopoldinen-Stiftung (see below). He adds that by 1922, the Society for the Propagation of the Faith had sent over $6 million to the United States—and that American Catholics had returned nearly $11 million to the society's French headquarters.

34.	For accounts that emphasize the preferences of some Catholic donors for ethnic or women's organizations, see Jay Dolan, *The Immigrant Church: New York's Irish and German Catholics, 1815–1865* (Baltimore: Johns Hopkins University Press, 1975), and Mary J. Oates, *The Catholic Philanthropic Tradition in America* (Bloomington: Indiana University Press, 1995).

35.	Canon Josef Salzbacher, *Meine Reise Nach Nord-Amerika* (Vienna: Wimmer, Schmidt, & Leo, 1845), pp. 354–57, translated and reprinted in Ellis, *Documents of American Catholic History,* p. 268. Non-Catholic students might also convert, Salzbacher added, and even if not, would likely defend Catholic institutions against nativist attack.

36.	*Presbyterian Review* XXXII, no. III (July 1860): 516–22.

37.	James F. W. Johnston, *Notes on North America, Agricultural, Economical, and Social* (Boston: Charles C. Little and James Brown, 1851), pp. 474–77.

38.	Irvin G. Wyllie, "The Search for an American Law of Charity, 1776–1844," *Mississippi Valley Historical Review* 46 (September 1959): 203–21.

39.	For an excellent brief discussion of these points see Norman I. Silber, *A Corporate Form of Freedom: The Emergence of the Nonprofit Sector* (Boulder, Colo.: Westview Press, 2001), pp. 20–25.

40.	"Trial of Mrs. Douglas for Teaching Colored Children to Read," from J. D. Lawson, ed., *American State Trials,* vol. VII, pp. 56ff, *Documents of American History,* 10th ed., ed. Henry Steele Commager and Milton Cantor (Englewood Cliffs, N.J.: Prentice-Hall, 1988), vol. 1, pp. 327–29.

41.	Henry C. Burdett, *Pay Hospitals and Paying Wards* (London: J. & A. Churchill, 1979), pp. 68–69, quoted in Edward H. L. Corwin, *The American Hospital* (New York: The Commonwealth Fund, 1946), pp. 61–62.

42.	For a detailed discussion of the failure of nonprofit organizations to secure adequate funding during the Great Depression, see David C. Hammack, "Failure and Resilience: Pushing the Limits in Depression and Wartime," in *Charity, Philanthropy, and Civility in American History,* ed. Lawrence Friedman and Mark McGarvie (New York: Cambridge University Press), pp. 263–80.

43.	For a fuller development of this point, see David C. Hammack, "Nonprofit Organizations in American History: Research Opportunities and Sources," *The American Behavioral Scientist* 45, no. 11 (July 2002): 1638–74, and "Growth, Transformation, and Quiet Revolution in the Nonprofit Sector Over Two Centuries," *Nonprofit and Voluntary Sector Quarterly* 30, no. 2 (2001): 157–73.

44. For excellent discussions of this process in social service organizations, see Steven Rathgeb Smith and Michael Lipsky, *Nonprofits for Hire: The Welfare State in the Age of Contracting* (Cambridge, Mass.: Harvard University Press, 1993), and Kirsten A. Grønbjerg, *Understanding Nonprofit Funding* (San Francisco: Jossey-Bass, 1993).

45. Council of Economic Advisors, *Economic Report of the President, 2001.*

46. On this point, see Silber, *A Corporate Form of Freedom.*

47. None of the comments on the proliferation of nonprofit organizations in the past thirty years notes that this is the consequence of the Civil Rights Movement, of *increasing* federal funding, and of *increasing* American prosperity.

48. Calculated from "Historical Tables" included in the Budget of the United States Government, Fiscal Year 1999, pp. 50–64, Budget of the U.S., FY 1999. Online via GPO Access, www.gpoaccess.gov/index.html, through 2000. This money goes for services provided by government agencies (state universities, community colleges, county hospitals, etc.) and by profit-seeking firms (technical schools, nursing homes) as well as by nonprofit organizations, but nonprofits have advantages in seeking these funds that have not decreased over this period. For the notion that federal funding *declined* under President Ronald Reagan, see, for example, Lester M. Salamon and Alan J. Abramson, *The Federal Budget and the Nonprofit Sector* (Washington, D.C.: Urban Institute Press, 1982). In fact, federal funding *increased* during the Reagan years. It is true that funds for direct social services, community organizing, and legal services were cut (as had also been the case under President Richard Nixon), and that the Reagan administration cut the CETA program whose "job-training" funds had allowed many social service and community development organizations to expand their staffs under President Jimmy Carter. It is also true that federal grants to college students grew more slowly than the economy in general, and than the cost and scale of collegiate education in particular. But Medicare, Medicaid, research, and job training funds grew more rapidly than the economy, and new administrative rules allowed Medicaid funds to pay for some services previously funded through federal social service and community development programs.

49. Smith and Lipsky, *Nonprofits for Hire*; Grønbjerg, *Understanding Nonprofit Funding.* Also relevant are Elizabeth Boris and C. Eugene Steuerle, eds., *Nonprofits and Government: Collaboration and Conflict,* (Washington, D.C.: Urban Institute Press, 1999); and Salamon and Abramson, *The Federal Budget and the Nonprofit Sector.*

50. On Nov. 26, 2002, consultant Dan Prives reported on the ARNOVA discussion list the total revenue of nonprofit organizations for each state for the previous year, according to the IRS master file (which excludes churches but includes church-related nonprofits that register as independent charities). When we divide state nonprofit revenue totals by total "state product," as reported by the Bureau of Economic Analysis of the U.S. Department of Commerce for 2001 (http://www.bea.doc.gov/bea/regional/gsp/), we find that the nonprofit sector accounts for 15 percent of state economic activity in most of New England; 10–13 percent in most of the Mid-Atlantic States; 9–11 percent in the Great Lakes and Northern Plains states; 5–8 percent in the South; 2 percent on the West Coast. The nonprofit sector also continues to vary significantly along regional lines. Nonprofits have always been most important in New England

and the Mid-Atlantic states, where many colleges and hospitals are private, and where many foundations, colleges, medical centers, and museums consider themselves to be national rather than local organizations. Nonprofits in the northeastern quarter of the United States are larger and interact with many more, and many more large, nonprofits in their immediate environs than do their counterparts in the South or in California.

51. For an overview of this data, see Lester Salamon, *America's Nonprofit Sector: A Primer.*

52. For excerpts from the Court's decision in *Rust v. Sullivan,* see Hammack, *Making the Nonprofit Sector in the United States,* pp. 474–81.

10 Philanthropy in Question

William M. Sullivan

9/11: A Defining Moment for American Philanthropy?

The tragic events of September 11, 2001 have had serious effects on American life in both its climate and the functioning of its institutions. In a variety of contexts, we are told, 9/11 has proved to be a defining moment, an event that has shifted Americans' perception of themselves and the world in some basic and continuing ways. Certainly, one of the surprising effects of the events was the sudden rise in positive attitudes about social solidarity and trust in government. Within months of September 11, however, while attitudinal measures remained higher than before the attacks on New York and Washington, these increases were not followed by comparable gains in positive civic behavior.[1]

One exception was charitable giving. Yet, here too the results were surprising, even disconcerting. After the terrorist attacks, there was a huge outpouring of contributions to charities that advertised themselves in the mass media as offering aid to the victims of the attacks. Huge amounts were contributed for the victims. Congress rushed into action to provide federal assistance to victims as well. Yet, in the months that followed, contributions to local charities around the country that had routinely aided the poor found that their usual donors failed to give. Americans' charitable sentiments seemed to be following the media spotlight.[2]

Shortly afterward, the national Red Cross found itself the object of intense public anger when it attempted to devote some of the 9/11 donations, which far exceeded what was needed in New York and Washington, to other operations. No matter that this has been a routine practice of most national charities for a long time, a practice that allowed such organizations to accumulate resources for rapid response to unexpected disasters. After 9/11 this was taken as somehow bad faith on the part of the Red Cross, resulting in the dismissal of its national director.[3] It seemed evident that the terrorist attacks brought out responses that ran very much against the grain of traditional American involvement with philanthropic giving, or at least what many had imagined that involvement to be.

Alasdair MacIntyre has pointed out that every ethic implies a sociology. Notions of how to live do not float entirely free of some basis in actual ways of living. What might be happening in the United States that could make intelligible the philanthropic responses to 9/11? Two features of those responses stand out. First, it seems that the mass media directed major attention and sympathy toward the victims—but also away from long-term commitments to established charitable organizations. Second, leaders of longstanding charitable organizations, notably the Red Cross, were attacked and forced from office, at least in part, for not following the (largely wasteful and irrational) preferences of the donors who were caught up in the mass response to the victims of the tragedy. There seems to be a common pattern underlying both these events. It resembles the familiar model of consumer choice. According to this view of human action, individual impulse, called spontaneity, can and ought to be valued more than commitment to organizations. Giving, then, need reflect only or mostly the donor's private sense of public need, and express a highly personalized sense of charity.

These developments add credibility to Robert Putnam's study in 2000 that documented a several decades-long shift in the way Americans relate to each other. Putnam argued that there has been a gradual but marked movement away from long-term, multipurpose connections toward "thin, single-strand, surf-by interactions." Putnam concluded that philanthropic giving had, like volunteering, become increasingly "one-shot, special purpose, and self-oriented."[4] This description, though penned well before the events of September 2001, helps make sense of the highly personalized, expressive accounts that donors gave media reporters in explaining their outpouring of one-time benevolence to the victims and their families. It may be possible, as Paul Schervish suggests in his essay in this volume, for individuals to make such giving an opportunity for personal moral growth. It is less clear that this understanding of philanthropy can contribute to greater solidarity or justice in American society.

While it remains unclear that 9/11 will emerge as a defining moment for American philanthropy, it certainly could be seen as a diagnostic moment. Such events demand rethinking the ethical criteria and operating rules for responding to national disasters. This is a task that ethicists have already begun.[5] However, it is also important to try to make sense of these responses, asking why they happened and what they might portend for philanthropy and giving in America. How, that is, should we understand them, and how can we relate these developments in our debates over philanthropy? These questions point toward another, more difficult issue: What, if anything, should we as concerned citizens try to do about these developments? These are the topics of this paper.

The approach in what follows is to place philanthropic activities within a conception of the American polity. This conception emphasizes that philanthropy is a major form of the larger category of civic engagement in the United States. Furthermore, the empirically strong connection between philanthropic work and religion is not fortuitous. Civic engagement of all stripes, like the polity itself, has been powerfully shaped over time by the formative influences of Protestant Christianity in America. These influences have not been simple or consistent, however. While patterns of civic life have changed over time in response to a variety of economic, political, and social forces, changes in the philanthropic imagination—the way Americans think about institutions and activities aimed at the general welfare—are to be understood in part as the result of struggle between differing conceptions of the nation, differences that have strong religious roots.

One fateful aspect of this imagination has been an inability to conceive the national state as a representative agency of the moral life of the nation. The events of September 11 and their aftermath only heighten the significance of this peculiar feature of the American philanthropic imagination. In addition, an influential segment of opinion has seized on the idea of philanthropic organizations as a "third sector," conceived as independent of both the profit-oriented market economy and the administrative state. This view resembles those theories of "civil society" that have imagined the institutions of civil society, especially the family, church, and school, as providing countervailing forces against the atomizing tendencies of market and state. I have criticized the adequacy of this view of civil society elsewhere.[6]

The persistence of this belief in the potency of a third force to rescue society from the vast forces of the market economy and government has obscured the situation more than enlightening it. So it is that the present reconfiguring of the polity toward a more unequal and divided society, although a development that bodes ill for many of the traditional patterns of philanthropic life, has so far failed to arouse a consistent ameliorative effort from our philanthropic organizations or their leaders. It remains unclear whether the "third sector" will emerge as part of a solution or simply as an adjunct of the larger problem.

Locating the Issue: Philanthropy as Civic Engagement in the American Polity

As in all other areas, our understanding of philanthropy is importantly determined by the concepts and categories we bring to bear upon facts and events. Philanthropy, organized private giving for social good, and charity are salient elements in American life. Yet they are not a single phenomenon but one that is multifaceted and complicated enough to resist simple definition.[7] It may be better to think of philanthropy as a "folk concept," somewhat like the American use of the term *profession*. A folk concept is an idea that denotes not a single reality but a whole range of perceptions that can only be understood by analyzing how the term is used, and by whom, over a particular period of time.[8] So, for example, the term is used rather differently to describe established philanthropic foundations than when speaking about the self-help practiced among groups that have experienced historical discrimination, such as African American churches. Philanthropy will be defined differently again when government seeks to classify and group organizations for the purposes of the tax code.

Such folk concepts are indispensable for making one's way in a given society, however. They help structure that society's cognitive map of important social phenomena. But they require analysis if we are to grasp the significance of what is being talked about. This is because we participate in a social life that embeds us in networks of interaction that reach far beyond the range of our experience. We therefore have to guide our lives according to how we imagine ourselves and the world we live in to be organized. Legitimate institutions rest upon the sense that there is at least some degree of mutual correspondence between the normative order and social practice. However, the ways in which a society organizes its basic activities greatly influence how members of that society imagine their world and its possibilities.

A number of social analysts have begun calling attention to ways in which American society at the turn of the twenty-first century has become markedly different from what it was a generation earlier. One of the key differences is a reversal since the 1970s of a trend toward a more even distribution of food, housing, and health care that began after the Great Depression and continued through the postwar decades.[9] Since the 1970s, not only has the gap between rich and poor grown dramatically, but it has been accompanied by increasing residential segregation of Americans by education and social class.[10] Interestingly, these trends toward inequality have not affected European nations to any extent like they have the United States.[11] While Europeans are by many measures less "philanthropic" than Americans, no European country tolerates the levels of poverty and its attendant morbid effects that have long marked the United States.

Over these same decades, many of the national organizations, especially political parties and voluntary associations through which local and national leadership communicated and hammered out policy, have shriveled or ceased to function as they once did.[12] These changes have spawned keen debate about the causes and likely consequences of these trends. Some see the problem as "too much of a good thing," in that democratized direct decision making has robbed many inherited institutions of authority and connective power.[13] Others, however, trace the weakening of institutionalized connections to the so-called Conservative Revolution of the past decades. On this view, the conservative ascendancy has worked to revive once-discredited policies of laissez-faire capitalism, thereby producing an inevitable return of plutocratic rule as in the Gilded Age of the nineteenth century or the Roaring Twenties.[14] Taken together, whatever their causes, these changes hold large-scale implications for the future of philanthropy.

Celebrants of a new era in the world of philanthropy, such as Peter Drucker, also point out that most of the action in our civil society today centers not on workers or excluded minorities but on the more affluent demographic segments of the population. Of course, relative affluence and philanthropy have always tended to go together, offset mostly by religious organization among the poor and working classes.[15] Yet, with wealth far greater and more concentrated at the top than a generation ago, and with elites less connected organizationally to their less affluent fellow citizens, the concentration of "spheres of effective citizenship" (Peter Drucker's phrase) among the upper 10 percent of the socioeconomic distribution represents a change of considerable proportions. In the proliferating nonprofit organizations that tend to define much of today's "third sector," affluent individuals can "exercise influence, discharge responsibility, and make decisions" that they feel less able to do in the corporate economy or in our money- and media-focused politics. Drucker sees this as the greatest positive contribution of the "counterculture of the third sector: here they are active citizens."[16]

Drucker is describing a genuine form of civic engagement. However, the perspectives of other analysts of this privileged group of citizens, such as Robert Reich and Richard Florida, make Drucker's happiness over what he discerned less clearly merited. Both Reich's "symbolic analysts," who occupy the upper fifth of the socioeconomic distribution, and Florida's more recently identified "creative class" workers look for guidance to an ethic of authenticity and personal expression.[17] As both analysts note, there is little in such a worldview to promote concern about relative social location, let alone a spirit of service to populations largely invisible from within the happy confines of symbolic analyst exurbs or creative class enclaves of revitalized "authentic" urban neighborhoods. In short, Americans continue to engage in philanthropic activity, in voluntarily doing good works. But who is doing this, in what contexts, and for or with whom, has been changing.

While American philanthropic activities seem to be morphing into a new configuration that makes old templates hard to apply, there are also clear points of continuity. Americans continue to engage the larger world beyond home and workplace in distinct ways, quite different in the main from those of comparable contemporary societies: Europeans, East Asians, or even Canadians. Americans share a uniquely strong and positive view of volunteering, of individual initiative in giving that is at once generous and interested in the moral uplift of the recipient. This is consistent with a heavy moral accent upon independence and self-support as key virtues upon which all are to be judged. Americans like their giving to be kept close to home. They are generally suspicious of leaders and elites, though not of the wealthy as such. By contrast, Americans have a comparatively weak notion of collective responsibility. Outside wartime, Americans are weak on collective action, except among and for the like-minded. Americans seem to have a difficult time making moral discriminations among interdependent entities. In a crunch, independence almost always trumps interdependence as an ideal and an ethic. Above all, perhaps, Americans are set apart by the combination of the strong valorizing of individual responsibility coupled with a fear and distrust of government.[18]

American involvement in philanthropic activities is part of larger patterns of social activity. This means that nonprofit and charitable activities are actually like dependent variables, parts of a larger context of social interaction whose development often shapes these activities more deeply than we have commonly imagined. One useful conceptual lens is to imagine philanthropy and charity as distinctive features of the American "polity." Used this way, polity is broader than formal government, with some of the connotation of a term like *regime*. It describes a society united and made distinctive by particular ways of organizing itself. Or, as Ronald L. Jepperson and John W. Meyer have used the term, a polity is a "public order, a system of rules that confer societal authority" on both persons and organizations. For example, in recent discussions of European and Japanese capitalism as contrasted with the American economy, it becomes clear that the American polity has "constructed" economic markets and persons as bearers of ever-expanding "rights," in distinctive ways, in areas such as labor contracts, equal access for the disabled, the rights of corporations, and so on.[19]

A polity is an institutional matrix that shapes a nation's sense of possible and proper ways of living. It thereby forms the basis for a certain way of imagining societal community. The utility of the concept becomes clearer when one compares taken-for-granted American assumptions about how life is and should be organized, or compares the American "public order," with those of other similar but distinct polities. For example, as long ago as the 1830s Alexis de Tocqueville was struck by how social problems that in France were always seen as the responsibility of the state became, in the United States, the object of "associations" voluntarily organized by citizens. Using Jepperson and Meyer's concept of a "polity," it becomes intelligible that, much later, Americans would persistently imagine that widespread poverty could (and should) be solved by voluntary activity and "associations," while the French (like most Europeans, Canadians, and Japanese) have seen poverty as a direct responsibility of the state. This is because the "rules" that confer "societal authority" in the American polity are different from those in the French or Canadian polities. Compared to common European standards, the United States is, like Japan, a clear outlier.

For the French, a strong national state is taken to be the essential basis for democracy. For Americans, the federal government is often perceived as one of the major threats to democracy. There are historical as well as cultural reasons for this difference in polity. "Europeans, congregating in cities . . . needed the state to create their democracy," notes Robert Wiebe, so that "everything hinged on controlling the state, which became invested with all kinds of conflicting hopes for security, order, and justice . . . [while] American democracy, thriving on suspicion of the state, invested far fewer hopes in it."[20] Ways of doing things obvious to citizens of one polity may not seem at all obvious to citizens of another.[21]

Seen from the perspective of the American polity, charitable organizations, such as the Red Cross, the United Way, as well as philanthropic grant-making foundations, are distinctive forms of civic engagement. They can be compared, but also contrasted, with such other modes of civic engagement as membership in mutual benefit societies such as religious organizations, fraternal or sororal organizations, unions, political parties, and professional associations. Especially since World War II, another organizational form, the nonprofit corporation, has proliferated, encouraged by federal tax incentives. The role of the national state has been critical here, though in typical American fashion, the rhetorical tendency has been to play this down, and to speak instead of an "independent sector," for example, even while most of its resources come directly or indirectly (because of the tax code) from the government.

The often noted importance such organizations have enjoyed is itself a major indicator of their centrality within the American polity. However, the evidence that Putnam has marshaled, as well as the history that Skocpol has uncovered, makes it clear that different types of organizations within the "third sector" have experienced very different fortunes. As we have already seen, the events of 9/11 have highlighted aspects of that shift. In broad outline, and while its specifics are still vigorously disputed, there seems plausible evidence for a general decline in voluntary organizations of the kind Skocpol calls "fellowship associations." These are membership groups, organized in local chapters but linked nationally, in which citizens participate and to which they contribute effort and dues toward the carrying out of good works. In contrast, present trends favor a whole new landscape of autonomous, tax-exempt nonprofit corporations. These are staffed by professionally credentialed personnel who administer services, or advocate for policies, and are mostly supported by direct-mail fundraising, government contracts, vouchers, or grants from other philanthropic foundations, supplemented by the sale of goods and services.

As the new landscape has taken form, and particularly since the 1970s, the range of possibilities for citizen participation has not so much disappeared as subtly but importantly changed character. The new forms of participation are more available to the more affluent, for example, and do not tend to create interaction or mingling across lines of income or residence. The traditional fellowship associations, from the Rotary to the Shriners or the League of Women Voters, were driven to recruit members as widely as possible so as to maximize dues. They also needed a constant supply of members to fill the slates of officers, often annually elected, who carried on the work of the organization in the absence of paid staff. Thus, recruitment was through diffuse webs of social connection, since individuals could be drawn to membership through a host of reasons that often made little reference to the organization's social contribution. However, once they became members, these individuals were drawn into the life of the organization, learning a variety of important civic skills in the process of "ruling and being ruled in turn." This is the pattern of American polity eulogized by Tocqueville. These organizations were largely segregated by race, gender, and often religion, but with common projects, they brought together a variety of citizens from a variety of classes and locales.

As an example, consider the way in which parental involvement in public schools has shifted over the last generation. The original Parent Teacher Association (PTA) was a classic, old-style membership organization, with a national membership organized into state and local chapters through which nearly every American public school participated. It was where professional educators and parents met on the grass-roots level and a key channel through which policy on education could be discussed, passed up and down the federated organizational chain, and implemented in a broadly consensual way. With the PTA's decline, other parent–teacher organizations (PTOs) have sprung up. These organizations, however, represent a very different model of voluntary participation. PTOs are not part of an interlinked, federated network, as is the PTA. The PTO is tied only to a particular school, and this at a time when schools themselves are becoming increasingly socioeconomically homogeneous. These new organizations have no connections to other schools, let alone to state or national bodies. They can play little part in educational policy discussion or formulation. Partly by default, policy making has become the preserve of professionals, narrowly based advocacy groups, and elected officials. As one commentator has summarized the change: "What was once a broad and inclusive civic arena has become a privatized and insular enclave."[22]

While these changes in the forms of "third sector" life need not be read as pointing toward an imminent evisceration of American civic life, they do indicate major changes in the forms and patterns of civic engagement, with consequently large implications for the future of the polity as a whole. There is no way to understand philanthropy apart from an effort to grasp the changing patterns of the larger polity of which it is part. Given this situation, how can we gain useful insight into the implications of these changes for thinking about, as well as strengthening, philanthropy in the broad sense?

Changing Patterns of the Philanthropic Imagination

In analyzing large-scale social change, most social science accounts, and many historical narratives, lay stress upon what are sometimes called *material factors*. It is important, however, not to lose sight of the way in which *ideal* as well as *material* factors intertwine in producing the "imagined communities" within which actual persons conduct their lives.[23] A strong example of such an integrated account has recently been provided by Charles Taylor, who has proposed a schematic narrative of the development of the modern polity, paying particular attention to shifts in meaning, especially religious meaning, as well as changes in the forms of organizations. By concentrating on the different routes toward more secular polities taken by the English-speaking, heavily Protestant societies, in contrast to the path of Catholic continental polities, Taylor has identified a historical trajectory that adds an additional dimension for understanding charitable and philanthropic activities.

Taylor begins his narrative with a depiction of a polity type that has been dominant throughout the world, including Europe prior to the Protestant Reformation. Drawing on the sociological research of David Martin, Taylor calls this first polity type "paleo-Durkheimian." This characterizes an understanding of society in which human social patterns make up a hierarchical order, a hierarchy that is thought to mirror and mediate a cosmic order of Divine ordination.[24] Taylor's nomenclature refers to Emil Durkheim's famous characterization of societies in which there is a strong contrast between sacred and profane, such that God or divinity is believed to be almost palpably present in specific places, times, rites, people, and institutions, as medieval Europeans viewed churches, holy days, the Mass, the clergy—but also kings. By contrast, profane reality exists only on the ordinary or mundane level of space and time. Sacred things participate in both the mundane and in a higher or "holy" dimension that reaches beyond the everyday world, so that they confer meaning on mundane life by connecting it to the "true" or transcendent order. The paleo-Durkheimian polity shares in the basic religious task of maintaining the proper relation between the two orders by hierarchically subordinating the secular to the sacred.

We might add a philanthropic gloss to Taylor's account of paleo-Durkheimian polities. Hierarchical polities are also holistic in that the whole is seen as more than the sum of its parts. As a social form, such polities can include very diverse types of people and groups who stabilize their relationships by ranking them according to status. In such a social order, philanthropy was conceived as benevolence on the part of a higher agent in the hierarchy toward a lower. The origin of the term *philanthropia* was in the well-institutionalized practice of private giving for social purposes by civic notables in classical antiquity.[25] As praised by hierarchical thinkers such as Plato, for instance, gratuitous giving was of the very nature of divinity at the top of the chain of being. Therefore human benevolence, especially when bestowed by the higher upon the lower, was seen as a kind of "imitation of God" within the mundane sphere.

The imitation of divine beneficence continued to be a powerful theme of religious teaching in the Christian, Jewish, and Islamic Middle Ages.[26] Charitable "foundations" for the purposes of education, healing the sick, burying the dead, and other pious works were conceived on this same model of giving away one's bounty in imitation of the self-giving of God. Even when, as in early Christian and Jewish conceptions, charity was practiced as a kind of collective mutual assistance within the religious community, what made the charitable act meritorious was its fidelity to the divine command to love one's (religious) neighbor.

Following the religious wars of the sixteenth century, however, Europeans began moving away from this kind of sacralized image of the world. The different paths by which they did so have given rise to two quite distinct families of modern polity. Taylor calls the first of these, exemplified in the Absolutist regimes of Catholic Europe, the "Baroque synthesis." Here, as in France of the Old Regime, the inherited paleo-Durkheimian order continued to be effectively "off limits" for question or criticism, but in other areas of life, such as commerce, law, and warfare, new kinds of "functional" justifications gradually became common. Finally, as the French Revolution and its many aftershocks around the Continent showed, this proved an unstable mix. The Baroque synthesis was replaced by polities in which a militant, total secularism attempted to unite a holistic sense of society with an egalitarian individualism.[27] Out of this cataclysmic step into modernity emerged the modern French sense of the state as the organizing center of society, charged with philanthropic responsibilities for the welfare of the whole yet guaranteeing individual liberty and equality.

By contrast, the English-speaking nations have followed a sharply different path into what Taylor calls a "neo-Durkheimian" polity. This is Taylor's account of the religious underpinnings of liberal polities of the English and American type. Here, too, development was through a violent overthrow of Absolutism in the English Revolution and Civil War of the 1640s, but after that, the polity developed in a more evolutionary manner. Most importantly, the age gave rise to religious pluralism and toleration rather than an ongoing struggle among rival systems of order. This development is Taylor's second major stage in the development of our more secularized, democratic world. The basic pattern is reflected in the American public order, the institutional context for the kind of philanthropy of civic membership that characterized American life during most of the past two centuries. However, it is a polity that, like civic philanthropy, is today under great strain. As we shall see, Taylor marshals evidence that complements the suggestions by Putnam, Skocpol, and others that we are witnessing the emergence of yet another kind of polity. However, this "post-Durkheimian" polity is at several points deeply subversive with respect to the inherited philanthropic practices and organization typical of the neo-Durkheimian order. The charitable responses to the 9/11 tragedy have thrown these tendencies into strong relief.

It is important for Taylor's argument that the liberal polity was still founded in a conception of sacred order, albeit one very different from the medieval or Baroque. At the founding of America, Christians and Deists agreed on the idea of a providentially ordered universe. While divinity was no longer seen as present in a special sacred dimension, God was revealed in the very design of the cosmos itself. Hence, Deists like Thomas Jefferson could speak confidently of a moral order "self-evident" to reason and divinely ordained by "Nature and Nature's God." Taylor notes, however, that this moral order "starts out from individuals and doesn't see these as set a priori within a hierarchical order . . . its members are not agents who are essentially embedded in a society that in turn reflects and connects with the cosmos, but rather it is disembedded individuals who come to associate together." It is confidence that divine design underlies the moral order of equality that enables members of such a polity to believe the pursuit by each individual of his or her good to result in the betterment of all.[28]

The liberal polity is thus imagined as both egalitarian and individualist, in that social order is believed to arise from volition of free and equal individuals. Its natural way of imagining political order is the theory of Social Contract, especially as it was given philosophical enunciation by John Locke. The American polity, based upon the sacredness of the moral order believed to be embodied in the U.S. Declaration of Independence and Constitution, thus empowered individuals to pursue their private aims, but also to associate for mutual benefit. In contrast to the sense of collective responsibility embodied in the state-centered polity of France, this American polity placed its confidence in the prospect that mutual benefit would result from the exercise of individual freedom, though it was understood that this freedom would have to be tutored and hedged in by institutions both religious and secular. One of the features of the emerging polity is the general repudiation of any such tutelary role for "forming" citizens by those of virtually all political persuasions.[29]

In a parallel way, the United States came to be seen as the anointed land of progress for the whole of humanity, the recipient of a special Providence because of its embodiment of the true moral order. Even today, one might note, it is official U.S. foreign policy that, though other kinds of regime may be tolerated for tactical reasons, there is really only one legitimate form of polity, that given paramount embodiment in the United States.

In these ways, Taylor argues, religion was "woven into" national identity. Church and state were officially separate yet closely linked through the notion of an overarching providential order. The result was the gradual identification of the American nation as a kind of church, a righteous people entrusted with a universal mission "under God." In the course of the nineteenth century, the various Protestant churches came to be seen as voluntary associations, then as "denominations" of a generalized, ecumenical Protestant Christianity. Individuals could migrate spiritually among these churches as among so many affinity groups without incurring charges of irreligion. This was a broad consensus and only Catholics and Jews remained outside it, though for both groups of immigrants, "assimilation" eventually meant remolding themselves to become as much like other "denominations" as possible. By the 1960s, Jews and Catholics could be described along with Protestants as adherents of the national or "civil religion," as Robert Bellah termed it.[30] The cultural resources that Jewish and Catholic moral traditions can bring to bear on questions of charitable giving (and fund raising) are demonstrated in the essays by Elliot Dorff and Paul Schervish in the present volume. Overall, however, the shapes of American religious and philanthropic imagination have continued to embody a distinctly Protestant cast.

Conflict within the American Philanthropic Imagination

Philanthropy, in the American version of this neo-Durkheimian polity, has been above all a matter of voluntary giving, an expression of individual moral conscience. It was emphatically not an affair for the national state. The state, in classic Protestant understanding, has been conceived as essentially an instrument, or even a necessary evil, needed to maintain the moral order, protect property, and provide defense. It has been only rarely seen by Americans, outside times of war, as the embodiment of some collective spirit of the nation. Yet the polity's very emphasis upon individual initiative and consent has given American philanthropy a distinctive cast. It has functioned as a form of civic action, a duty imposed by the moral order, an expected feature of membership in the American polity. Its aim has been not just, or even not so much, the relief of distress as the fostering of those qualities of individual initiative and responsibility that are, as we have seen, essential aspects of the public order.

Within this broad agreement, however, the nation's philanthropic history, like so much else, has been riven by a clash between what E. Digby Baltzell called "two Protestant Ethics" that fought over differing conceptions of "authority and leadership."[31] Out of this conflict among Protestants representing competing traditions of "authority and leadership" came the twentieth-century landscape of philanthropy. In essence, the division was between a Calvinist ascendancy, rooted in New England culture, that espoused a holistic understanding of the polity as more than the sum of its parts—as having a "common good"—as well as a belief in the need for leadership on the part of public-spirited elites, versus a majority of more sectarian Protestants who distrusted any hierarchy and thought individualistically and privately.

The moral outlooks of the two tendencies differed markedly. The Calvinist tradition of stewardship through a calling was more hospitable to the civic republican ideal of magnanimity, which promoted leadership with a wide vision and a strong sense of public responsibility. For this ethic, philanthropy as literally love of humanity was expressed through the idea of "public service," meaning leadership for the community's good, often through politics. In contrast, the sectarian ethic was focused on personal diligence, moral purity, and neighborliness. These were less conspicuous virtues and sometimes gentler ones, but as Baltzell shows, they rarely led to the creation of institutions for public purposes or to public stewardship.

Following the Civil War, a New England-inspired institution-building elite impulse played a leading role in transforming the United States into a major industrial, urban power. A kind of "establishment" or "national class," rooted in the new industrial economy, succeeded in placing itself at the head of this process of nation building. This establishment developed a vast network of self-perpetuated boards of a myriad of philanthropic, educational, and cultural institutions that operated to nurture a new sense of national purpose and solidarity.[32] The cultural foundation for these works was an ethic of "stewardship" according to which individuals, especially those blessed by God with talent, wealth, or position, were held responsible for undertaking leadership in the service of the whole community. This spirit of stewardship by the wealthy and cultivated, sometimes resembling the *noblesse oblige* of European polities, found institutional embodiment in the modern professions and their espoused ethic of disinterested social service. While relying on private initiative, it was an ethic heavily circumscribed by a republican sensibility of collective responsibility.

Much of the growth in social capital analyzed by Robert Putnam was the long-term consequence of the work of the adherents of this version of the Protestant ethic that we might call "elite stewardship." However, while these efforts were in part stimulated by expansion of the national government during the Civil War, their direction was always toward private, voluntary stewardship rather than government direction or action. This movement reached its climax in the years before the Great Depression in Herbert Hoover's ideal of the "associative state," in which initiative and largesse were to remain essentially private, though orchestrated through the expertise housed in the Executive Branch of the national state.[33] In contrast, the more direct interventions by the federal government from the New Deal forward never achieved a consensual acceptance as permanent elements of an enlightened polity.

The ascendancy of that ethic of public-spirited elites, and its adherents, was always challenged by the more "populist" version of the American imagination.

This other Protestant ethic espouses an undiluted egalitarian and voluntarist image of the ideal polity. In many ways always the majority position, particularly in the heartlands of the old Confederacy, this Protestant ethic has also promoted hard work and moral responsibility. But it has seen these things as primarily the individual's own responsibility. Populist Protestants have also sought the moral uplift of their nation, and have at various times even been willing to enlist the distrusted national state to help them do this, but their attention has been on the redemption of the individual and on protecting enclaves of the elect from the ungodly. The spirit of this ethic of sectarian uplift has been largely anti-institutional. Even when undertaking public work, adherents of this ethic have tended to remain close to "home," serving the like-minded. Outreach was to convert, rarely to take responsibility for those outside the elect.

The description of the two ethics given by Baltzell and others recalls Ernst Troeltsch's famous contrast between the church and the sect as historical forms of social organization in the Christian church. For Troeltsch, the Christian ideal has always contained two poles. One pole receives expression in what he called the *sect*. Here, "communal forms rest on the principle of a mature, free, conscious decision by the adult individual, on the constant control of faith and morals," so that the religious community is seen as an "association" of free individuals. In this understanding of Christianity, argued Troeltsch, "divine law is more important than sacrament," while individual achievement is decisive rather than grace, so that the [sect type] has congregational discipline and the expulsion of the unworthy."[34] The great strength of the sect type has been energy and renewal. Its negative legacy has been an indifference and cruelty to those considered outside the circle of light.

By contrast, the *church* for Troeltsch is a manifestation of an organic understanding of the Christian community as itself a vehicle of divine presence in the world. It has never been entirely absent in any Christian movement, but in American history it had an attenuated presence. It has been strongest among Anglicans, Lutherans, and New England Calvinists. The church is an accommodation on the part of Christians with the worlds of nature and history. It places fewer demands upon believers but incorporates them all, at whatever state of adherence they may be. As a consequence, the church type "corresponds to the Christian conception of grace . . . and the objective holiness of all, even amid personal sinfulness . . . while the idea of subjective perfection recedes into the background." While the sect is simply an association of individuals, the church understands itself to be "an institution of salvation, a work of God and not humans, a miraculous establishment endowed with divine truths and powers of salvation that is not produced and constituted by the its members . . . and which bestows on its members an indelible character."[35] This understanding of institutions as wholes greater than the sum of their parts and as embodying trans-individual moral meanings has been one of the most persistent legacies of Christendom to modern European nations. In the United States, however, this viewpoint was only rarely extended to a morally positive view of state action.

To put this contrast another way: the sect attempts to separate itself from the world, enforcing that separation by making high demands upon individuals for various kinds of achievement. But it provides little support beyond pervasive discipline. Hence, there is the penchant of the sectarian imagination for testing and expulsion as a way to maintain purity and organizational morale. By contrast, the church type inclines toward including the world, or at least toward accepting many of its basic features, making fewer demands on individuals. The church type therefore depends upon an elite leadership, members who embody the ideals of the community to a high degree and are responsible for the welfare of that entire community. The church polity provides a variety of ways for remaining connected with the community it encompasses.

American versus European attitudes toward poverty, state action in the economy, the welfare state, even toward morality in general resonate with these distinctions. But in America, the predominance of the sectarian form of religious life has strongly colored the philanthropic imagination, even while the organizations through which that imagination has mostly worked have been heavily shaped by the elite adherents of the more church-like forms of Protestantism. However, as we have seen, neither moral view fully legitimated the national government as an agency of collective responsibility except as an emergency measure. Indeed, today's arguments over "faith-based" (i.e., religious) charity clearly fit the sectarian pattern of uneasiness about giving outside the community of believers or those being directly invited into the life of faith. That so much of federal welfare spending has long been through "faith-based" religious organizations has been mightily obscured by the resonance of sectarian religious discourse in American public life.

Despite these important differences, the peculiar political heritage of the nation has remained nearly unanimous in regard to the national government's role in society. There has persisted, in contrast to other industrial nations, a lack of willingness, or perhaps even an inability, to fully legitimize the national government as the major agency for charitable and philanthropic works. Some currents of political thought in the twentieth century Progressive movement did valorize the state as an agency of moral purpose, but even after the experiences of the Great Depression and World War II, Americans found it difficult to accept such a conception. In fact, the federal government has since World War II become the largest funder, as well as the major allocator, of philanthropic resources. However, this role of funder and allocator has not been complemented by the direct provision of goods and services.

On the contrary, federal resources have been channeled through a vast and confusing system of grants, vouchers, loans, and gifts. Most of the charitable aid provided by the "independent" charitable organizations is actually government-funded. Yet, it has proved politically unpopular to describe the tight, and growing, interdependence of the government and the "private, nonprofit" sector in clear terms.[36] Here the European heritage of Catholic Social Teachings can provide a useful corrective. As John Langan makes clear in his essay in this volume, the Catholic intellectual heritage presents a way of defending the autonomy of the small-scale and the local that is at the same time sensitive to their embeddedness within the larger political entity of the nation. This kind of thinking is badly needed to offset some of the myopia of the American polity's distinctive religious heritage. As long as Americans persist in the fiction of believing they have an independent philanthropic realm, it will be impossible to understand the real dimensions of "philanthropy" in the United States in ways that might allow for a more rational discussion, let alone better disposition, of these issues. The United States remains in many ways a nation that embodies many church-like patterns of integration while attempting to think with the soul of a sect.

After Tocqueville: An Alternative to Civic Philanthropy?

The patterns of American philanthropy have been changing dramatically. September 11 simply provided a revealing glimpse of how they have been changing. The world of intense civic organization that had been built up through most of the twentieth century is in decline. It may not disappear, but it is surely much less a determining factor of American life than it was three decades ago. This much is clear from the work of Putnam and Skocpol. The now-decaying civic infrastructure provided a voluntary mass political socialization into the practices of American democracy while carrying out a variety of charitable works. The elite boards and organizations may survive. But their connection with the old fellowship associations is what will be missed. In effect, though not always by intent, those organizations, like the political parties, the religious bodies, and the unions, provided civic education as well as training in the charitable uses of wealth for public benefit. As much by political necessity as by design, citizens had to assemble coalitions across economic divides in order to accomplish these ends. The newer forms of nonprofit enterprise are typically much narrower (more "focused") in both aim and constituency, with a correspondingly narrower potential for mobilizing citizens across class lines.

As an indication of what this means, recent studies of giving by wealthy entrepreneurs in the information and communications technology industries suggests "an orientation to locally-based 'hands-on' philanthropy that would be more amenable to measurable and tangible outcomes." This, argues Peter Dobkin Hall, "may well be expressive of the distaste for conventional forms of civic engagement" among such generally young stars of the "new economy."[37] Putting aside the glamorous evocation of a "new economy," this is the pattern of a familiar American moral vision: that of the ascetic Protestant sect, now secularized.

As we have seen, the sectarian moral imagination is hostile to "distant" organizations and suspicious of "elites" who presume to take leadership and responsibility. As the emphasis upon "outcomes" in the new philanthropy portrayed by Hall reveals, the new "social entrepreneurs" dutifully obey the old sectarian admonition to take a relentlessly "no nonsense," instrumental approach to good works as a matter of moral principle. But this moral imagination is also reluctant to engage with those who are different from the "like-minded."

Hence its preference for the "hands-on" and the local. All this is happening precisely as the mediating and countervailing forces within the American polity have weakened significantly. For example, from the late nineteenth through the mid-twentieth century, the conflicts between the two American ethics and their social bases were mediated and finessed through the federal structure of the fellowship associations that Skocpol has studied. Their decline has coincided both with a growth of social and economic inequality and the loss of the cohesion and prestige of the former Protestant establishment.

In imagining our future, Charles Taylor has hazarded an outline of what the emerging "post-Durkheimian" polity may look like. He notes that after World War II, and especially during the affluent 1960s, individuals in all the advanced nations experienced a great increase in the amount of personal consumption and private space available to them. For the first time in history, a mass "youth market" appeared in the form of a music and clothing industry oriented to the new social category of youth. But among all sectors of the population, television and new opportunities for individual expression and experiment weakened the older disciplines of mutual help in favor of individualized projects for "realizing tastes, needs, and affinities." The new "culture of authenticity" placed great emphasis upon "living out one's own realization of humanity" in ways previously possible only for elites or artists. The religious consequence has been the now-familiar opening up of a great pluralism of "spiritual paths." But the collective effects have meant that "the sacred has been uncoupled from political allegiance," with the consequence of "destabilizing Durkheimian identities" within a culturally "fractured world."[38] This is recognizably the same social reality and cultural horizon described by analysts such as Reich and Florida. Its *leitmotiv* has perhaps been captured by sociologist Robert Wuthnow's title, *Loose Connections: Joining Together in America's Fragmented Communities.*[39]

These trends are surely affecting the evolution of philanthropy in the American polity. The new kind of civil society that is developing in the United States is marked, as we have noted, by increased polarization of wealth and education, together with a thinning out of the old institutional integuments of political parties and national fellowship associations. The emerging kinds of philanthropic activity, such as those celebrated by Peter Drucker, focus more on private spaces and involve mostly the more affluent demographic segments. The "counterculture" of this "third sector" that Drucker describes includes a form of active citizenship. But it is a citizenship of the like-minded (and similarly comfortable) who "volunteer" or seek to help others "authentically," that is on their own terms, without the counterbalancing disciplines imposed by membership in institutions with national constituencies. It is a social sector that is highly integrated with the state and yet thinks of itself as "independent."

Taking these ideas together, we might conjecture that we are headed toward a philanthropy that would largely satisfy the subjective needs of some of the upper middle class to "do good," while feeling significant as citizens, without significantly affecting social and economic relationships within the larger polity. Such a civil society would be no longer of the sort Tocqueville saw as the social ecology of democracy. Built around highly focused nonprofit organizations run by professional staff, philanthropy would do little of the work of civic education that the older fellowship associations provided for the less educated and less affluent. It is likely to provide far less experience of cross-class cooperation toward common ends. In short, such a new configuration of the "voluntary sector" may do good works and provide services, but it will cease to fulfill philanthropy's inherited nation-building function. The problem, however, is not only to deal with whether the decline in the old, Tocquevillian civic space is irreversible. The more serious worry is whether there *is* any alternative.

It is not clear that one is available. The underlying direction of the American economy is now marked by a continuing inequality. This is written off today by many influential national figures, despite significant evidence to the contrary, as simply an inevitable price to be paid for economic growth.[40] These tendencies are complemented in the realm of politics by what has been termed the "the new American consensus: government of, by, and for the comfortable." At the core of this consensus, argues historian John Higham, a critic of the earlier "cult of consensus" during the 1950s, "is something more than self-protection and distrust. I think of it as a kind of privatism that denigrates the public sphere. The emergence of widespread indifference, somewhat flecked with disgust, is the most distinctive phenomenon of the present day. I don't think there's ever been anything like it."[41]

A systematic denigration of the public sphere, widespread indifference "flecked with disgust": this is hardly an auspicious climate for a rebirth of concern for one's fellow citizens who are distant or different in education, culture, race, or income. Americans are an optimistic as well as personally generous people, who have rarely been interested in collective introspection or self-criticism. It therefore seems almost *outré* to raise the following question: Could philanthropy, and the American polity, be entering a period of crisis without alternative? Could 9/11 and the national response to it represent not a new birth of collective spirit and attention to the world's needs, but a reinvigoration of sectarian anger at outsiders and a refusal to think beyond accepted pieties? Could American society at present be trapped within a moral imagination that is unable to translate its fundamental intuitions about human dignity and responsibility into realistic and constructive institutional forms suited to an increasingly interdependent world?[42]

Only future events, and our collective political decisions, can answer these questions. However, a few things do seem clear. The U.S. polity has fewer institutional mechanisms for ensuring social justice and national cohesion than Europeans can call into action. Nearly everything, in our polity, finally does hinge on the "hearts and minds" of the citizenry. So the need is clear: a renewal of the idea that citizens in our democracy share a collective responsibility to make the distribution of both rewards and risks more just. But the premise, both practical and moral, is social solidarity. As we have seen, however, the major trends in national life are undercutting what solidarity exists and inhibiting new developments. Ideologically, tradition of elite stewardship has weakened, while sectarian uplift is mostly indifferent to the practical conditions for solidarity beyond the like-minded.

For leverage in this effort, there is no "independent" or "third" sector to turn to. That sector is itself a site of conflict among these same forces. Indeed, without a new, positive conception of citizenship that acknowledges partnership between civil society and government, especially the national government, the drift toward a more segmented—and stratified—polity seems inevitable. Breaking out of this drift will require an expansion of the collective moral imagination. There are parallels in our past that give grounds for hope. But past experience strongly suggests that such hope must be based upon expansion and reform in the polity itself, in a social and political movement of great size and scope yet rooted deep in the social soil. America's religious and political traditions contain ideals that could, once again, rescue us from the vice of sectarian phobia and obsession. Here lies the open opportunity—and great responsibility—of philanthropic leadership. This is indeed a "culture war" worth fighting. But whatever the outcome of that long-running conflict among American ethics, one other thing is all too clear: within the emerging privatized public order, the future of philanthropy cannot be either civic or just.

Notes

1. Robert Putnam, "Bowling Together: The United State of America," *The American Prospect*, February 11, 2002, pp. 20–22.
2. Winnie Hu, "Outpouring for Sept. 11 Groups Mean Less for Food Banks," *The New York Times*, November 21, 2001, section B.
3. See Deborah Sontag, "Who Brought Bernadine Healy Down?" *New York Times Magazine*, December 23, 2001.
4. Robert Putnam, *Bowling Alone: The Collapse and Revival of American Community* (New York: Simon and Schuster, 2000), p. 184.
5. For example: David H. Smith, "Clarity about Charity: Who Gets What after September 11?" *Christian Century*, April 10–17, 2002, pp. 18–20.
6. William M. Sullivan, "Making Civil Society Work," in Robert K. Fullinwider, ed., *Civil Society, Democracy, and Civic Renewal* (Lanham, Md.: Rowan and Littlefield, 1999), pp. 31–54. See also Christopher Beem, *The Necessity of Politics: Reclaiming American Public Life* (Chicago: University of Chicago Press, 1999).
7. For example, see the "Introduction" by Robert L. Payton to the volume *Giving: Western Ideas of Philanthropy*, ed. J. B. Schneewind (Bloomington and Indianapolis: Indiana University Press, 1996), pp. ix–xv.
8. For "profession" as "folk concept," see Eliot Freidson, *Professionalism Reborn: Theory, Prophecy, and Policy* (Chicago: University of Chicago Press, 1994), pp. 20–23.
9. See Isaac Shapiro and Robert Greenstein, *The Widening Income Gulf* (Washington, D.C.: Center for Budget and Policy Priorities, September 1999).
10. For example, see Robert C. Reich, *The Future of Success* (New York: Alfred Knopf, 2001).

11. For data into the mid-1990s, see Claude Fischer et al., *Inequality by Design: Cracking the Bell Curve Myth* (Princeton, N.J.: Princeton University Press, 1996).

12. Theda Skocpol et al., "How Americans Became Civic," in *Civic Engagement in American Society,* ed. Theda Skocpol and Morris P. Fiorina (Washington, D.C.: Brookings Institution Press, 1999), pp. 27–80.

13. For example, Fareed Zakaria, *The Future of Freedom: Illiberal Democracy at Home and Abroad* (New York: W. W. Norton, 2003).

14. Kevin Phillips, *Wealth and Democracy: A Political History of the American Rich* (New York: Broadway Books, 2002).

15. Sidney Verba, Kay Lehman Schlozman, and Henry E. Brady, *Voice and Equality* (Cambridge, Mass.: Harvard University Press, 1995).

16. Peter Drucker, *The Realities in Government and Politics, in Economics and Business, in Society, and World View* (New York: HarperCollins, 1989), p. 9. In fairness to Drucker, his rhapsody was penned at an earlier phase of the trends commented upon above.

17. Robert B. Reich, *The Wealth of Nations: Preparing Ourselves for Twenty First Century Capitalism* (New York: Alfred Knopf, 1991); also Richard Florida, *The Rise of the Creative Class: How It Is Transforming Work, Leisure, Community and Everyday Life* (New York: Basic Books, 2002).

18. These, of course, are gross generalizations. However, the general themes are well documented. For a sample of literature on the topic, see Seymour Martin Lipset, *American Exceptionalism: A Two-Edged Sword* (New York: W. W. Norton, 1996); Herbert Gans, *Middle Class Individualism: The Future of Liberal Democracy* (New York: The Free Press, 1988); Robert N. Bellah, Richard Madsen, Ann Swidler, William M. Sullivan, and Steven M. Tipton, *Habits of the Heart: Individualism and Commitment in American Life,* revised ed. (Berkeley and Los Angeles: University of California Press, 1996); Alan Wolfe, *Whose Keeper? Social Science and Moral Obligation* (Berkeley and Los Angeles: University of California Press, 1989).

19. Ronald L. Jepperson and John W. Meyer, "The Public Order and the Constitution of Formal Organizations," in *The New Institutionalism in Organizational Analysis,* ed. Walter W. Powell and Paul J. DiMaggio (Chicago: University of Chicago Press, 1989), pp. 204–13, p. 206. See especially Ronald L. Jepperson, "Political Modernities: Disentangling Two Underlying Dimensions of Institutional Differentiation," *Sociological Theory* 20, no. 1 (2002): 1–32.

20. Robert Wiebe, *Self-Rule: A Cultural History of American Democracy* (Chicago: University of Chicago Press, 1995), pp. 182–83.

21. For elaboration of cross-national comparisons on this and a host of other issues, see Seymour Martin Lipset, *American Exceptionalism.*

22. Peter Dobkin Hall, "Philanthropy, the Welfare State, and the Transformation of American Public and Private Institutions, 1945–2000," Working Paper no. 5, The Hauser Center for Nonprofit Organizations, John F. Kennedy School of Government, Harvard University, 2002, p. 38. Also see Susan Crawford and Peggy Leavitt, "Social Change and Civic Engagement: The Case of the PTA," in Skocpol and Fiorina, *Civic Engagement,* pp. 249–96.

23. The now-classic source of this idea is Benedict Anderson, *Imagined Communities: Reflections on the Origin and Spread of Nationalism* (London: Verso, 1991; 1983).

222 *William M. Sullivan*

24. Charles Taylor, *Varieties of Religion Today: William James Revisited* (Cambridge, Mass.: Harvard University Press, 2002), pp. 64–66. Taylor is drawing upon David Martin, *A General Theory of Secularization* (Oxford: Basil Blackwell, 1978).

25. As discussed by Scott Davis, "Philanthropy as a Virtue in Late Antiquity and the Middle Ages," in *Giving: Western Ideas of Philanthropy*, pp. 1–23.

26. See, for example, Arthur O. Lovejoy's classic *The Great Chain of Being: The History of an Idea* (New York: Harper and Row, 1960; 1936); see also Werner Jaeger, *Early Christianity and Greek Paideia* (Cambridge, Mass.: Harvard University Press, 1961).

27. Taylor is here following David Martin, *Secularization*. See Taylor, *Varieties of Religion*, esp. pp. 12–99.

28. Taylor, *Varieties of Religion*, p. 67.

29. Michael J. Sandel, *Democracy's Discontent: America in Search of a Public Philosophy* (Cambridge, Mass.: The Belknap Press of Harvard University Press, 1996).

30. Taylor, *Varieties of Religions*, pp. 73–79. The reference is to Robert N. Bellah, "Civil Religion in America," *Daedalus* 96, no. 1 (1967): 1–21.

31. E. Digby Baltzell, *Puritan Boston and Quaker Philadelphia: Two Protestant Ethics and the Spirit of Authority and Leadership* (New York: Free Press, 1979).

32. Wiebe, *Self-Rule*, pp. 144–50.

33. See: Joan Hoff Wilson, *Herbert Hoover: Forgotten Progressive* (Boston: Little, Brown, and Company, 1975).

34. Ernst Troeltsch, *Religion in History*, ed. James Luther Adams (Minneapolis: Fortress Press, 1991), p. 221.

35. Ibid., p. 220.

36. The key research was done by Lawrence Salamon and colleagues. See Lawrence Salamon, "Partners in Public Service: The Scope and Theory of Nonprofit-Government Relations," *The Nonprofit Sector: A Research Handbook*, Walter W. Powell, ed. (New Haven: Yale University Press, 1987).

37. Hall, "Philanthropy," p. 37.

38. Taylor, *Religion Today*, pp. 88, 95, 106.

39. Robert Wuthnow, *Loose Connections: Joining Together in America's Fragmented Communities* (Cambridge, Mass.: Harvard University Press, 1998).

40. That inequality is not a trade-off for growth but rather an obstacle is argued by Jeff Madrick in *Why Economies Grow: Forces that Shape Prosperity and How We Can Get Them Working Again* (New York: Basic Books, 2003).

41. Nicholas Lemann, "The New American Consensus: Government Of, By, and For the Comfortable; or, The Smallness of Centrism," *New York Times Magazine*, November 1, 1998, p. 70.

42. For elaboration, see Robert N. Bellah, Richard Madsen, William M. Sullivan, Ann Swidler, and Steven M. Tipton, *The Good Society* (New York: Alfred Knopf, 1991). The author is grateful to the members of the seminar on "Moral Issues in Doing Good" for much valuable criticism and many useful suggestions in the writing of this paper. In particular, David Hammack was forceful but gentle in pressing an alternative point of view, while David Craig and David Smith each suggested valuable ways to clarify important parts of the argument.

Postscript: An Ongoing Conversation

David H. Smith

Individually and collectively the essays in this volume raise more questions than they settle. In this short postscript I want to underscore a few of them.

A recurring issue is the question of just how much we can and should do for each other. At least three answers to this question are at or just below the surface of these essays. One answer keys on the value of self-respect and says, in effect, that any improvement in one's lot worth having must be a product of one's own effort. A better life is not something that one can simply give to someone else, no matter how much someone may want to offer that gift. Something like that seems to have been Booker T. Washington's view, and there is a kind of tough-love candor about it that is very attractive.

A second view agrees that people must work for the improvement of their own situations but sees a larger role for others in that process. Schools can be built, external funding sought, living conditions and basic hygiene improved. In this view, initiative or intervention from outside is possible and perhaps even necessary; gifts of resources and opportunity may be essential. Washington's whole career shows that he did not entirely reject that view, but we see this stance more clearly in the work of Jane Addams in her focus on creating community among helpers and those helped, and the concept is clearly focused in David Craig's notion of "giving and taking."

Yet a third option is to see government as a different *kind* of outside helper. Actions by governments at the local, state, or federal level to help people in trouble are not disrespectful in the way private charity is, because at some basic level governments—at least democratically elected governments—are not just "them" but reflect the will of the community. When I accept help from government, I do it as a citizen and as a matter of right conferred on me by *my* representatives. We see public education this way in the United States. William Sullivan sees this attitude toward government in the Progressive era a century ago, but bemoans the loss of civic or public responsibility and involvement today.

It is hard, if not impossible, entirely to abstract a discussion of the ethics of philanthropy—that is, of doing good on a grand scale—from this background question of social and political philosophy. David Hammack's essay makes plain just how much the nonprofit sector is sustained by public funding, whether directly or indirectly. In fact, the public service and welfare economy in the United

States is much more of a mixed economy than is usually supposed. Of course, the question of the proper role of governments is bitterly contested terrain in the American polity, and something of that diversity is reflected in the views of our contributors. Our discussions may model a fresh way to join some issues constructively, if we begin with the assumption that we want to help each other and then discuss just how best to do that, individually and collectively. Certainly more thoughtful philosophical and theological writing about the political economy of giving needs to be done.

A second issue these essays raise concerns the fact that most philanthropy today is mediated through large organizations. Individual gifts, even very large ones, are usually combined through the United Way, the social outreach budget of a religious community, or the Red Cross. The effect is to put the individual donor in the position of evaluating alternatives, perhaps using a criterion such as the "focused fairness" that Patricia Werhane recommends. Whom can I trust to do what in my judgment most needs to be done? Who will be a good steward of my resources? How can I get information that will help me to choose whom to trust? Fortunately or unfortunately, individuals wanting to help out today find their choices among possible recipients of their financial gifts at least as difficult as choices among new digital cameras or audiovisual components. The number of options is bewildering and the differences among them are often unclear. Individuals have to make some decisions about the communities or authorities they will entrust. We open this question in our volume and several authors join the issue. But as a practical matter it remains vexing. Trust and verify? But how to verify?

This matter relates to yet a third complex of issues, those concerning the donor's motivations and expectations. Among others, the essays by Schervish and Werhane in this volume are at pains to point out that some aspect of concern for oneself is a legitimate part of a decision to give. Giving need not be purely sacrificial or devoid of all gratification to the giver. There is nothing wrong about wanting to feel good about doing good! Nevertheless, there are better and worse reasons for giving, ranging from a desire to improve one's image or assuage a guilty conscience through genuine compassion and concern for those in need. Many donors want to be involved personally, but as a practical matter this may be impossible or even counterproductive. As someone selects among possible recipients of her benevolence, she has to factor in her convictions about the role she herself wants to play in the giving and be clear about what her own motives are for wanting to give. Introspection is as important as inspection of targets of assistance, but not much attention has so far been focused on this process. Corrupt motives leave traces on gifts, limiting their helpfulness.

Religious organizations strive for some level of holiness, or purity, despite the fact that like all organizations they are riven with issues of power imbalance, disagreements about how to acquire support, and plain old human cussedness. But their expectations of themselves—and the expectations others have of them —raise particular problems. One clear problem is the extent to which their caring should focus outside the circle of faith. Another is special standards for their own behavior: just what does the demand for purity require? Philip Turner opens the first of these issues and Elliot Dorff the second in their essays in this volume. One effect is to raise the question of the extent to which a religious congregation is in fact a philanthropic organization, committed to the help of *others*. In one of our conversations, someone remarked that 20 percent of the funding of religious organizations is philanthropic while the remaining 80 percent is essentially the funding for a social club. No true religious organizations would admit the accuracy of this characterization, for the description fits poorly with their ways of understanding themselves. What are the standards that should control religious giving—by individuals and congregations? In what ways should a religious community be constrained by its religious identity and sense of mission?

These are only some of the issues that we found our work opened. We could not be more aware that we have only scratched the surface of them—or that there are many issues of great importance that we have left untouched. For example:

- With the exception of part of Paul Pribbenow's essay, we have given very little attention to the work of *philanthropoids*, a term of art that denotes professionals in the philanthropic industry itself—fundraisers, managers of the investment portfolios of philanthropic organizations, foundation executives. Yet these persons find themselves facing major conflicts of loyalty and in positions of considerable power and influence.
- We have given no attention to corporate philanthropy, the support of various charitable and other nonprofit organizations by businesses and corporations. Yet such giving is important to philanthropy in the United States today.
- Indeed, we have given very little attention to the role of charitable foundations, organizations that have played—and continue to play—a major role in our collective response to problems of human welfare.
- As we acknowledge in the Introduction, we really are not in agreement about a definition of philanthropy. We are clear that it is not tied just to the "nonprofit sector" and that there are forms of doing good that can be defined as *philanthropy* only if we strain our ordinary usage of words. We never, however, frontally take on the question of the relationship between philanthropy and political advocacy. Support for Greenpeace, for example, entails commitment to a kind of advocacy that support for an art gallery does not. What difference does that make?
- We give no attention to forms of help or goodness that may be found outside the world shaped by Christian and Jewish traditions, or to radically contrasting voices within those traditions. A reader of this volume will look in vain for a discussion of distinctive issues that may arise in the world of Islam or Buddhism, or with ethnic groups, such as African American or Native American communities.

We make no apologies for these omissions. One can only do so much in any one book. We hope that our work will prove as challenging and provocative to readers as work on the project did for all involved. In fact, future work that attends to these omissions, or corrects the reflections we present here, will be viewed by us as acts of goodness. We may not enjoy the result, but it will signal to us that we did good—even if not by doing as well as we should.

Contributors

David M. Craig is Assistant Professor of Religious Studies, Indiana University—Purdue University Indianapolis.

Elliot N. Dorff is rector, Sol & Anne Dorff Distinguished Service Professor in Philosophy and co-chair of the Bioethics Department at the University of Judaism in Los Angeles.

David C. Hammack is the Hiram C. Haydn Professor of History and a member of the Faculty Council of the Mandel Center for Nonprofit Organizations at Case Western Reserve University, Cleveland.

Amy A. Kass is Senior Lecturer at the University of Chicago and Senior Fellow at the Hudson Institute.

John Langan, S.J., is the Joseph Cardinal Bernardin Professor of Catholic Social Thought at Georgetown University, Washington, D.C.

Paul Pribbenow is President of Rockford College in Illinois.

Paul G. Schervish is Professor of Sociology and Director of the Center on Wealth and Philanthropy at Boston College, and National Research Fellow at the Indiana University Center on Philanthropy.

David H. Smith is Nelson Poynter Senior Scholar at the Poynter Center for the Study of Ethics and American Institutions at Indiana University Bloomington.

William M. Sullivan is Senior Scholar at the Carnegie Foundation for the Advancement of Teaching in Palo Alto, California.

Philip Turner is retired dean of The Berkeley Divinity School at Yale University.

Patricia H. Werhane has a joint appointment at DePaul University, Chicago, where she is the Wicklander Professor of Business Ethics, and at the Darden School, University of Virginia, Charlottesville, where she is the Ruffin Professor of Business Ethics.

Philanthropic and Nonprofit Studies

Dwight F. Burlingame and
David C. Hammack, general editors

Index

distribution of aid, 89–92, 93–96, 207

diversity: and concept of good, 60; and egalitarianism, 172; at Hull-House, 45; and moral distance, 77–78; and nonprofit organizations, 183–184, 193–194

domestic violence, 66–67, 71

donors: benefits derived from giving, 5, 155, 163; imposition of standards, 77–78; language denoting, 58, 61, 76–80; sources of donations, 107–113. *See also* recipients of gifts; relationships

Dorff, Elliot, 61, 103–122, 180, 214

double hermeneutic of social analysis, 149

Douglas, Margaret, 192

Drucker, Peter, 207–208, 219

Dryden, John, 127

DuBois, W. E. B., 19, 28, 39

Durkheim, Emile, 150, 211–213, 214, 219

duty: to aid, 89–90, 96; to avoid harm, 89, 91, 93; to beneficence, 89, 96; civic duty, 42–43; to fairness, 96; Kant on, 11, 89, 100; and relationships, 115; of religious institutions, 121, 132

Dyke, C., 91

East Africa, 128, 138, 140, 142

economics: economic citizenship, 160, 161; and inequality, 94, 220; and nonprofit institutions, 106–107, 116–117; and solidarity, 176

education: and Addams, 41–42; alumni funds, 188; as central capability, 63; civic education, 220; as civic right, 224; and consumption philanthropy, 60; funding for, 83, 186, 187, 197–198; giving aimed at, 69–70, 71; and "legacies," 117; and nonprofit organizations, 190–192; polarization in, 219; segregation in, 207; and self-sufficiency, 191–192, 195; student grants and loans, 184, 193, 194, 195, 202; Teach for America program, 76–77; and Washington, 23–32

effective demand, 157–158, 159, 161

effectiveness, measuring, 96, 97

efficiency, measuring, 96

egalitarianism, 172, 212, 213, 216

egoism, 59, 88, 96, 99, 168

Egypt, 133

elderly citizens, 186

emotional life, 63, 67, 68

empathy, 44

employment. *See* work and workers

empowerment, 151–152

England, 197

Enlightenment, 105, 127, 135

Enron, 113

environment: control over, 63, 67, 68; environmental issues, 68, 71, 82

Ephesians, 142

equanimity in resource distribution, 207

ethics: of identification, 154–155, 156, 157, 159; of responsibility, 44. *See also* morality

ethnicity, 63, 226

Europe, 207, 208, 209, 212, 217

evaluation of projects, 93–94

evangelism, 129–135, 138, 140–143, 189–190

excellence, promotion of: and central capabilities, 70; and distributive principles for philanthropy, 92; independence associated with, 77–78; and language of giving, 76; and leading a good life, 72, 73; and prioritizing giving, 69–70

existentialism, 103

Exodus, 151–152

fairness in philanthropy, 84–98, 115–116

faith-based programs, 75. *See also* religion

family: as central capability, 63; familial metaphors, 156, 158; identification with, 156; obligations to, 115; role of, 82

fear, living in, 21

federal funding, 186, 193, 194, 204

fellowship associations, 210, 219

financial capacity for charity, 163–164

First Amendment, 195

fistula, 86–87, 91–92, 97–98

Florida, Richard, 208, 219

focused fairness, 84–98

folk concept, philanthropy as, 206

food: distribution of, 207; food-aid programs, 90–91, 93; food stamp program, 91, 193; nourishment as central capability, 63

Foucault, Charles, 145

foundations, 58, 59, 226. *See also* nonprofit organizations

France, 209, 213

Francis of Assisi, Saint, 170

Frankena, William, 166

freedom, 63, 151

fundraising: history of, 187–188; and philanthropic relationships, 48; as profession, 40, 47, 49–51, 226

generosity, 1–2, 156

Gentiles, 136

Germany, 171–172

Gershom, Rabbenu, 119

G.I. Bill, 193, 194

Giddens, Anthony, 149

Gilleman, Gerard, 155

117; purposes of organizations, 47; and recognition for philanthropy, 59. *See also* ethics
mores, respect for, 90–91
Moses, 151–152
motivations for giving: control or correction, 5; gratitude, 8, 154, 155–156; love, 8–9; mercy, 69–70, 72, 73, 78; purity of, 167–168; recognition, 58–62; religion, 8, 9–10; self-interest, 225
museums, 186
Muslims. *See* Islam
Mussolini, Benito, 173
mutual benefits, 213

naïveté in philanthropy, 98
naming of foundations and institutions, 58, 59
National Council of Churches (NCC), 135–136, 137
National Defense Education Act, 193, 194
national initiatives, 173, 174
National Institutes of Health, 184, 193
National Science Foundation, 184, 193
Native Americans, 184, 226
natural resources, 68
needs: of donors, 5; material needs, 29, 31; perceptions of, 5, 78; satisfaction of, 32; scope of, 2; Toner on, 153, 157, 159, 164
neo-Durkheimian polity, 212–213, 214
Neusner, Jacob, 106
New Deal, 12, 184, 215
New England, 215
New York, 192
New York City, 186
New York City Tract Society, 190
New York Times, 114
New Zealand, 104
Nicomachean Ethics (Aristotle), 57, 151
Nigeria, 97–98, 133
Nixon, Richard, 202
Nobel Peace Prize, 39
noblesse oblige, 215
nonprofit organizations: autonomy of, 192–197; changes in, 12; and civil society, 79; and communities, 106; and donors, 194–195, 196; employees, 186–187, 195; and ethical issues, 107–121; and funding, 107–113, 192–197, 202–203, 224–225; goals of, 69; as intermediary, 183; and Judaism, 61, 103–107, 117–121; naming, 58, 59; and Nussbaum, 62; and philanthropy, 48, 49; preferential treatment in, 113–117; proliferation of, 209–210; regulatory agencies, 192, 195; in the U.S., 183–184, 186–197, 220
nourishment. *See* food

Nozick, Robert, 175, 180
Nussbaum, Martha: central capabilities concept, 11, 62–63, 66–67, 82, 179; and a good life, 58, 70, 80, 81; on minimal thresholds, 70, 78; on states' responsibilities, 73
nutrition. *See* food
Nygren, Anders, 8

"The Objective Value of a Social Settlement" (Addams), 46
objectivity and nonprofit organizations, 115
obligations in giving: and moral compulsions, 4; and nonprofits, 196; and reciprocity, 79; and religion, 135–141, 142, 225–226
Ochs, Robert, 156
O'Fahey, R. S., 134
Oliver, Roland, 129, 132
On Liberty (Mills), 175
opportunities, improving, 92, 93, 95. *See also* excellence, promotion of
optimism, 39
organizations, work of, 46–51, 60. *See also* nonprofit organizations
orphans and orphanages, 186, 187, 188
Orphan Society of Philadelphia, 188
Ostrander, Susan, 60
outreach programs, 66
Oxfam, 134, 140

paleo-Durkheimian polity, 211–212
Parent Teacher Association, 13, 210–211
Parent Teacher Organizations, 13, 210–211
parochialism, 91, 92
passions, 99
paternalism, 61, 91, 95, 96
patronizing attitudes, 5–6
Paul (biblical), 136–137, 167
Payton, Robert, 6, 40
Peabody, George Foster, 188
Perkins, Thomas, 189
Perkins Institution and Massachusetts Asylum for the Blind, 189
personal responsibilities, 72–74
Philadelphia, Pennsylvania, 186
philanthropists. *See* donors
philanthropoids. *See* fundraising
philanthropy: Addams on, 48, 51; benefits derived from giving, 155, 163; and charity, 166–168; defining, 6–7, 120, 127, 226; etymology, 127
Philip Morris Company, 111–113, 124
Pietists, 184
Pius XI, 171, 172, 179
planning giving, 65

Sullivan, William, 204–221, 224
Summa Theologiae (Aquinas), 175–176
sympathy, 90
syndicalism, 172–173

takers. *See* recipients of gifts
talents, gifts of, 58
Tanzania, 134
taxes, 72, 119
Taylor, Charles, 211, 212–214, 219
Teach for America, 76–77, 78, 79
telephone solicitations, 64
Teresa of Calcutta, 6
teshuvah (return), 109–110, 111, 113, 124
A Theory of Justice (Rawls), 94
The Theory of Moral Sentiments (Smith), 88, 160
third sector, 208, 210, 211, 219, 221
Thornton, L. S., 137
thought, capability of, 63, 65, 66, 68, 71
Tillich, Paul, 8
time, gifts of, 58
Tocqueville, Alexis de, 154–155, 188, 209, 210, 219–220
Tolstoy, Leo, 39
Toner, Jules, 153, 154
totalitarianism, 171–172, 174, 178
Toynbee Hall, 43
traditions, 95, 97
Troeltsch, Ernst, 216
true needs, Toner's concept of, 153, 157, 159, 164
Tucker, Alfred, 131
Turner, Phillip, 6, 61, 127–144, 180, 226
Twenty Years at Hull-House (Addams), 41, 42, 46
tyranny of the gift, 4
tzedakah (justice), 61, 106, 120–121, 185

Uganda, 128, 131, 133, 134
ultimate purposes, 149, 158–159, 160
Union of the Soviet Socialist Republics (former), 104
United Kingdom, 2, 139
United Nations, 74
United States: charity and, 2–3; moral health of, 159; and nonprofits, 183; secular philosophy, 104. *See also* September 11 attacks
United Way, 209, 225
universalism, 160
Up from Slavery (Washington), 19
U.S. Supreme Court, 195
USA Freedom Corps, 17

values: coercion, 91; differences in, 90, 96, 97; in organized philanthropy, 48, 49; stress on giving, 1–2; value-rational action *(wertrational)*, 149
vices connected with altruism, 91
Victims' Compensation Fund, 6
Victorian age, 132
Virginia, 192
vocations, 41
volunteers and volunteerism: and moral citizenship, 159; and nonprofit organizations, 49, 187, 196; and preferential treatment, 113, 115, 116; Putnam on, 205; views of, 208
voucher programs, 194, 196

Washington, Booker T., 17–34; and Addams, 39; criticisms of, 18; education of, 23–27, 34; family, 27; influence of, 10; on self-help, 19–20, 20–21; on self-respect, 179, 224; in slavery, 21–23, 32–33; at Tuskegee, 26–31
Wayland, Francis, 191–192, 195
wealth: and Addams, 45; after World War II, 193; Carnegie on, 44; contributions of the wealthy, 120–121, 218; New Testament on, 168; prosperity in U.S., 193, 194, 207; regard for wealthy, 208, 218; and spirit of stewardship, 215; wealth gap, 207, 219. *See also* poverty
Weber, Max, 149
welfare, 12, 17–18, 224–225
Werhane, Patricia, 84–98, 178, 225
wertrational (value-rational action), 149
Western European countries, 104
Western liberalism, 103–104
"widow's mite," 6
Wiebe, Robert, 209
wisdom, virtue of, 151
Wollstonecraft, Mary, 84, 92, 98
women and nonprofit organizations, 183, 184, 193, 196
word choices, 61, 76–80
work and workers: and independence, 31; job training programs, 184, 193, 202; nonprofit organizations' employees, 186–187, 195; philanthropy as common work, 39, 40, 47, 48, 50, 52; and syndicalism, 172
Worldcom, 113
World Health Organization (WHO), 84, 87, 92
Worldwide Fund for Mothers Injured in Childbirth (WFMIC), 86
Wuthnow, Robert, 219

zweckrational (instrumentally rational action), 149

DAVID H. SMITH has recently retired as the Director of the Poynter Center and is Emeritus Professor of Religious Studies at Indiana University. Smith was the co-editor, with Robert Veatch, of the Indiana Series on Medical Ethics, for which he co-authored *Early Warning: Cases and Ethical Guidance for Presymptomatic Testing in Genetic Diseases.* He is author of *Entrusted: The Moral Responsibilities of Trusteeship.*